THE STORY OF **GOD**, **THE WORLD** AND **YOU**

GLEN SCRIVENER

First published in Great Britain in 2014
Reprinted in 2015 (twice), 2017, 2018 and 2019.

British Library Cataloguing in Publication Data

A record for this book is available from the British Library

ISBN: 978-1-909611-94-8

Designed by Jeremy Poyner

Printed in Denmark by Nørhaven

10Publishing, a division of *10ofthose.com*
Unit C, Tomlinson Road, Leyland, PR25 2DY, England

Email: info@10ofthose.com
Website: www.10ofthose.com

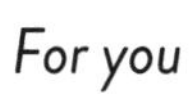

For you

CONTENTS

1
WELCOME

> 'I don't know [what I think about God]. We've never been introduced!'
>
> —*Noel Coward*

> 'Come and see.'
>
> —*Jesus, John 1:39*[1]

You made it, well done! So glad you came out, especially at this hour. Let me take your coat. Yes, the signs are shocking around here; people are always missing the entrance. No, that's true, we forget how it looks from the outside. I know ... But you're here now and you're very welcome. What can I get you to drink?

If Christianity is a house, consider this book an exercise in hospitality. I'm inviting you to view Christian faith from within. I'm not interested in throwing stones at the other houses – bashing other belief systems. And I'm not trying to build stepping-stones that take you progressively from your house to ours. Actually I don't think it works like that – I'll say why in a minute. Call me lazy if you like but I'm just going to throw open the doors, stick on the kettle and see who comes.

Don't get me wrong, I don't expect you to *believe* in Christianity as we begin – far from it. I'm presuming you're *not* a Christian and that right now you consider it to be, to some degree, naive, nuts, nasty or naff. That's fine – we pretty much view ourselves that way, if the truth be told. All

I'm asking is that you let me give you 'the grand tour'. Let me show you Christianity from the inside.

As I make this invitation, I realise that I'm asking a lot. I'm aware that the view from the outside can be off-putting.

From the outside looking in

If you've peered into the yard, you've probably seen the household pets – a motley bunch. There's the:

- Labrador Pup Christian: excitable, exhausting, endless enthusiasm but – bless 'em – they seem happy.
- Scared-y Cat Christian: awkward to a fault, serious-minded, scrupulous, petrified of living but, still, they're no harm to anyone.
- Giant Tortoise Christian: ancient, slow-moving, with constantly raised eyebrows and superiority etched in their faces. But if we ever have to endure another Blitz, they'll show the way.
- Ostrich Christian: head in the sand lost in their own world of religio-babble, but it seems meaningful *to them*.
- Bearded Dragon Christian: thick skin, fire in their bellies, thumping their Bibles, praying for Armageddon. But hey, with them around, the rest of us can feel progressive.

I would love to tell you there is no truth to these caricatures. But we all know that caricatures have some basis in fact. Perhaps you have met one or two of these specimens? I've met several. But I assure you that most Christians are not like this. And faith in Jesus does not condemn you to a caricature. It ought to make you more truly yourself. One of the dangers, though, of viewing things 'from the outside' is the danger of stereotyping. If you stay at a distance, you won't understand Christians.

More than this, if you remain 'on the outside', you won't understand Christian beliefs either. Imagine piecing together your knowledge of Christian faith using only your Internet news feed. You would be left with more questions than answers:

- Are Christians a majority pleading minority status? Or the other way around? Or both?
- Do they want their morality on the statute books? Or special exemptions for their churches? Or both?
- Do they want freedom of speech for themselves? Or blasphemy laws for the rest? Or both?
- Are their leaders desperately old fashioned? Or desperately trying to be 'relevant'? Or both?
- Are their men distressingly unmanly? Or distressingly anti-women? Or both?
- Are they priggish sex-deniers? Or obsessed by the subject? Or both?

The view from the outside can be confusing, ugly even. And beyond these mixed messages, what is the core of the faith? What comes through the cultural noise? Not a lot. Only arcane views of sex and society and a vague remembrance that somewhere, somehow it has to do with God – whoever God is.

The view from the outside is bleak. And to be honest, if that's Christian faith, I want no part of it. Not only do I find many of the views above objectionable, not only do I cringe at the contradictions in so much Christian communication, I also despair that any of these issues are considered the heart of the matter. In so many cases these issues relate to true Christian faith the way football hooligans relate to 'the beautiful game'. They are distractions at best if you want to understand the thing itself.

This is why I'm inviting you inside. None of those externals get at true Christianity. I assure you, when you enter the real thing, it looks quite different. But actually that's always the way. When it comes to anything important, the view from the inside is your best hope of understanding it.

The view from within

Lots of things are only understood from within. The future is a good example.

In 1878 the Chief Engineer of the British Post Office, Sir William Preece, made this confident assertion: 'The Americans have need of the telephone, but we do not. We have plenty of messenger boys.'

Seven decades later here's the Chairman of IBM, Thomas Watson, with a similarly poor prediction: 'I think there is a world market for maybe five computers.'

Half a century on Clifford Stoll wrote a, now famous, 1995 *Newsweek* article about another newfangled technology. It was entitled 'Internet? Bah!'

It's easy to laugh at predictions made in the past. It's much more difficult to put ourselves in their shoes. How could they have foreseen the new world ahead? Actually you have to enter that world to understand it.

There are other 'new worlds' that are like this. Do you remember your childhood views of love and relationships? How does a seven-year-old grasp 'falling in love'? Typical parental advice goes something like: 'You'll know it when it happens.' This rarely satisfies the seven-year-old, but it's true nonetheless. These things must be entered to be understood.

I suggest to you that beliefs are very much like this. If I tell you Jesus has turned my world upside down, that now I see God, the world and myself in a new light, how does that sound to you? Some will say, 'Glen's got religion.' Others will cry, 'Brainwashed!' Still others will think, 'That's a nice crutch if you need it.' But, from where I'm sitting, none of those descriptions fit. From my perspective I've entered a new world, seen the future, fallen in love, that kind of thing.

So if you ask me about my Christianity, I'm liable to give some infuriating answers:

- 'What's the Christian position on such and such?' you ask. 'Let me tell you a story,' I'll say.
- 'Why should I trust it?' you ask. 'Try it on for size and you'll see,' I'll say.
- 'Can't you just give me an overview of Christianity?' you ask. 'You ought to view it from within,' I'll say.

Going inside out

Before you throw your hands up in exasperation, let me reassure you. I'm not trying to flee reality and take refuge in a Christian bubble. I have found – as have millions of others – that this story gives you an expanded vision of the world, not a diminished one. You see the Christian story claims to be *the* story – the one that explains every other.

It's a tale that begins before every other beginning. A God who is three and one. A cosmos born of community. A catastrophe unleashed at a stroke. A tragedy entered by love. A Creator made creature and killed. A Corpse conquering death by dying. A Lord with scars, rising to rule. A world invited to share God's life. A universe renewed and redeemed.

This is certainly a strange story and you might think that belief in this tale condemns you to the loony fringe. But actually the story at the heart of Christianity is *every* story. There's a golden age of innocence; mistrust; betrayal; unrequited love; a fall from grace; murder and intrigue; a pit of despair; a Hero's epic journey; a fight to the death; victory through sacrifice; and a happy ending complete with wedding and singing. That's like all our stories. But the Bible says it's God's story too. In fact – here's the claim I want you to consider – the Bible says it was God's story first. And this story makes sense of our little stories. Push through the strangeness and you'll find that everything becomes more familiar. Come into the

Christian story and it will send you out again with renewed passion and engagement.

Could that be true? Well here's the invitation – come on over. You won't understand it from a distance, so take the tour. Enter the story and figure out whether you think *this* is the Story of stories. Look to the Hero and decide whether he might be the Hero of heroes. If he is, then you haven't shrunk your world; you've opened it out.

Look to the Hero and decide whether he might be the Hero of heroes. If he is, then you haven't shrunk your world; you've opened it out.

Let me also reassure you, as you 'take the tour', that I'm not trying to avoid your objections. This is not a bold attempt to silence dissent from the outset. Actually I want to take your questions seriously. You'll notice from the contents page that I devote the last chunk of the book to addressing frequently asked questions. We'll be thinking about the following:

- OK, but is it true?
- Is the Bible trustworthy?
- How does a good God fit with evil and suffering?
- How does a loving God fit with judgement?
- How can anyone join the church with all its hate, its history and its hypocrisy?
- What about other faiths?
- Why are Christians so weird about sex and sexuality?
- Aren't believers anti-science?

These questions – and dozens more – are great to ask. But they're difficult to answer when we're both stood outside, so I'm inviting you in. Hopefully you will see how the Christian story itself answers the questions, maybe alters the questions, maybe even alters the questioner. But, first things first, let's explore the basics of the Christian faith.

The Grand Tour

Here's the structure of the book. In the next chapter I'm going to introduce you to the Christ at the heart of Christianity. Maybe you've grown up learning Bible stories, or maybe you've never clapped eyes on a Bible. I'm going to assume no knowledge so we can allow the Jesus story to strike us afresh.

Once we refocus on Jesus, I want to show how he recasts our vision of God, the world and ourselves. In particular, we will major on God's THREE-ness, the world's TWO-ness and our ONE-ness. That probably won't make a lot of sense right now, but you'll pick it up as we go along.

To stretch the 'house' analogy to breaking point, Jesus will be our entryway, 3-2-1 will be the highlights of the grand tour and then we'll sit down with a cuppa so you can ask your questions. Is that OK?

Well then, let's begin at the beginning. In the case of Christianity, the clue is in the name. We must begin with Christ.

• COMING UP IN CHAPTER 2 •

The next chapter is a bit like a drive through the country. I'm taking you through the life of Jesus at speed. If you focus on the close-up details, it will all be a blur. If you breathe in the air and look to the horizon, you should enjoy the ride.

As we travel along you may have a bunch of questions, like 'Who does Jesus think he is?' or 'Why on earth does he do this?' or 'What is the point of that?' But those questions are for later. THREE will answer the 'Who?' question, TWO will answer the 'Why?' question and ONE will answer the 'So what?' question. This chapter is simply about the 'What' – what is the Jesus story? There won't be a lot of interpretation or commentary. The point is not to get a grip of everything but to get a feel for it.

Everything I say is found in the Bible's four biographies of Jesus – Matthew, Mark, Luke and John. At points the quotes are slightly more paraphrase than translation, but only slightly. The references are in the footnotes – please do look them up and read them for yourself. Luke 15:11, for example, means that the Bible quote can be found in the book of Luke, chapter 15, verse 11.

There's a lot of ground to cover and not much time, so buckle up, here we go ...

2

JESUS: THE WAY INTO THE STORY

If God is not like Jesus Christ, he ought to be.

—Lord Byron

The Son is the image of the invisible God.

—St Paul, Colossians 1:15

Starting in the stable

Born in a shed, laid in a feeding trough, Jesus began his earthly life as he meant to go on. The Christmas scene is so strange. But it's the perfect introduction to the strangeness of Christ.

If the ancient prophecies can be trusted, there in the manger – the feeding trough – lies the infant God. His newborn flesh is smacked to elicit that precious first breath. A mess of mucus, blood and wriggling limbs, he is wrapped in rags and placed on the straw, ready to receive his worshipping visitors – foreign dignitaries and farm labourers alike.[1]

Others are threatened by the competition. King Herod orders a mini-

genocide to destroy any rivals to the throne. His teenage parents must act quickly. Scooping up the King of Kings, they flee to Egypt.[2]

After years on the run, this dirt-poor family settles back in Galilee, a northern backwater of Israel – a tiny oppressed nation under the thumb of mighty Rome. The people are downtrodden but proud. Some speak of a military coup. Others, more schooled in the Scriptures, hope for the Messiah – the true King – to bring God's long-promised kingdom. But what could possibly overpower the reigning empire?

From what we know of the time, Jesus would have walked along roads sometimes lined with Roman crosses. On them hung his countrymen: a warning about what rebels can expect. Such was the end for many a would-be Messiah.

Joseph, his adoptive father, taught Jesus his trade. He was a builder, and Jesus worked at that for the great majority of his adult life. Then, aged 30, this unschooled nobody from Galilee makes a public announcement. In his distinctive northern accent he proclaims that the long-promised kingdom has come. And he's it.[3]

He quickly assembles an unlikely following of no-hopers and miscreants: ill-educated fishermen; despised tax collectors; prostitutes; criminals; political zealots; and notorious 'sinners'. Within a few short years he has changed the world forever.

This travelling preacher never graduated from the recognised academies, never accepted political office, never entered religious orders, never joined the military. He never founded a school, never fathered a dynasty, never wrote a book, never lead an army, never had an ounce of earthly power. He was butchered as a blasphemer in his thirties yet today he commands more allegiance than any human has or could. Billions call him Lord. Not bad for a kid born in a shed.

An unlikely launch

Jesus was a public relations disaster area. Anyone employed to maintain the brand integrity of 'Messiah Ministries™' would soon resign with nervous exhaustion.

For his launch onto the world stage he chooses a National Failures Convention. We'll see more on this in the next chapter but, in brief, let's picture the scene. Crowds are lining the banks of the Jordan River and Jesus' cousin, John, is baptising waifs and strays. 'Baptising' means giving someone a ritual wash. It's a sign of the spiritual cleansing we all need deep down. The only qualification for this washing is the acknowledgement that you need it.[4]

Jesus shows up to the Failures Convention and promptly dives in the water. It's a marketing disaster for Team Jesus. It looks for all the world like he too is a spiritual failure. But he doesn't seem to mind. He's happy to be counted among the messy people. This is his idea of a launch event.[5]

His inaugural address is just as strange. Back in his local synagogue, Jesus is invited to give the Bible reading. As the scroll of the prophet Isaiah is handed to him, he chooses a section where the Messiah is speaking:

> God's life-giving Spirit flows through me to proclaim good news to the poor, freedom for the prisoners, sight for the blind, liberation for the oppressed. All God's grace and blessings are available through me.[6]

How do you follow such a reading? Jesus simply says, 'The wait is over. Here I am!'[7]

The people are thrilled. The Messiah has come. But soon they realise this is not the Messiah they had wanted. He's far too gracious for their liking. As Jesus begins preaching, he declares just how far God's blessings extend. The Spirit flowing from *this* Messiah is for the poor and the pariah – even those of the surrounding nations.[8]

The people are furious. There are limits to the love of God, surely. They don't want a Messiah overflowing to the nations, to the unclean, to outcasts. This Messiah demolishes their carefully maintained systems. They can't have that.[9]

The congregation soon turns lynch mob and Jesus' inaugural address ends with him escaping an early martyrdom. It's a sign of things to come. Jesus brings to the world an unbounded offer of life and liberation. To the poor, the prisoners, the blind and the oppressed he is received gladly. To the rich, the strong, the religious and the comfortable he provokes anger and violence.

Something's building

Undeterred, Jesus sets about recruiting for his kingdom – first stop: the docks. He picks three fishermen, renaming one of them Peter, meaning 'the rock'. Peter was anything but a rock – he was impulsive and bullish. Yet within a few years Peter will be Christ's chief spokesman – chosen not from a house of prayer or a house of learning, but chosen from a fishing boat.[10]

Jesus' next recruit? A leper. According to the ancient Scriptures this man was spiritually unclean and contagiously so. Day after day the world flees from this man. Jesus reaches out and says, 'Be clean.' He doesn't run from bad contagions; he spreads good ones.[11]

Something is building. Here is the long-promised kingdom: a builder-turned-rabbi, three unemployed fishermen and an ex-leper. Who's next?

Jesus is teaching in a house bursting at the seams with fascinated enquirers.[12] The religious policemen – called Pharisees – catch wind of this new kid on the block. They travel from miles around, some from the capital, Jerusalem, to investigate. Pushing their way through the crowd, they *sit* at the front. Picture the room – a heaving crowd of common folk and these elder statesmen, seated, cross-legged, cross-armed, their whole posture screaming: 'Alright Galilean, what have you got?'

At that moment, pieces of roof cave in and four faces peer down. They've brought their paralysed friend to see Jesus. This was the only way through. So they lower their friend on a mat through this makeshift skylight.

We're not told whether the Pharisees rose to make room. But if they were scandalised by the cheek of the roof-crashers, they are outraged by Jesus' response. Seeing the desperation of these men, Jesus declares, 'Friend, your sins are forgiven.'[13]

Wherever Jesus sees faith (or desperation – it all seems the same to him), he has forgiveness on a hair trigger. There and then he unloads a heaven of blessings on the man. It's much more than the paralysed man bargained for and far more than the Pharisees could stomach: 'Only God can forgive. Who does he think he is?'[14]

Yet Jesus not only claims to dispense the blessings of God, he delivers in full view of them. 'Up you get,' he tells the man. 'Safe journey home. Don't forget your mat.'[15] The crowd are astonished as the man rises and walks out into the sunshine.

Jesus simply speaks and new life springs up. Here is a serious contender for Messiah. The people are delighted. The Pharisees are livid. Nonetheless, the kingdom bursts in – relentless and unmanageable. It crash-lands on planet earth as a builder-turned-rabbi, three unemployed fishermen, an ex-leper and a former paralytic. Who's next?

This is a real shock. Jesus spots the most hated man in the province – a turn-coat villain called Levi, later known as Matthew. As an ancient 'tax collector', Levi was about as depraved as it's possible to be: socially, morally and spiritually. *Socially* he was a collaborator with the Romans; *morally* he was a white-collar criminal, stealing from his own people; *spiritually* he had betrayed the God of Israel. The masses despised him as a traitor. The religious denounced him as 'unclean'. Jesus recruits him without a second thought. 'Follow me,' he says, and now *everyone* is scandalised.[16]

What kind of recruitment policy is this? Jesus' kingdom is unlike any seen before. There is nothing careful, calculating or containable about this movement. Frankly it looks like an almighty free-for-all.

That night Levi holds a dinner party to celebrate his new path. Jesus is the guest of honour. The house is filled with outcasts of every stripe. Outraged, the Pharisees gatecrash the party to complain about the guest list (which is an odd tactic for gatecrashers). They ask: 'Why do you eat with tax collectors and sinners?'

From the heart of the room, Jesus replies, 'It's not the healthy who need a doctor; it's the sick. I haven't come for "the righteous"; I've come for "sinners".[17]

Now press pause. Study the scene. The religious police are trying to get in on Jesus' party. They want to make sure he is enforcing proper recruitment procedures. They want the riff-raff out. Jesus remains resolutely at the heart of the party and it is *he* who pronounces the judgement. He is for the outcast, the marginalised and the depraved. And he stands against the most respectable men of the day.

If the religious do not recognise their own sickness, they can slink away. And when they go, press play, let the music strike up again. They leave God's Messiah to feast with sinners.

Why? Because Jesus is a Doctor for the sick, a Liberator for the oppressed,

Jesus is a Doctor for the sick, a Liberator for the oppressed, a Saviour for sinners.

a Saviour for sinners. That's the kind of kingdom he reveals. That's the kind of King he is.

If you want to find Jesus, look for a dinner party. 'I have come eating and drinking' is one of his mottos. 'Heaven is a feast,' he's saying. 'And I'm extending the invitation.'[18]

The last are first – the first are last

At one dinner Jesus is the guest of a Pharisee called Simon.[19] In walks a prostitute. She knows Jesus. She loves Jesus. Everyone can see there has been a history between them. It's not what they think, nothing scandalous has happened, but *something* has gone on. And the prostitute is overwhelmed with gratitude. Ignoring the other guests, she rushes towards him and falls at his feet, a blubbering wreck. She kisses his feet, washes them with her tears, dries them with her hair and perfumes them with the most expensive ointment. No-one knows where to look – except Jesus. He simply receives her gift.

Jesus has no thought for his reputation. He doesn't seek to 'set the record straight' though all eyes are on him. He doesn't, for a second, distance himself from this woman. He is not ashamed of her and he refuses to embarrass her, though she has made the whole room squirm.

To an outraged Simon, Jesus has only words of challenge. To the woman, there's only blessing, forgiveness and salvation. 'This man welcomes sinners, and eats with them!' cry his enemies.[20] He's 'a friend of ... sinners!' they splutter.[21] The Pharisees consider these to be slurs. Jesus wears the accusations with pride.

Here is the kingdom foretold by the prophets: a realm for the poor, the oppressed, the blind and the lame. Here is the King who comes for the uneducated, the unclean and the unnoticed. Here is Jesus, exploding all categories, dismaying the careful and disgusting the respectable. A holy man hugging lepers. A righteous man feasting with sinners. A pure man kissed by prostitutes.

On the other hand, how does Jesus consider the pompous and the powerful? He rounds on them with volley after volley of the most devastating polemic. Just listen to his scorching denunciations. The religious are like:

- Swine trampling on pearls.[22]
- Wolves masquerading as sheep.[23]
- Mansions built on sand.[24]
- Bad yeast, infecting the batch.[25]
- Tutting optometrists with a plank of four-by-two in their eye.[26]
- White-washed tombs, dead on the inside.[27]
- Food critics, choking on a camel but complaining about the fly in their soup.[28]

According to Jesus, these moralisers pile heavy loads on the people, never lifting a finger to help them. They commission fanfares to accompany their charitable donations. They choose street corners for their babbling prayer times. They even disfigure their faces to 'hint' at their pious fasting. Finding true goodness in these religious leaders is like trying to pick grapes from thistles or figs from thorn bushes.[29]

Jesus places the religious elites, thinly disguised, into his most famous stories. Perhaps you know the tale of 'the Good Samaritan'. Before that charitable stranger comes to the aid of a dying man, it's the *priests* who cross the road to avoid him.[30]

You may have heard of 'the Prodigal Son' – the story of a young boy who runs off with the family wealth. As Jesus tells the story, the father welcomes home his young tearaway but the 'elder brother' seethes with rage. That's what the Pharisees are: stuck-up elder brothers, fuming at a father's mercy.[31] So many of Jesus' stories (he calls them 'parables') are told *against* the holiest-looking men on the face of the planet.

Jesus actually coined the term 'hypocrite'. Before, it was simply the word for a masked actor. Yet Jesus applies it to the religious elites of his day. Hypocrites! Like a gleaming goblet, says Jesus, brilliant on the outside, mildew and maggots on the inside. Hypocrites! To those who claim to be heaven's gate-keepers, Jesus asks, 'How will you escape from hell?'[32]

Yet to the weak and marginalised, to those who admit their spiritual poverty, he's a Shepherd for lost sheep; a Doctor for the sick; a Ransom for captives; Bread for the hungry; a Fountain for the thirsty; and a Friend for the friendless.[33] He forgives the guilty; restores the shameful; frees the bound; leads the lost; heals the sick; and raises the dead.

Love him or hate him

Little children flock to him; the religious want rid of him. Those in need want him near; those in power want him dead. Notorious 'low-lifes' hang off his every word, but so do the religious authorities. They try desperately to catch him in some theological blunder. He never makes one.

Jesus' comebacks under pressure have become famous: Give 'to Caesar what is Caesar's, and to God what is God's'. '... all who draw the sword will die by the sword.' 'Let any one of you who is without sin be the first to throw a stone.'[34] He silences the pretentious and exhilarates the poor.

Yet nothing is done for show. As Isaiah predicted, this Messiah 'does not cry aloud in the streets';[35] he hires no Public Relations consultants, calls no press conferences, seeks no fame. In a phrase which Jesus coins himself: he never 'lords it over' people.[36]

Isaiah had said, 'He won't snap off a reed, no matter how battered. He won't snuff out a candle, no matter how smouldering.'[37] The Saviour of the world is tender with the broken, gentle with the bruised and patient with the weak. Yet at the same time he wields almighty power.

In his presence sickness flees, limbs strengthen and backs straighten. The lame walk, the blind see, even the dead are raised to life. Jesus is like a walking, talking garden of Eden – a sphere of paradise on earth. With him wrongs are righted, darkness is dispelled and everything that's twisted gets smoothed out again.

The world put right

For 12 years a woman has suffered continual haemorrhaging.[38] She has spent everything on doctors and only gotten worse. She hears that Jesus is in town and remembers an old prophecy about the Messiah – healing is 'in his wings'.[39] So she presses in with the rest of the crowd, just to touch the hem of his robe (or the 'wing' of his robe as the Jews called it). All she wants is a zap-and-run. She grabs the hem. And like sunshine into a valley of deep shadow, it happens. She's whole again. She feels it. He feels it too. He stops.

'Who touched me?' asks Jesus.[40] Such a stupid question from such a smart Teacher. Who touched him? Everyone touched him. Everyone always touches him. He's in constant danger of being crushed. But Jesus refuses to be an impersonal dispenser of heavenly goodies. He wants a face-to-face encounter. 'Who touched me?' he asks.

Trembling, the woman tells Jesus everything. He hears her whole story, looks her in the eye and calls her 'Daughter'. He even commends her for her faith – though it was so meagre, so impulsive, so born of desperation. If we were being unkind, we might say her faith bordered on the superstitious. Nevertheless, Jesus praises her, blesses her and says, 'Go in peace.'[41]

No-one is simply a face in the crowd for Jesus. No-one is an anonymous beneficiary. No-one is an awkward encumbrance. This is all the more remarkable when you understand the context. Jesus is heading somewhere as this woman grabs hold of him. He is on his way to save a life.

A 12-year-old girl lies at death's door.[42] She is the daughter of perhaps the most important man in town – the synagogue ruler. This ruler has been begging Jesus to hurry home and heal his little girl. There isn't a minute to lose. It's *then* that Jesus brings the scene to a maddening halt. He wants to know who touched him.

And as they all wait for Jesus to have his precious face-to-face, word comes from the ruler's home: 'Your daughter is dead.'[43] Here is the father's hell-on-earth scenario. Here is everything he's been battling for weeks. But now the fight is over. The adrenaline sours. Four words have destroyed his world.

Yet Jesus meets them with five of his own: 'Don't be afraid, trust me.'[44] What kind of man says, 'Don't be afraid, trust me' to a freshly bereaved father? Jesus does. Without wavering he leads the man home, throws out the grieving relatives and sits on the end of the girl's death bed. Taking her hand, he says, 'My daughter, it's time to get up.' Instantly she rouses as though from an afternoon nap. While the household erupts with awe and amazement, Jesus simply tells them, 'Give her something to eat.'[45]

There is absolutely nothing flashy about Jesus. He makes no fuss. He has no need for approval or acknowledgement. He simply gets on and saves both 'daughters' – the haemorrhaging woman and the little girl – in his own way and in his own time. Nothing hurries him; nothing daunts him; nothing thwarts him.

We 'race against the clock', bound by that ultimate limit on our lives: death. He seems oblivious to any such limit. He simply moves from need to need at his own pace, with his own priorities – priorities which are infuriatingly different to ours. He is baffling, exasperating, unmanageable, but unwaveringly good.

He is the Lord who serves.

The powers he wields are not 'displays of the supernatural'. He never commands mountains to blow their tops like volcanoes. He never makes donkeys to tap-dance and sing show tunes. He never sets off a heavenly fireworks show to draw a crowd. The miracles aren't there to show 'who's the boss'. Far more they show what *kind* of 'boss' Jesus is. He is the Lord who *serves*. He heals the sick, cleanses lepers, feeds the hungry and raises the dead.

Whatever you think about the possibility of miracles or the truthfulness of these accounts, at least recognise this: they are not parlour tricks done to impress. This is God's kingdom breaking in, not to overawe us but to restore and heal us. Jesus wields his power, not to keep us down but to raise us up.

These were Jesus' actions; his words were equally authoritative.

Messiah complex

What do you say about a humble man claiming to be God? These claims were not mad scribblings in his journal that were unearthed posthumously. They were integral to his teaching, tripping off his tongue as a matter of course.

According to Jesus, he is the one Bread of life, without whom we starve. He is the one Light of the world, without whom we walk in darkness. He is the one good Shepherd, without whom we're lost. He is the one Way to God, the one Truth of reality, the one Life that is truly life.[46]

He can't speak of judgement day without putting himself at the centre of our cosmic conclusion – he is the Judge. He can't set eyes on Jerusalem without lamenting the way they've treated him for the last millennia. He can't mention Abraham without saying how terrific it was when they met – 2000 years earlier.[47]

When a follower asks how he can see God, Jesus directs him, 'Right here. Keep looking at me. The Father is in me and I am in the Father.'[48] Jesus is always conscious of, and always articulating, a unique bond between himself and 'the Most High'.

While praying out loud, Jesus reminisces with the Almighty about their glorious companionship *before the world began*.[49] He thinks of himself as *very* old – as old as the God he's praying to. At one point he prays, 'you loved me before the creation of the world'.[50] This eternal bond is a union of love. That's why he almost never calls God 'God' – he is 'Father'. And Jesus is his unique 'Son'. He's an eternal chip off the old block: the Father's beloved, his executor and his heir.

Apparently the Father has committed everything into his hands: life, salvation, judgement, the cosmos even.[51] At least that's what Jesus keeps insisting. Whatever Jesus does, he assures us he is doing only what the Father has told him to do – only what the Father has shown him beforehand.[52] He speaks only the words the Father has given him. When he acts, he is performing God's work of re-creation. When he speaks, he is pronouncing God's verdict. When he blesses, it is God's blessing. When he forgives, it is the undiluted forgiveness of God himself. As far as Jesus is concerned, to see him is to see God. Our response to him is our response to God.[53]

As far as Jesus is concerned, to see him is to see God. Our response to him is our response to God.

Jesus continually declares himself to be 'sent' into the world. Not *born and raised in Galilee. Sent.* From *heaven*. Sent from the loving embrace of his Father. Sent to save the world.[54]

Separated by centuries of Christendom, it is difficult to hear these claims with their original force. 'Yeah,' we concede, 'Jesus *would* say that, after all he was *Jesus*.' But that misses the point. Jesus wasn't *Jesus* when he said this stuff – not in the popular consciousness. To them he was a self-taught preacher standing up in the middle of history, claiming he got all things started in the beginning and that he'll wrap all things up at the end. On the face of it he's a complete nobody to anybody, but he claims to be *the* Somebody for everybody.

Today we speak about 'having a messiah complex'. Jesus had the original condition. And just when people wanted to ask him, 'Who do you think you are!?' he rounds on them and asks the same question: 'Who do *you* think I am?'[55] Divine? Demonic? Deranged? He forces us to extremes.

I don't know how you consider Jesus today. It's astonishing to me how people manage to have lukewarm opinions of Jesus, labelling him a 'spiritual man', 'good teacher' or 'proto-hippy'. It's popular to think of Jesus as a nice Jewish boy, suitable to take home to mother. In reality there was a time his own family tried to get him sectioned.[56] Those in his presence were forced to extreme conclusions. Some were persuaded he's from heaven; others were convinced he's from hell. But those who saw him first-hand could find no earthly explanation for him.[57]

He owns divine titles; accepts divine worship; performs divine acts; pronounces divine verdicts; and makes divine oaths.[58] In short, he walks around planet earth like he owns the place.

Such almighty self-assurance infuses all his words – his moral teaching included. Speaking as the proprietor of planet earth, Jesus is never shy of sharing his vision for the good life.

The good life

'Forgive,' he commands.[59] 'That's sweet,' we think (because we've forgotten how gut-wrenchingly unbearable it is). When we realise he means business, we respond, 'I tried that once, but they hurt me again, so ...'

'So forgive again,' he insists.

'Well now, hang on, Jesus,' we protest. 'Haven't you heard of moral hazard? Let's not be doormats here. How often should we forgive?'

Peter puts a hypothetical figure to Jesus: 'Up to seven times?'[60] That's Peter for you – too keen by half. Who forgives the same person for the same crime seven times?

Jesus replies, 'I tell you, not seven times, but seventy-seven times.'[61] It's a Jewish way of saying 'endlessly'. When it comes to forgiveness, we should offer free, unlimited downloads.

And while we're left gasping, he moves on: 'Oh, and don't worry. Ever. About anything. Don't worry about tomorrow; your wealth; your health; your body; your clothing; or where your next meal is coming from. Look at the birds, do they look worried?'[62]

'Umm ... well, Jesus, birds don't have bills to pay. Can we get serious for a minute?'

But Jesus is serious – in the most carefree way. He is proclaiming *his* kind of life for all to see. And it's free – wildly, bafflingly, frighteningly free. 'Don't give a second thought to tomorrow. Tomorrow has enough worries of its own. Do you think your heavenly Father has forgotten you? He has numbered the hairs on your head. When did worrying add a single hour to your life? And anyway, what's the worst that can happen? They can only kill you.'[63]

As we are reeling from the 'don't worry' thunderbolt, he strikes again ...

'Love,' he demands, and we breathe a bit easier. 'OK,' we think, 'finally something in our grasp.' But it's not. Don't 'love the world', he says.[64] What does that even mean? 'Love the actual people who cross your path, no matter how different or disagreeable they are. Don't just love people who love you back. That's hardly worthy of the name. Love the unlovely and unloveable. Love your enemies.'[65]

'Enemies?' we gasp.

'Yes,' he insists. 'Pray God's richest blessings for them. Find ways to do them good and serve them.

'If someone slaps you on one cheek, stand your ground and offer them the other. If a soldier forces you to carry his pack for a mile, take it two miles. If someone sues you for your coat, offer them the shirt off your back. Give without boundaries, without bitterness, without bargaining.[66]

'And don't climb the ladder,' he goes on. 'Don't be upwardly mobile. Everyone is trying to get out from under, to get on top, to get ahead. Not you. You should sink to the bottom, give up your rights, be the servant of all.'[67]

'Sweet sentiments,' we sigh. 'You're right, Jesus, we must have a spirit of self-giving.' But he won't let us spiritualise it ...

'Giving yourself means giving your stuff – your possessions, your money. Give to anyone who asks you. Don't keep accumulating, upselling, upscaling and upgrading. Sell your possessions; give to the poor. Lend without hope of repayment. Your life does not consist in the stuff that you own. That stuff ends up owning you. Give it away.'[68]

In all his teaching he is basically saying, 'Unfurl those folded arms. Receive from the Father then pour out to the world. Freely receive; freely give. Open yourself out. Extend yourself into the world in self-giving love. This is freedom.'

We think of service and freedom as opposites. In Jesus we see how they coincide. He is completely given over to others and completely in possession of himself. What he tells us to do, he embodies in himself: 'If you want to find yourself, give yourself away.'[69]

He is completely given over to others and completely in possession of himself.

Jesus urges us to ignore the constraints that frame our vision of life. He wants us to give as though unconfined by wealth, health, danger or death. To live without slavery to worry, greed, lust or pride. The way of Jesus means not holding back, not shutting down, not clinging on. He exhorts us to be the person with nothing to lose, nothing to prove, nothing to hide, nothing to fear.

This is the good life as preached by Jesus: completely poured out; completely free; completely terrifying. At every point we want to say, 'Nice idea, Jesus, but life doesn't work like that.'

And essentially he responds, 'I know *your* life doesn't work like that. But mine does. And if my life and your life don't match up, who has the problem?'

Jesus constantly teaches that we have the problem – a deep one. The good life doesn't come out of us because the good life isn't *in* us – not naturally. He teaches that we are like bad trees producing bad fruit.[70] He puts it another way: our hearts are like dirty fountains.[71] They spew forth selfishness and lies. Our very being is corrupted at its source. Jesus even calls his closest friends 'evil'.[72] He loves them. He is completely for them. But he calls it how he sees it. Apparently we're doing it wrong. And our wrong *doing* reveals a wrong *being*.

We spend our lives protecting and justifying ourselves. He spends *himself* in complete abandonment. Our folded arms are at odds with his arms-wide offer. And therefore Jesus opposes our kind of life – in the strongest possible terms.

Jesus never tries to meet us halfway. He doesn't lower the bar. His teaching is not: '*Do your best* to forgive. Try and love *a little more.* Don't worry *so much*.' There can be no compromise – no coalition government – in his kingdom. Our kind of life is at odds with his. It is cursed. It must be judged.

Judgement's a-coming

'There's a fire on the way,' he remarks without a hint of regret. 'It will consume the whole earth and how I wish it were already blazing.'[73] He speaks as though the fire has been shut up inside him, as though he has been keeping it back for far too long. But it won't be withheld forever.

'It will all be rubble,' he says, switching the metaphor from furnace to building site. 'First God's House, the Temple, will come down. But that's just the beginning. The whole earth is scheduled for demolition. Not one stone will be left on another, not one nation at peace with another. Rocks and realms and relations will be flung apart.'[74]

Or – yet another angle on it – there is a poisoned chalice to be passed around the human race. It is a cup of judgement for all to drink.[75]

Jesus speaks of judgement relentlessly. He is strongest on the subject whenever he encounters the self-righteous. But it's a universal reality to be reckoned with. Judgement is coming, root and branch.

Judgement isn't his *final* word on the world. Jesus speaks of immeasurable hope beyond the judgement. Just as the wrecking ball gives way to the builder and decorator, so judgement paves the way for new life. Beyond the birth pains, there's birth! Beyond the demolition, there's a renewed earth. Beyond the poisoned chalice is a feast.[76] The blazing language turns, at points, into sunshine language.[77] But there's no getting around it. The path to life goes through death: Jesus is adamant about that.

Yet, of all his teaching on judgement, the greatest shock is this: Jesus stands at the head of this cosmic shakedown. He is not simply the dispenser of judgement, he is its chief *victim*!

He is not simply the dispenser of judgement, he is its chief victim!

From his baptism onwards we see how Jesus joins us in our predicament. He's not the kind of Lord who will 'wash his hands' of our problems. Instead he dives into the whole sorry mess to take responsibility for it. Therefore, with all the judgement the world deserves, it will be Jesus himself who shoulders it. *He* has the supreme 'baptism of fire' to undergo.[78] *He* is the true temple, the House of God, to be torn down.[79] *He* must drink humanity's cup of judgement.[80] *He* is the sacrifice for the sins of the world.[81] Jesus is the Judge who is judged.

Just before his crucifixion Jesus says, 'Now comes the judgement of the world ... Now I am lifted up from the earth.'[82] He speaks of the world's judgement converging on him. He pictures himself as an almighty human shield bearing the coming onslaught.

Judgement's a-coming. There's no escaping it. But Jesus makes it his life's work to endure this himself. Through his cross he sets himself up as a refuge for the weak, a shelter from the storm, a safehouse for the world.

According to Jesus, his godforsaken death is not an unfortunate twist of fate. It is the reason he was sent.[83] He *must* go to Jerusalem for where else can a true martyr die?[84] He *must* be betrayed by his own people. He *must* be handed over to the Romans. He *must* be mocked, flogged and killed. He *must* suffer and after three days he will rise again.[85] The Messiah has a death wish and he won't be talked out of it.

Destined to die

The night of his arrest Jesus gathers his friends for a final meal.[86] He is hours from an excruciating execution. They don't know it, but he does.

Someone has forgotten their middle-eastern manners – no foot basin has been provided. No matter, the Son of God will do it. He leaves his place of honour at the table, takes off his robe, puts on an apron and kneels at each of his friends' feet. As he washes and pats them dry, Peter's skin crawls. Only the lowest of slaves took this job. 'Don't you dare wash my feet, Master. I should wash yours!'[87]

But Jesus is adamant. He will show them his love to the last – the love of a Master become Slave. On his knees he shows them the true extent of his earlier claim: 'I only ever do what I see my Father doing.'[88] Here is the stature of deity: stooping to serve – and to feed.

Jesus is adamant. He will show them his love to the last – the love of a Master become Slave.

Later that night Jesus breaks bread in his hands saying, 'This is my body – broken apart for you.' He pours out red wine saying, 'This is my life-blood – emptied to fill you.'[89] It all proclaims his death so powerfully – but the disciples aren't getting it.

After dinner he takes them to a garden overlooking Jerusalem. There they see him as never before. His face is twisted in anguish. His sweat, mingling with burst blood vessels, drips crimson from his face. 'I'm overwhelmed with sorrow,' he confides. 'It's killing me. Please pray at my side.' And when he prays, he falls on his face crying, 'Father, my Father, there must be another way. Not *this* cup. Please not *this* cup.'[90]

While he agonises, his friends sleep off their dinners. Soon they will all desert him and Peter – the 'Rock' – will crumble under the slightest pressure. Three times this night Peter will deny even knowing his master.[91] There is no help for Jesus. Only he can drink the cup. Only he can enter the furnace. Only he can take this judgement on the cross.

Through his prayerful wrestling, Jesus rises ready to meet his fate, and to meet it with an other-worldly poise.

The betrayer, Judas, arrives.[92] He has brought an armed mob from the temple. Jesus responds to his friend the way he will to every accuser this night: with perfect stillness and a disturbing sincerity. 'Are you betraying me with a kiss, Judas?'[93] Like a mirror, Jesus reflects back to his enemies their own groundless evil.

The Judge of all is led away in chains and brought before hastily assembled courts.[94] Six 'hearings' in four locations are held this night. The whole scenario is an artist's dream. Finally, humanity has hold of its Maker. Finally, he's been brought in for questioning. Yet the court-room drama does not unfold to plan.

The one in the dock is silent and unimpeachable. It's his accusers who are exposed. They employ illegal, night-time hearings, false witnesses, torture and intimidation. The more they seek his guilt, the more they reveal their own. Repeatedly they put the question to him: 'Are you the Messiah?'

Jesus answers variously: 'Is that your own idea? ... You have said so.'[95] Jesus never plays the part of the accused. He is constantly seeking to draw a confession from his prosecutors. Yet when he has had enough, he seals his own fate.

'Are you the Messiah, the Son of the Blessed One?' they demand.

'I am!' replies Jesus.

And so they cry, 'Blasphemy!'[96]

This is the crime for which he is executed. When humanity judges its Maker, every charge is thrown out of court but one. His unforgiveable sin is *to be who he is*. For this he must die.

But, of course, this is what Jesus had been saying all along: he must die. And he must die precisely as these kangaroo courts had 'determined'. Here is a condemned man, silently calling the shots in his own execution.

The Roman soldiers, to whom he is delivered, twist a crown from thorns and beat it down onto his skull. They dress him in a royal robe and offer mock homage. In their abuse they cannot help but hail him as King.[97] They blindfold him and take turns in punching him. 'Prophesy!' they taunt, 'Who hit you?'[98] Yet even as he's beaten the prophecies of old are being fulfilled. Seven centuries earlier Isaiah had predicted this moment:

> He was despised and rejected by mankind,
> a man of suffering, and familiar with pain.
> Like one from whom people hide their faces
> he was despised, and we held him in low esteem.
> Surely he took up our pain
> and bore our suffering,
> yet we considered him punished by God,
> stricken by him, and afflicted.
> But he was pierced for our transgressions,
> he was crushed for our iniquities;
> the punishment that brought us peace was on him,
> and by his wounds we are healed.
> We all, like sheep, have gone astray,
> each of us has turned to our own way;
> and the LORD has laid on him
> the iniquity of us all.
> He was oppressed and afflicted,
> yet he did not open his mouth;
> he was led like a lamb to the slaughter,
> and as a sheep before its shearers is silent,
> so he did not open his mouth.[99]

The Scriptures are coming true. This unholy torture of a 'dead man walking' unfolds according to the most ancient plan.

Jesus carries his cross through a jeering crowd.[100] At the place of execution he is nailed to the cross-beam and hoisted naked into the sky.[101] Every Jew knew the meaning of this death. The Old Testament had proclaimed that those lifted up on a pole were dying the death of the godforsaken.[102] Here was a blasphemer, condemned under God's curse.

The crowd hurls abuse: 'He saved others, but he can't save himself! He's the king of Israel! Let him come down now from the cross, and we will believe in him.'[103]

Jesus responds as he had taught his followers. He prays, 'Father, forgive them.' This was the first of seven, now immortal, 'words' from the cross.[104] His second word is addressed to the condemned man beside him: he promises him paradise. Next he commends his mother to the care of his friend, John. Then he prays an ancient psalm, expressing his godforsaken anguish. He pants with thirst. He prays another psalm, to commend his spirit to his Father's care. And, with his final breath, he bellows one last word: 'Finished!'

It seems an absurd end to an absurd life. A naked man chokes to death in front of a mocking crowd and his final cry is triumph. 'Paid!' you could translate it. Or 'Mission accomplished! ... I did it!' says the bleeding victim.

The man with a Messiah complex has his death wish fulfilled. A spear is thrust up into his heart, just to make sure.[105] The corpse who claimed to be Creator is taken from the cross and wrapped in grave clothes packed with 30 kilograms of spices. That Friday afternoon he is laid in a tomb. The entrance is sealed with a giant stone.[106] Jesus is dead and buried.

After the darkness, light

Few people get to spoil their own wake. If the opportunity fell to me, I'm sure I'd overdo it: 'Boo!' I'd say. And, 'Ta da!' And, no doubt, '... the look on your face!'

By way of contrast, the day Jesus defeated death was a day of sublime understatement. When the 'big reveal' came, he played it very cool.

On the Sunday after crucifixion a follower called Mary Magdalene hurries to the tomb at first light.[107] She is there to pay her respects but, shockingly, the tomb is empty. She concludes what anyone would suppose: someone has stolen the body! Jesus approaches from behind, asking, 'Woman, why are you crying?'[108] She mistakes him for the gardener and continues her enquiries. Finally Jesus identifies himself. He doesn't speak his name, he speaks *hers*: 'Mary!' And the world of this mourner – and all mourners – is transformed.

In the afternoon a crestfallen couple are returning from Jerusalem to their hometown.[109] They had known and followed Jesus. They had hoped he was the One. In all likelihood they had watched him die. A stranger joins the conversation. 'What are you discussing?'[110] he asks, innocently. They begin to tell the tale that had gripped Jerusalem that weekend.

By this stage most of us would have cracked. With a flourish, we would surely end the sorrow with a grand unveiling. But as with Jesus' life, so beyond death, he resists the hype. He doesn't end the sorrow but enters it. And then, without fanfare, he rehearses the Bible's story with them. 'Didn't the Messiah *have* to endure this suffering and *then* rise again? Isn't this exactly what the Ancient Scriptures have been saying all along?'[111] Through a Bible study and through breaking bread with his friends, Jesus reveals himself. No sooner does the penny drop than Jesus departs. Yet he leaves them with hearts burning and hope renewed.

Later that day the disciples are holding a tense prayer meeting.[112] They are in fear for their lives. Their leader has been executed, perhaps they are next. Jesus arrives, speaking his favourite post-resurrection greeting. 'Peace!' he says, which never fails to disquiet them![113] Here is the Master they had denied and deserted that very weekend. The man they had left for dead has tracked them down from beyond the grave.

Understandably they are speechless. So Jesus says it again: 'Peace!' He shows them his nail-scarred hands. He points to his spear wound. These battle scars are badges of honour. They are proof of a love that had taken him to hell and back. When the disciples see it – when they see *him* – they are overwhelmed. Peace had endured hell for them. Peace had tracked them down. Peace had upended every certainty, turning guilt to grace and death to life. Nothing could ever be the same.

Jesus does not return from the grave to exact vengeance – the very opposite. He comes through death in order to share his victory.

And so for 40 days Jesus continues to appear to his friends. At every point foolish, faithless and failed people are met with undeserved grace. To the despairing couple, Jesus gives heart-melting Bible truth. To 'Doubting Thomas', Jesus gives proof of his death-defying love.[114] For Peter, Jesus cooks breakfast and restores this deserter in full.[115] Jesus does not return from the grave to exact vengeance – the very opposite. He comes through death in order to *share* his victory.

These encounters are not hallucinations. Jesus appears to whole multitudes at once, 500 on one occasion. They are not ghostly apparitions. He eats many a meal, goes for long country walks, enjoys fishing with friends and barbecues on the beach. For Jesus 'life after death' is not *less* real; it is not *less* earthy or physical. He comes through death to give us a foretaste of the future. The 'life after death' which Jesus pioneers is about feasting joy, physical hope and face-to-face relationships.

The aftermath

In the six weeks following his resurrection Jesus commissions his followers to spread the news: 'Go, tell the world – sins are forgiven, lives are made new and the world is put right in me.'[116] Such an earth-shattering message is entrusted to a small band of unschooled peasants. With Jesus returning to heaven, these complete unknowns mouth off about a crucified Jew back from the dead.

Thousands believe.[117] In the very city where Jesus taught, died and was buried, the followers proclaim his empty tomb. None can refute the facts. The tomb is empty, the Scriptures have been fulfilled, the Messiah has come and the world is turned upside down.

Within a few hundred years the empire that crucified Jesus will hail him as Lord; the penniless preacher will become the central figure of human history; and his band of followers will grow to the largest sociological movement the world has ever known.

History written by a loser

Twenty centuries ago Jesus said, 'I will build my church; and the gates of hell shall not prevail against it.'[118] If you were present to hear the forecast, you would probably consider it lunacy – a particularly conceited lunacy too. Today more people will follow Jesus than at any prior moment in history. Tomorrow will break the record again. As will the next day. From Burma to Brazil and from Britain to Botswana, the world remains captivated by Jesus.

No-one needs to explain the legacy of a great warrior, a great politician or a great writer. Their impact is easily understood. But what about a nobody followed by no-hopers? What about a poor Jew crucified in disgrace? If history is written by the winners, how is it that a loser like Jesus towers above the rest?

Historian Philip Schaff has said:

> Jesus of Nazareth, without money and arms, conquered more millions than Alexander, Caesar, Mohammed and Napoleon; without science and learning,

> he shed more light on things human and divine than all the philosophers and scholars combined; without the eloquence of the school, he spoke words of life such as were never spoken before nor since and produced effects that lie beyond the reach of orator or poet; without writing a single line, he has set more pens in motion and furnished themes for more sermons, orations, discussions, works of art, learned volumes, and sweet songs of praise than the whole army of great men of ancient and modern times.[119]

'Jesus is Lord'

You have now heard something of the Jesus story. We had to go fast and the events were a blur, but everything you have read is taken from the original eye-witness records.

Perhaps you're not yet convinced that these Gospels are God's word, but at least be assured that these are the earliest, most thorough accounts. If we are to do business with the foremost figure in world history, *these* are the histories we must consult.

In chapter 7 we will consider the trustworthiness of the Bible a little more but if you want to put these documents to the test, you can do no better than reading them for yourself. From now on I'll finish each chapter with a suggested reading from John's Gospel. John is the fourth biography in the New Testament and was written by Jesus' closest companion. As you read, ask yourself: What do I make of Jesus?

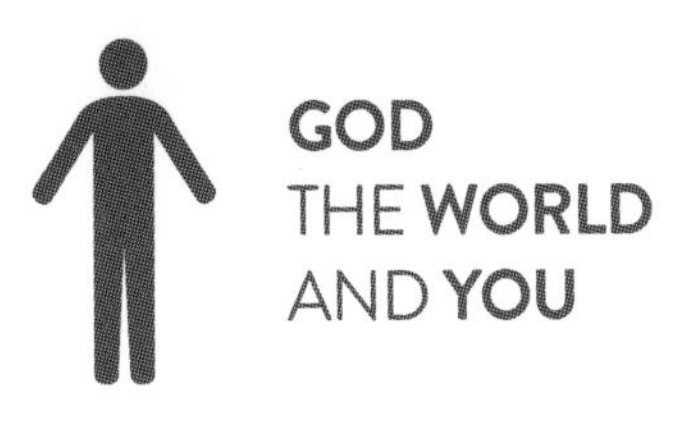

According to Christians Jesus is the lens through which everything comes into focus: God, the world and ourselves too. We become Christians when we recognise Jesus as the key to it all. The shorthand for this confession is 'Jesus is Lord'.[120] To say Jesus is 'Lord' means to recognise Jesus at the centre of everything. It means:

- Jesus is the true Revelation of *God.*
  Whatever else God is like, we recognise Jesus as his true image.
- Jesus is the true Ruler of *the world.*
  We have seen him go through death and out the other side to resurrection and we trust him to take the world through that same journey.
- Jesus is the true Master of *our lives.*
  He's not just a Lord for the world; he is *my* Lord – the One who has captured my heart and directs my life.

'Jesus is Lord' has all those connotations and it is the fundamental confession of the Christian.

15 years ago I still remember reading through the Gospels and being captivated by the person of Jesus. In him I saw a towering greatness and a stooping love that won my heart. I found myself believing. I couldn't have given you a detailed explanation of my beliefs. All I knew was that Jesus was insanely brilliant. He was *it*, he was *the One*, he was *ultimate*, *tops*, *numero uno*. I didn't know the phrase yet, but I had come to believe that Jesus is Lord.

I wonder how you respond to the phrase 'Jesus is Lord'? Perhaps it sounds strange, abstract or religious. Perhaps it sounds like a power play. To the Christian it sounds like good news. It means God is utterly Christ-like. It means the world is ruled by One who has loved me to death. It means my life is in safe hands forevermore. 'Jesus is Lord' is not a truth designed to drive us down into grovelling submission. 'Jesus is Lord' is the most liberating, joy-filled message imaginable.

In the next three chapters we're going to tease out the good news that Jesus is Lord. First we will see how Jesus stands at the centre of our vision of God – in particular he shows us God's THREE-ness. Then we will see how Jesus stands at the centre of our view of the world – in particular he reveals the world's TWO-ness. Finally we will see how Jesus stands at the centre of our own lives – he gives us our ONE-ness. Don't worry about those numbers for now – all will be revealed. The point is that Jesus is the heart of it all.

If you have been attracted to the person of Jesus thus far, I invite you to consider the most wonderful possibility: could it be that *this person* really defines reality? He *says* he does – could he be telling the truth?

- Might *this person* be God – and the kind of God who is actually worth knowing?
- Might *this person* have the final word in our world?
- Could *he* be the answer to our deepest personal longings?

If you start answering yes to those questions, watch out. You may just be becoming a Christian.

 **Watch this video: *three-two-one.org/Jesus***

Optional reading: John chapters 1–4

- 'The Word' is a title for Jesus (1:1; 1:14). Why do you think Jesus is described as God's *Word*?
- What kind of God does Jesus reveal?
- How is Jesus portrayed in these chapters?
- Jesus comes across some very different characters in these chapters. How does he respond to them?
- What do you think it would be like to meet Jesus?

• COMING UP IN CHAPTER 3 •

If the last chapter was a race through the countryside, this chapter is more like a ride in a hot-air balloon. Having dashed through the story of Jesus, now we rise up to get a bit of perspective. In particular we're asking this question: 'What kind of God does Jesus reveal?'

Here's our answer: God is a loving union of THREE. Jesus is the Son of God and he introduces us to his Father and to his Spirit. These are the THREE – the Father, Son and Holy Spirit – and they are unbreakably intertwined. According to Jesus, God has always been an eternal union of love.

Is that true? Is it possible? Does it even make any sense? Read on ...

3

GOD IS A LOVING UNION OF **THREE**

> The universe we observe has precisely the properties we should expect if there is, at bottom, no design, no purpose, no evil, no good, nothing but blind, pitiless indifference.
>
> —*Richard Dawkins*

> Underneath are the everlasting arms.
>
> —*Deuteronomy 33:27*

'God' is the slipperiest word in existence. Thousands of definitions vie for our attention, so where should we turn for clarity?

That's right, Ricky Gervais. Here he is explaining his atheism:

> Since the beginning of recorded history … historians have catalogued over 3700 supernatural beings, of which 2870 can be considered deities. So next

> time someone tells me they believe in God, I'll say 'Oh which one? Zeus? Hades? Jupiter? Mars? Odin? Thor? Krishna? Vishnu? Ra? ...' If they say, 'Just God. I only believe in the one God,' I'll point out that they are nearly as atheistic as me. I don't believe in 2870 gods, and they don't believe in 2869.[1]

What do you make of his argument? I think it's an excellent point. Thor, Zeus, the gods of ancient Egypt – no-one believes in them today. With regard to a whole pantheon of deities I am an atheist, and so are you. So why cling onto *any* gods? Why not be done with the lot of them?

Gervais is saying that *all* of us are sceptics. Even the most ardent 'believer' is also an unbeliever – and with good reason. There are countless gods who are unworthy of our trust. Let me pluck one at random from the history of religions: Coatlicue, the Aztec creator god. She wears a skirt of writhing snakes and a necklace of human hearts. She gave birth to gods and mortals but was later killed by her offspring. Do you believe in her? I thought not. Gervais is right: you and I are atheists with regards to her – and with regards to thousands more like her.

The question is not so much 'Do you believe in God?' The question is 'Which god do you believe in?'

Therefore the question is not so much 'Do you believe in God?' The question is '*Which* god do you believe in?' And even if you're an atheist, this question is worth considering.

Which God?

Tom Wright was a college chaplain at Oxford University. Quite often a student would declare to him, 'I don't believe in God.' Wright had a great response: 'Oh, that's interesting. Which god is it you don't believe in?'

The student would look a little puzzled but Wright would press them to describe the God they doubted. Often the student would paint a picture of some lonely individual, high on power, low on personality – a kind of celestial CCTV camera, always watching, ever ready to smite. Wright would listen to the description, then say, 'I'm not surprised you don't believe in that god. I don't believe in that god either ... I believe in the god I see revealed in Jesus of Nazareth.'[2] In this book we are letting Jesus shape our view of reality – that is, Jesus shows us God, the world and ourselves. Therefore this chapter will not be an argument for 'some kind of God', it's specifically about 'the Jesus-God'. I'm borrowing that phrase – 'the Jesus-God' – from an Iranian woman I met a couple of years ago. In Iran she had gotten hold of the Gospels – the stories of Jesus. The more she read, the more she began to think: *here* is a God I can believe in. Thrilled by the prospect that God might be like Jesus, she came to England to learn all she could from the Bible. After years of study she made this conclusion, 'God cannot be the God of the Ayatollahs. He must be "the Jesus-God".' She had it just right. You see a Christian is not someone who loves the *idea* of God. To be honest, the *concept* of deity leaves me stone cold. Confessing 'belief in some kind of god' is about as appealing as marrying 'some kind of carbon-based life form'. Who cares about 'spouses *in general*'; it's *my Emma* who has won my heart. In the same way, who cares about 'God'? 'Which god?' is always the question. The Christian can happily own the words of Lord Byron: 'If God is not like Jesus Christ, he ought to be.' We're not fans of deity, we are believers – specifically – in 'the Jesus-God'.

So Ricky Gervais has it right: believers are also sceptics. There are many gods we reject – consciously so. But there's a flipside to this truth: sceptics ought to admit that they are also *believers*.

We're all sceptics – we're all believers

Imagine a debate between different political views. There's a believer in fascism off to the right (obviously), a communist (you guessed it) to the left, a monarchist trying to have her way and a republican opposing her. A military dictator paces the room while a democrat is eagerly seeking some consensus. No-one agrees. Everyone harbours deep concerns about the positions of the others. They may all *believe* in their view of the world, but it's also true to say that everyone in this room is a sceptic.

Picture the scene then as a young anarchist enters the room. He notices the disagreements and thinks he has found a cunning way forward. In a loud voice he announces to the room: 'My friends, you are all sceptical of each other. I encourage you to go one scepticism further: be an anarchist.' At this point the room erupts in laughter. Everyone knows (except, it seems, the anarchist) that anarchism is itself a point of view, and one which the others are deeply sceptical of. Each person in that room – the anarchist included – holds certain beliefs and each person harbours certain doubts. No one is a pure sceptic.

It's the same when it comes to God. Disbelief in some kind of god does not mean you hold no beliefs. It means you hold *other* beliefs. Ricky Gervais doesn't believe in any of the 2870 recorded gods, but he does hold a view called 'materialism'. I don't mean that he's obsessed with material possessions – that's a different kind of materialism. I'm talking about the conviction that the material universe is *all there is, was or ever shall be*. I put it in religious-sounding language because, to my ears, it's a religious-sounding belief. To be sure, it doesn't sound like Christianity, but there have been plenty of religions that explain our world according to primeval powers that are less than personal.

I happen to be sceptical about materialism (for reasons I'll touch on shortly). I don't buy it. Personally I think *Jesus* is Lord. Having encountered him in the Gospels, I've become a believer in Jesus and a sceptic about materialism. For an atheist it's the other way around. But here's the issue: the atheist has not swept aside all faith commitments. They aren't actually any more sceptical than a Christian. An atheist might disbelieve in a thousand visions of reality, but in so doing they embrace their own position. That's just life: we're all sceptics; we're all believers. So, contrary to popular opinion, the world does not divide into 'believers' on one side and 'unbelievers' on the other.

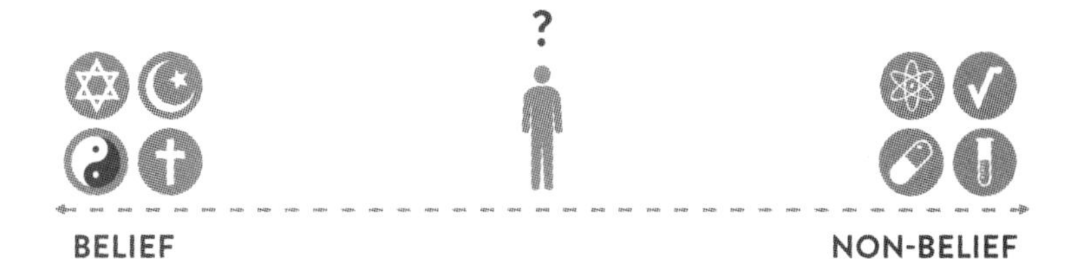

So often we think of belief and unbelief as a spectrum along which we line up – with religions standing together at one end and atheists standing together at the other. But while the picture is a popular one, it completely fails to account for the question 'Which god?' or, if you like, 'Which vision of reality?' I might be a believer *or* an unbeliever depending on what I'm asked to believe.

I am part-sceptic, part-believer – and so are you. We all embrace some views of the world and reject others. If you ask me, the picture is much more like this:

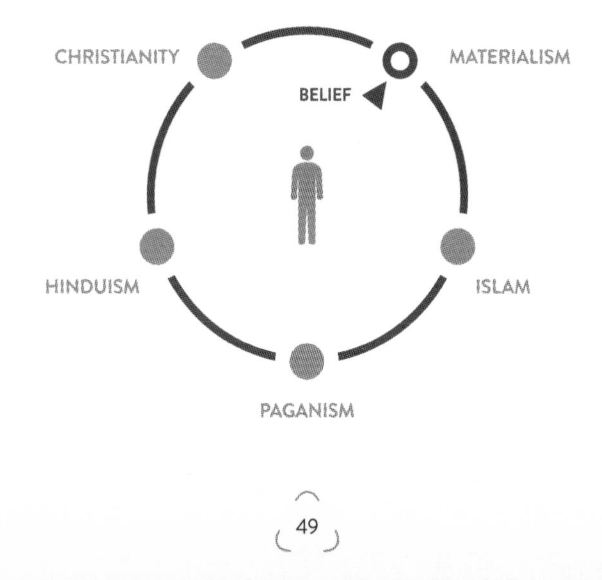

You and I believe in some things. We are sceptical of other things. That's the nature of truth, of reality, of humanity. There's no getting around it.

The question is always 'Which god?' Or, if you don't like the religious tone, put it another way: 'What is the deepest principle of reality?' What's underneath it all?

What is underneath it all?

Let's get down to brass tacks. Beneath our day-to-day lives, is there any purpose in life? Beyond our brain chemistry, is there real meaning? Behind our personal and cultural choices, is there an ultimate goodness? Or, if you dig down far enough, do we merely find physics and chemistry, with nothing deeper? When you boil it all down, is this world basically shaped by impersonal forces and material causes?

Stephen Hawking relates a famous story about what is underneath it all:

> A well-known scientist (some say it was Bertrand Russell) once gave a public lecture on astronomy. He described how the earth orbits around the sun and how the sun, in turn, orbits around the centre of a vast collection of stars called our galaxy. At the end of the lecture, a little old lady at the back of the room got up and said: 'What you have told us is rubbish. The world is really a flat plate supported on the back of a giant turtle.' The scientist gave a superior smile before replying, 'What is the turtle standing on?' 'You're very clever, young man, very clever,' said the old lady. 'But it's turtles all the way down!'[3]

The woman could think of nothing more ultimate than these turtles. On the other hand, Bertrand Russell – the famous atheist who is supposed to have given this lecture – thought there was nothing more ultimate than the material universe. For him it's impersonal matter and energy all the way down. Richard Dawkins agrees. In the quotation at the beginning of this chapter he tells us what he thinks is 'at bottom' in the universe: 'nothing but blind, pitiless indifference'.

The firmest, most foundational reality in the universe is the love of God.

What do you think is at bottom? What goes all the way down? I'm guessing you don't go for the turtles thing. Do you buy the 'blind, pitiless indifference' foundation? What do you think is the deepest reality in life?

An ancient song from the Bible gives this answer: 'Underneath are the everlasting arms.'[4] According to the Bible, it's actually love 'all the way down'. The firmest, most foundational reality in the universe is the love of God.

Could that be true? It is if 'the Jesus-God' is God.

Introducing 'the Jesus-God'

How do you respond to hearing of God's love? Perhaps it sounds like a cruel joke in a suffering world. Perhaps it sounds like wishful thinking. Perhaps it sounds like a cheesy platitude to be posted on the Facebook walls of the gullible. Is there any justification for the claim – made in a million pop songs – that love is the greatest thing?

Yes there is. We've been talking about him all along.

Showing up in the middle of history we have a man who claims to *be* deepest reality. He says he has come from above, he was there in the beginning and he will wrap it all up at the end. Ordinarily we dismiss such people as madmen or liars. But this man seems entirely credible. The rest of his teaching has shaped civilisations – I don't think he was mad. The rest of his life pulsates with self-giving love – I don't think he was bad. Perhaps then he can be trusted. If so, we have a window onto life's ultimate foundation. When we look at Jesus, what picture of God do we see?

Let's return to a scene we touched on in the last chapter: Jesus' baptism.

This was his grand unveiling – a public launch event at the Jordan River with hundreds in attendance. The people were there to be washed in a religious ritual. It was a confession to God and the world: 'I am a mess,' 'I'm a failure,' 'I'm filthy and I need a bath.'

He's joining us in our failure, so we can join him in his family.

We all know that there is a mess *out there* in the world. These people were confessing to a mess in their own hearts. So they came to be washed – that is, to be baptised. Stunningly, while they were all confessing to their filth, the Son of God shows up. And he doesn't judge them, he joins them. He lines up with the messy people – shoulder to shoulder with all the moral failures – and he gets baptised. What is he doing? He's joining us in our failure, so we can join him in his family. The Gospel-writer Luke describes the scene:

> When all the people were being baptised, Jesus was baptised too. And as he was praying, heaven was opened and the Holy Spirit descended on him in bodily form like a dove. And a voice came from heaven: 'You are my Son, whom I love; with you I am well pleased.'[5]

Normally heaven is *closed* to us. We don't naturally have an angle on divine realities but here God is opening up to us and the picture we see is both strange and wonderful. When 'the Jesus-God' opens up, we see a loving union of THREE.

Here is the Christian vision of God and it's utterly unique. For Christians, God is a Father loving his Son (Jesus) and filling him with his Spirit. At first glance we see THREE, but look closer and we understand how completely united they are. We see Jesus, but instantly we see that he is the Son of a Father and filled with his Spirit. We notice the Spirit, but the Spirit seems to be flowing from the Father to the Son. We hear the Father, but the Father is sending his Spirit and rapt in delight for his Son. When we understand each person, we realise how utterly dependent they are on the other two. They are THREE, but these three are *one* – forever united in love.

At the Jordan River we see what it looks like when heaven is 'opened'. This is what there has *always* been. Before there was a world, there were these THREE in perfect harmony.

The night before Jesus died, he prayed publicly. Addressing his Father, he said, 'you loved me before the creation of the world'.[6] What's deeper than the universe? What's the foundational principle of existence? Jesus says he was there before the universe began. What was it like? According to Jesus it was a Father pouring out love to his Son in the joy of the Holy Spirit. If you could open up heaven and look inside you would see precisely what they saw at the baptism: Jesus the beloved Son of the Father, filled with the Holy Spirit. The deepest reality of all is this union of love.

Perhaps you have heard the word 'Trinity'? That's what we're talking about here. Trinity is just a word that squashes 'Tri' and 'unity' together. The Tri-unity (or Trinity) is the loving unity of these three: the Father, the Son and the Holy Spirit. The word is not so important; its significance is cosmic: it means that love really is ultimate. The universe has come from love, been shaped by love and is made for love.

Perhaps you think this is an exercise in wishful thinking. Maybe Christians just want a father-figure so have dreamt him up and thrust him into the heavens as some almighty 'Sky Daddy'. That's essentially what Freud thought.[7] But Christianity is not about dreaming up a god and sticking him in heaven. It's precisely the other way around. Jesus is the one from heaven who comes to us with an unparalleled view of God. 'The Jesus-God' is not a God we would have imagined by ourselves. No-one would *invent* 'the Trinity' as a religious comfort blanket. Jesus brings to the world the strangest and most surprising vision of God.

But once we understand it, THREE helps us make sense of our lives. Again, it's a case of pressing into the strangeness and finding an even deeper familiarity. When we draw near to this odd belief in 'Trinity', we find it clarifies rather than complicates. Let me show you how ...

When we draw near to this odd belief in 'Trinity', we find it clarifies rather than complicates.

In the next few pages I want to explore how a belief in THREE makes sense of our world. To make the point I'm going to contrast belief in THREE with two other beliefs: atheism and theism (that is, belief in a god). First I'll tell you why I am not an atheist, then I'll tell you why I am not a theist. This section isn't about 'throwing stones' at other beliefs, it's just an explanation for why I couldn't live with atheism or theism myself. If you ask me, belief in the THREE is something else. Let me show you what I mean.

Why I am not an atheist

Whatever you believe, I'm sure you *live* as though truth, beauty, goodness, joy, love, and so on are the deepest realities in life. When we get a taste for these things, it feels like life. When we experience the opposite, it feels like death.

We live as though people are more important than prawns and prawns are more important than pebbles – we live as though personal reality is ultimate. Regardless of beliefs, we all agree that relationships trump *things*, right? And yet Richard Dawkins wants to tell us that 'at bottom' there is 'no evil, no good, nothing but blind, pitiless indifference'.

Notice the choice of words there – Dawkins has been quite deliberate. He knows that we want someone to see. We want there to be compassion and love at the heart of reality. But Dawkins says these are not ultimate: they boil down to biology; and biology boils down to chemistry; and chemistry boils down to physics.

Does it stop there? Are there yet more turtles underneath? What does physics rest on?

Some have spoken of the universe spontaneously creating itself: the whole cosmos propped up by nothing, absolutely nothing. As miracles go, this would be unparalleled. Everything from nothing? Christians believe in the virgin birth of Jesus but this would mean the virgin birth of the cosmos. In fact, it's the virgin birth of the cosmos but without a virgin, without anything. Here would be the greatest conjuring trick ever pulled: nothing up the sleeve, no sleeve, not even a magician. Just pure magic, out of nowhere. Literally. Since this is a more absurd proposition than all the religions in the world have suggested, most people back off from 'absolute nothing'. If you hear people talk about the universe coming from nothing, dig around and you'll find there are some very significant somethings in their 'nothing'.[8] Actually they believe in impersonal forces 'all the way down'.

While we're thinking about what's 'all the way down', let's face a common objection put to Christians: 'If God made the world, who made God?' This question is perfectly sensible when asked about the kind of gods Ricky Gervais mentioned earlier. Thousands of gods do indeed have origins stories – they are created by other gods, powers and natural processes, sometimes in quite nauseating ways. *Those* gods do indeed rest on the back of other, more ultimate, beings. But the God of the Bible claims to be 'Maker' not 'made'. He is beginningless or, in other words, the God of Jesus goes 'all the way down'.

This may be a difficult concept to understand, but I would argue it's actually the simplest and most elegant solution to a problem faced by all. Whatever we believe, we have only two options about the nature of reality: either the universe rests on nothing (which is absurd) or there is *something* that is beginningless – *something* that goes 'all the way down'. Maybe it's turtles, maybe it's impersonal forces and matter, maybe it's the God of love. For Christians, *the* foundational reality is the THREE: 'Underneath are the everlasting arms.' Frankly all other candidates for 'what's underneath' seem unfit for purpose. What other foundational reality is strong enough to support the world and fruitful enough to shape what we see?

We all recognise that the most profound realities in our experience are personal relationships, meetings of hearts and minds and encounters with beauty and bliss. For the Christian this makes perfect sense – these realities *are* the deepest realities because 'God is love'. On the atheist account, foundational reality is impersonal, amoral and non-rational. Therefore there are huge questions that remain unanswered: how could life emerge from non-life? How could minds emerge from matter? Why on earth would we trust them if they did emerge via mindless processes? But perhaps, most troubling of all, if ultimate reality is impersonal, why are any of these things – persons, minds, logic, language, laughter and lemon drizzle cake – considered to be 'progress'? The primacy of love, which we all believe in, is completely undermined by the impersonal foundations of atheism.

Perhaps here the atheist will point out that love and goodness aren't the only realities we see in the world. We also see cancer, genocide and earthquakes. Isn't that proof that love is *not* ultimate after all?

Well let's think for a second: Why are we outraged by evil and suffering? We *are* outraged. We *should* be outraged. But why? This question is easy to answer for the Christian but difficult for the atheist. Remember what Dawkins said: 'at bottom ... [there is] no evil, no good'. For him evil and good are surface-level experiences, not deeply connected to the way things actually are. The nastiness of this world might be unpleasant, painful, grotesque or maladapted to survival. But if, at bottom, there is no evil and no good, then for Dawkins those things are not *wrong* – not on the deepest level.

Yet when we experience the horrors of this world, we experience them as *evil*; we feel that they should not be; we cry out for a solution, for justice; and we grieve them as realities that don't belong. Therefore, even as suffering strikes, the Christian view is not disproved but upheld. For the Christian, evil can never be 'one of those things'. It is a profound violation of the way life ought to be.

When Christians say 'God is love', they don't then conclude that 'everything is lovely'. It's not. But the God of love makes sense of our outrage at everything that is unlovely. He gives us the right to call a bad world 'bad'. There is much more to be said about suffering in chapters 4 and 8, but for now the point is simply this: the God of Jesus helps us to understand our *experience* of both good and evil. This God allows us to make sense of the goodness of good and the evil of evil.

This God allows us to make sense of the goodness of good and the evil of evil.

Finally, on the subject of atheism, consider for a moment how you would argue for materialism. What points would you seek to score and on what basis? What elements would you hope to be persuasive in the debate? Surely if it's going to be a meaningful conversation, the critical factors will be things like reason, truth, rhetoric, emotion, personality, and so on. Yet what do you notice about these factors? None of them are material. The materialist – even while proclaiming materialism – depends decisively on immaterial realities to do so. They are very welcome to make these appeals to reason and the like, but every time they do, they bear witness that mindless matter is not ultimate. We all defer to immaterial realities like logic, language and love, but those realities make best sense on the Christian view since, for Christians, minds and hearts go 'all the way down'.

Now, in the interests of fair play, let me turn my attention to theism. You see I don't think theism is any kind of solution to atheism. Theism means belief in some kind of god, but I'm really not interested in 'some kind of god'. As we've already seen, the real question is 'Which god?' And theism *in general* gives answers that are just as barren and unsatisfying as atheism.

Why I am not a theist

If you take a generally religious person and ask them, 'What is underneath it all?', you will find answers like 'God' or a 'Higher Power'. They might well have Freud's Sky Daddy in mind or maybe a whole bunch of supernatural beings. At this point they qualify for the title 'theist' – a believer in a god or gods. I too qualify for that label, but I don't usually wear it because that might give the impression that I like the notion of gods *in general*. I don't really. Maybe it's because I'm a 21st-century westerner, but I've never warmed to the idea of 'the supernatural', and I'm not alone.

The late Christopher Hitchens would often train his considerable rhetorical firepower on belief in God. He expressed profound revulsion at the idea of anyone submitting to some power in the sky:

> [It is] a totalitarian belief. It is the wish to be a slave. It is the desire that there be an unalterable, unchallengeable, tyrannical authority who can convict you of thought crime while you are asleep, who can subject you ... to total surveillance around the clock every waking and sleeping minute of your life ... and, even worse and where the real fun begins, after you're dead. A celestial North Korea. Who wants this to be true? Who but a slave desires such a ghastly fate?[9]

Hitchens described himself as an anti-theist. For him belief in God was not only unfounded, it was unethical. If God existed, thought Hitchens, it would be a bad thing – a celestial North Korea.

If you take the time to listen, Hitchens makes some excellent points. Hear the language – 'unalterable, unchallengeable, tyrannical authority ... surveillance ... slave'. What is Hitchens taking aim at? Actually he's talking about the God of generalised theism – a God defined by power. What is most relevant about this God is that he is bigger than us. What is most incumbent upon us is that we bow.

Does that sound attractive? Not at all. Does it sound like Jesus and the God he reveals? No. But does it sound like a lot of generalised theism? Absolutely.

Ask a general God-believer – whether they go to church, synagogue, mosque or nowhere at all – about the God they believe in. To get specific, ask this question: 'What was your God doing before the foundation of the world? Wind back the clock as far as clocks can be wound ... before people, before planets, before protons. Go back before the world to the time when it was just God and now think: what was your God doing?'

I ask this question quite a lot. Here are the answers I get: 'He was bored. He was lonely. He was contemplating himself. He was planning creation.' Almost everyone thinks of God as a solitary individual – even Christians, who should know better.

But let's explore this sterile belief for a minute. The Bible says God 'inhabits eternity'.[10] That's a nice phrase. But then think about a *solitary* God 'inhabiting eternity'. Before the cosmic clock has started he has no-one and nothing beside him, just his own thoughts for company. This God knows nothing of relationship, nothing of back-and-forth or give-and-take. Before the universe – imagine it – all of reality consists of this God in splendid isolation. Such a God might be immense, supreme and powerful. But this God cannot be *loving*. Love worthy of the name requires more than one person. An eternity doting on yourself is no-one's definition of love – that would be infinite narcissism. Yet the solitary God is an eternal egotist.

If such a God wants to love, he will have to make others. Once he has created the world, the possibility for love emerges, but it is only a possibility. He might choose to love us. But equally he might not; it's his *choice* that is foundational, not his love. For such a God, love is not his eternal nature even if, occasionally, he 'tries on love for size'.

Now think of our relationship to such a God. If God is defined by supremacy then *we* must be defined by submission. Our 'place' with this God could never be 'at his side'. No-one can be at the side of this God. The only place we could fit would be *beneath* his almighty rule. No wonder Christopher Hitchens was an anti-theist. 'Who wants this to be true?' asks Hitch. 'Who but a slave desires such a ghastly fate?'

Not me. Not the Christians I know. If Hitchens is taking aim at *this* God, I'm with him. You cannot put a name tag on cosmic power and call it 'God'. Such a God would be monstrous. With such a God we might be delivered from meaninglessness but we'd be delivered into slavery. For this reason I am not simply 'a theist'. Not every god is good news. Many gods simply dominate, subsume and enslave.

Now, if you *insist* on calling me 'a theist' I won't get too upset – there are ways in which the shoe fits. But if I'm allowed to identify myself, I will generally resist the label because I have no commitment to *the idea of god*. I'm like the woman who has never particularly supported *marriage* but is happily wedded to her husband. She's doesn't love *marriage* – she loves *him*. Other Christians may take a different view, but for me it's 'Jesus or bust'.

Jesus gives us something utterly unique – an 'ultimate reality' that has come, personally, to share and to serve. Theism *in general* does not have this. In some religions, 'God' remains infinitely aloof – unseen and unmoved. In other religions, one of their lesser deities may have fought some battles or displayed courage or sacrifice. Yet if you ask *who* are these deities, we are not talking about the supreme being. And if you ask *when* this self-sacrifice occurred, you will be told that it happened in dream time, in a mythological time and space. Not so with Jesus. God the Son was crucified under the Roman Governor, Pontius Pilate, on – scholars believe – 7 April, AD 30. If that date is off, it's not off by very much. The point is that Jesus reveals the highest God who has genuinely come down, not 'to be served but to serve, and to give his life as a ransom for many'.[11]

When Jesus shows us ultimate reality, he does not speak in terms of supremacy but service. When he reveals life before the beginning of the world he does not show us loneliness but love.

When Jesus shows us ultimate reality, he does not speak in terms of supremacy but service.

The Christian claim is this: the ultimate pulse of reality is unbreakable and unending love. The claim is unique to Christianity because no other religion has this kind of God. The God of Jesus is a loving union of THREE – the Father, the Son and the Holy Spirit. This belief makes all the difference. If God was merely a power over us, then we would simply have to bow. But what if God is a family of love opened out to us? Then we are invited to share.

Contrary to Hitchens' view, Christianity is our one hope of *escaping* slavery. You see both the atheist and the theist face the same problem. For both of them power is ultimate. For the atheist it's sub-personal forces that determine reality. For the generalised theist it's a sub-personal deity that determines reality. With both beliefs we are overpowered. Only Jesus can assure us that love is ultimate.

Three and One

As we conclude this chapter let me repeat: Christians do not believe in three Gods. It's not as though the Father, the Son and the Holy Spirit are three separate beings who have decided to club together. When Jesus describes the unity he shares with his Father and the Spirit, he says that they are 'in' one another.[12] They are bound together in ties of inseparable love and they simply *cannot* be apart. Think about it: without the Father, the Son would stop being Son. Without the Son, the Father would stop being Father. Loving union is not a hobby for the THREE. They *are* one. They have not found that they 'work well as a team'. They do not have three separate lives. They have only one life – a life together, a life of love.

This is why the Bible can say, 'God is love'.[13] It doesn't just say that God is loving. He is, but this truth goes far deeper. God *is* love. He is a Father forever loving his Son in the intimate bond of the Spirit. Love is not simply what he does, it is who he is and who he has always been.

We all feel like love is the greatest thing. The Christian says, 'I know why! Because the greatest thing, God, *is* love.' The best things in life really are personal connections, meetings of minds and meetings of hearts. If we think the universe is *basically* material, or if we consider everything to be ruled by raw power, we won't understand it. But if we let Jesus show us reality, we learn that, beyond and beneath the material realm, there is a personal realm. The God of THREE provides the grounding for everything we value in life – relationships, goodness, truth, beauty and love.

Friedrich Neitzsche was an atheist who famously proclaimed that 'God is dead.' Yet at one point he speaks of the God he might be prepared to consider: 'I would only believe in a god who could dance.'[14]

I'm with Friedrich. I'm not interested in the power play of a distant God. Neither can I follow the chaos of many disparate gods. But what about a God of give and take, of back and forth? What about the God who is love?

For nearly two thousand years Christians have spoken of the 'round dance' of the Father, Son and Holy Spirit.[15] Here is a God who not only *can* dance, he *is* a united movement of love.

The rest of this book will unfold how the THREE relate to the world and to ourselves. We will see how the Son has come to link arms with us in order to draw us into his own life – he joins us in our failures to bring us to his family. The Christian is someone who, as it were, stands with Jesus in the Jordan River. As we admit our failures and come to him in that place of honesty, we enter into the most astonishing 'circle of trust'. We become united to the Son of God. Suddenly his Spirit is our Spirit, his Father is our Father and the love of God is ours. The heavens are opened, not merely to satisfy our curiosity but to receive us with joy.

The Trinity is not a mystery to be puzzled at from a distance – it's the good news that 'God is love' and we're invited.

Watch this video: ***three-two-one.org/God***

Optional reading: John chapters 5–8

- How does Jesus speak of himself and his Father?
- How does Jesus speak of his mission?
- What does Jesus seem to want from people?
- How are people responding to Jesus? Why?

• COMING UP IN CHAPTER 4 •

Last chapter was like a high-altitude balloon ride – we thought about lofty ideas such as the Trinity, eternity and 'ultimate reality'. Now we're going to come crashing down to earth again. Our next chapter is about TWO. We're going to learn this fundamental truth: the world is shaped by two representatives.

First we will think about Adam: a story of failure and despair; a story we recognise all too well – we live it every day. Then we will consider Jesus: the 'second Adam'. We will explore how the Jesus story answers the Adam story and what it means for the world.

So then, let's go back to the beginning to see a promising set-up and a desperate fall ...

4

TWO: THE WORLD IS SHAPED BY **TWO** REPRESENTATIVES

> You can choose your friends but you sho' can't choose your family, an' they're still kin to you no matter whether you acknowledge 'em or not, and it makes you look right silly when you don't.
>
> —*Harper Lee,* To Kill a Mockingbird

> You must be born again.
>
> —*Jesus, John 3:7*

In 1787 my ancestor Ann Forbes stole 10 yards of printed cotton from a London market. In other words, she was a convict, and she sailed on the First Fleet from Portsmouth to Botany Bay. This is part of how I came to be Australian. Without Ann Forbes – and without her crime – I would not be the person that I am.

In England this kind of thing might be considered a skeleton in the closet or a blight on the family tree. In Australia it is a badge of honour. All my Australian friends wish they were descended from genuine convicts. So I proudly declare: I am the offspring of a thief. In fact, when you think about it, much of my life is the product of one theft.

Initially Ann was sentenced to death for her crimes, yet good sense prevailed. It dawned on the authorities that colonising Australia might require some females. Banking on Ann's breeding potential, they commuted her sentence to seven years' transportation. She more than repaid their faith by the way. In Australia she produced 10 children that we know of. They in turn produced 150 grandkids. I'm biased, I know, but I'd say those are some good genes.

Of course when Ann was saved from the hangman's noose, many considered exile to Australia a fate worse than death. If you ask me, she left the set of *Oliver Twist* and wound up on the set of *Home and Away*. She died a quite prosperous farmer north of Sydney and the biography of her life is called *Transported to Paradise*. Who says crime doesn't pay?

Every now and again I think about Ann's experience. It's not just a history lesson, it's personal. The day she was spared from execution, my life was saved. The lives of 6000 descendants depended on that one decision. I realise this is an odd way to think about it, but it's true.

And – let's pursue this strange line of thought a little further – when Ann was transported to Australia, I was, if you like, carried across the ocean too. Seven generations of us 'became Australian' in this one event. Everyone in our extended family owes their existence and identity to one person, one crime and one exile.

Decisions, decisions

You will have stories like this in your genealogy. At one stage your family line jagged off in a new direction. One of your forebears sailed across an ocean, or fathered an illegitimate child. They moved to the big city to find work, or survived the war. Perhaps they left the convent, or turned down the rich man's proposal, or ran away with the servant. At the time these decisions and twists of fate seemed like a personal affair. In fact they have shaped the course of history – family history anyway. These events have determined our lives for better or for worse.

Thinking like this doesn't come naturally to us these days. We like to feel that we determine our own lives. If we meet at a party, you're going to tell me who you are by telling me your choices: you choose to like this music; you choose to like this film; you chose that city; you took this job; you married that person. These are the decisions you have made. And they're important. But how much of our stories are shaped by the decisions of others, about which we had no option?

Think of my family tree. Because of Ann Forbes – and thousands of others – certain realities were fixed in place centuries before my birth. I didn't choose *where* I was born, or *when* I was born. I didn't choose my nationality, my culture, my family, my gender, my genetics or my upbringing. And yet these influences have shaped me at the deepest level.

If I was born in France in the 13th century, would I still be *me*? Even if I had the same genes, what else would I have in common with my alternative French self?

Our choices *are* important. They mould our stories – at least a bit. But our stories are so much bigger than us and bigger than the decisions we have made. This isn't scientific but let me guess at some statistics: I reckon 90 per cent of my life has been determined by the choices of others. The other 10 per cent has involved choices I've tried to make *but they never came off*. Even when I've tried to lay hold of my circumstances and take a big step, it's been thwarted or redirected or has led to completely unintended consequences.

John Lennon said, 'Life's what happens to you, while you're busy making other plans.' That certainly rings true in my life. So much of life simply happens to you. We just don't have the power over our lives that we like to imagine. The story of me – and the story of you – is caught up in a story far grander and far older than anything we can control.

The story of me – and the story of you – is caught up in a story far grander and far older than anything we can control.

In this chapter we're thinking about that bigger story. Here we're exploring the truth of TWO: the world is shaped by two representatives.

The Bible begins with the story of Adam. Just like Ann Forbes, he failed and was exiled from God's presence. Now we are caught up in his failure and exile – our story is shaped by his. Thankfully, Jesus is 'the second Adam': the one who joins our family to pioneer a new kind of life. Adam took us down into death and disconnection; Jesus offers us life and reconnection. These are the TWO representatives who shape the world. Let's think about the first representative: Adam.

Bear with me

In the pages that follow I'll be talking about Adam and Eve (and the biblical book of Genesis, 'the garden of Eden', 'the forbidden fruit', 'Satan', the works!). Perhaps you're thinking, 'We're all modern people now, why bother with these ancient stories? If we've got Darwin's *Origin of the Species*, why do we need Genesis?'

In chapter 13 we will think about science more generally but for now we should realise that for thousands of years people have thought about these biblical stories and discovered profound truths that go deeper than the science books. Certainly Genesis is not a scientific manual and was never meant to be. We ought to read texts in the way they were intended. More than this, humanity has had many scientific theories about our origins over the centuries (and we will have many more), yet all throughout the millennia people have found these biblical stories to contain wisdom that goes beyond the mechanics of physics and biology.

Right now I'm giving you 'the grand tour'. Later on you can figure out what you want to do with the story. I hope you will discover what millions have found down through the ages – though they've held many different scientific beliefs – the world comes into focus when we look through these biblical lenses.

Where it all began

Genesis chapter 1 is a majestic introduction to the Bible. I highly recommend reading it – in fact now would be a great time to read Genesis chapters 1–3. The next few pages will refer to these passages at length.

In a sentence let me summarise Genesis 1: in the beginning a good God made a good world and placed humanity at the head of it. Notice how the three main players – God, the world and ourselves – are related. Humanity is the climax of creation, standing over the world and under God. Whatever else we get from the Bible's opening chapter, that is central.

In verse 26 the THREE say to one another: 'Let us make mankind in our image.' The THREE want to make an 'image' of their life in the world, but what could possibly look like God? Answer: a union of love. So they make humanity as 'male and female' in order that they might 'be fruitful and increase in number' (verse 27–28). The human race is created as a counterpart to God. We are meant to look like God's united life, but even deeper than that, we are meant to share in it.

In Genesis chapter 2 we see the same truth but told from a different angle – we zoom in on Adam. Everything in the story depicts Adam as a representative. His name simply means 'man' (i.e. humanity). From the beginning we're being told that Adam's story is our story. He is an 'everyman' – in fact *the* 'everyman'. He is given rule and responsibility over the earth – once again his kingly role makes us think of him as a representative.[1] In time Adam is also given a queen – Eve.[2] It was the original 'match made in heaven' and, upon meeting her, Adam bursts into the world's first love song.[3]

Genesis 2 ends with a picture of peace, intimacy and joy: 'Adam and his wife were both naked, and they felt no shame.'[4] Harmony with each other, harmony with God, harmony with nature – when God's representative does his job, all is well. But then, as with all the great stories, things fall apart.

His fall – our fall

Genesis chapter 3 is often called 'the fall'. It tells of the downfall of one couple – Adam and Eve – and yet in this one downfall we see a cosmic catastrophe. The garden of Eden is a microcosm – a world in miniature – and Adam is 'humanity', he's the ultimate 'everyman', he's *me*. This is important to know because, as modern people, we can often view Genesis 3 as a quaint tale, suitable for olden days and simpler folk. But if we hold this story at arms' length we will miss its power. We are meant to see *ourselves* in this ancient drama.

In this section we will travel through the story of the fall, highlighting six aspects of the Adam story and showing how they continue to shape us today. Under each heading we see this truth: what *he* did, *we* do.

1. SUSPICION

The issue of trust is at the heart of Genesis 3. The chapter opens by introducing a wise and powerful creature: 'the serpent'. The Bible does not present him as 'a talking snake' – more like a dragon actually![5] He is an angelic creature who was supposed to be guarding the couple.[6] Later in the story he is named as Satan or 'the devil', but God did not create him devilish. He fell, just as Adam and Eve did. In Genesis 3 we see it happening.

The serpent's opening gambit begins to sow doubt into the mind of the couple: 'Did God really say, "You must not eat from any tree in the garden"?'[7] No, God did not say that. In Genesis chapter 2, God had said, 'You are free to eat from any tree in the garden.'[8] The emphasis is on *freedom*. God had placed only one restriction on Adam and Eve – just one forbidden fruit.[9]

There was no other rule to obey and no other boundary to keep. Adam and Eve could do anything and go anywhere in the world. So why does God draw this particular line? Answer: the forbidden fruit provides an opportunity for trust. Without this prohibition there was no way for Adam and Eve to show their love or dependence. With the forbidden fruit they can demonstrate their allegiance to (or rebellion against) the Lord – not through legal obedience, religious rituals or grand quests, but by *refraining* from a single activity. It's the simplest way possible for humanity to say to God, 'We trust you.'

Therefore their trust becomes a target for the serpent's temptations. He seeks to paint God as a miser: 'God knows that when you eat from it your eyes will be opened, and you will be like God.'[10] 'It's a power play,' the serpent effectively says. 'God is keeping you down. He is hoarding the best for himself and throwing you the scraps. He doesn't have your best interests at heart. He can't be trusted. Don't depend on his provision, grasp at life for yourself.'

This seed of suspicion will grow in Adam until it becomes full-blown rebellion. But it starts in the heart: Adam begins to doubt God. With every tree hanging heavy with fruit, with a garden paradise around him and with a marriage made in heaven before him, he should have seen only bounty. Instead he fixated on the boundary – the one boundary in all the world. Somehow he infers a grudging God who cannot be trusted. Therefore, suspicious of God, he takes what he wants unlawfully.

It's the same with us. We're born into the world screaming. We have a primal fear that our needs will not be met. This is quite understandable

We are suspicious of God and suspicious of his motives.

physically, but the Bible insists it's a spiritual truth too. None of us are born trusting that God is a bountiful and generous Giver whose every 'No' is pronounced only for our greater good. We are suspicious of God and suspicious of his motives. If we think he's there at all, we imagine that he doles out blessings with a teaspoon and a scowl.

Even as we listen to the Genesis story, we find ourselves crying out, 'But why the forbidden fruit?' It rarely occurs to us that the garden was the most liberal, rule-free existence humanity has ever known. Just one boundary proves too many for us. We conclude that the whole set-up is deeply suspicious. And this leads to ...

2. SELFISHNESS

If God cannot be trusted, there's a very willing candidate for God's job: ourselves.

> When the woman saw that the fruit of the tree was good for food and pleasing to the eye, and also desirable for gaining wisdom, she took some and ate it. She also gave some to her husband, who was with her, and he ate it.[11]

Because they are not *trusters*, the couple become *takers*. They want what they want, when they want it and to hell with God, to hell with his warnings, to hell with the consequences. We are the same. Exhibit A: a report from the Minnesota Crime Commission in 1926. This is starkly put and it doesn't, by any means, capture the totality of our nature, but it's hard to argue against:

> Every baby starts life as a little savage. He is completely selfish and self-centered. He wants what he wants when he wants it: his bottle, his mother's attention, his playmate's toys, his uncle's watch ... Deny him these and he

> seethes with rage and aggressiveness which would be murderous were he not so helpless.

This isn't the whole story, but it's part of our make-up. Our first instinct is self-preservation, self-protection and self-promotion. Of course as we grow we realise that others don't respond well to our naked savagery, so we moderate these instincts. We learn to 'play nice'. But notice *why* we play nice – it serves our interests better!

I find it happening in the most mundane ways. A friend tags me in some Facebook photos. I click through to shots of our group holiday and for whose face do I scan the pictures? The woman who I say I love more than anyone else in the world? My friends who I haven't seen in months? Or do I fix immediately on my own ugly mug before declaring that it's not a great likeness because – yet again – the photographer has failed to capture my 'boy band' good looks? Yep, it's the latter. My wife, who maintains an admirable zeal for truth, will often remind me, 'See that, Glen? *That* is how you look. *All the time!'*

Of course then I feel deflated and am very tempted to declare to the world, 'I'm so ugly! I hate myself!' But obviously I don't hate myself at all in that moment. I'm actually hopelessly enamoured with me. I just think I deserve to look better than I do.

I think of myself and my own interests far more than the interests of others. I lavish care and attention on myself that I wouldn't dream of offering to others. In short I put myself first in a thousand different ways. And even when I 'put myself down', it springs from an unhealthy self-focus.

Selfishness besets the children of Adam. But, ironically, grasping after 'what I want' does not lead to self-mastery but to slavery.

3. SLAVERY

Contrary to all their expectations, Adam and Eve's rebellion did not liberate them, it limited them. They got what they wanted but it didn't expand their horizons, it actually shrank their world.

> Then the eyes of both of them were opened, and they realised that they were naked; so they sewed fig leaves together and made coverings for themselves.
>
> Then the man and his wife heard the sound of the LORD God as he was walking in the garden in the cool of the day, and they hid from the LORD God among the trees of the garden.[12]

I'm sure Adam and Eve had anticipated the 'eye-opening' wonders of the forbidden fruit but in the end the only thing their eyes were opened to was their nakedness. So they covered up and they hid. Imagine the scene: covering up with *fig leaves*, a ridiculous outfit; hiding from *God*, a ridiculous proposition. They cut such a pathetic figure yet such a familiar one.

This is what *we* do. We fixate on *something* to give us the meaning and significance that ought to come from God. Suspicious of God's love, we selfishly grasp at *things* to make life work. We imagine that they will satisfy the hunger in our souls. In essence these *somethings* become little gods for us – gods like money, or popularity, or experiences, or achievements. We feel like *if we get THIS, our eyes will be opened!*

We live for people's love. We live for people's respect. We live for the weekend. But all these little gods make us anxious – because they might fail us, and we might fail them. If our god is our career, we'd better not lose our job. If our god is good looks, we'd better not get old. If our god is family life, everyone had better be happy and healthy.

Everything is uncertain when these things are our *gods*. And so we live anxious lives, trying to please gods that are always demanding more from us. The biblical word for this is 'idolatry'. But it doesn't take a wooden statue to involve you in idolatry.

Human beings are always taking the good things of this world and turning them into god things. But the gods of this world never satisfy you when you get them – not fully. And they don't forgive you when you fail them. Nonetheless, we're suckers for idols. It's slavery.

Here's another feature of Adam's race ...

4. SELF-JUSTIFICATION

When God confronted the couple about their sin it became a comedy masterclass in blame-shifting:

> 'Have you eaten from the tree from which I commanded you not to eat?'
>
> The man said, 'The woman you put here with me – she gave me some fruit from the tree, and I ate it.'
>
> Then the Lord God said to the woman, 'What is this you have done?'
>
> The woman said, 'The serpent deceived me, and I ate.'[13]

Adam blames both God and his wife in a single sentence. Eve blames the serpent. No-one owns their guilt. And not much has changed since.

George Carlin, the American comedian, used to joke about our self-justification on the roads:

> When driving, everyone who goes faster than you is a *maniac*; everyone who drives slower than you is an *idiot*. I've noticed it myself. When I'm driving, I shake my head in disbelief at pedestrians who step out into traffic. Within minutes I've parked the car and do exactly the same. Whether driving or walking, one thing stays the same: I'm in the right.

We are inveterate self-justifiers. When we mess up, we *might* say sorry but there's usually an excuse coming at the end. So much of what spoils our world is not our human badness, it's our human *right*-ness. The greatest evils of history have been justified as serving a greater good. Everyone has their reasons. Everyone's just doing their best. No-one's trying to be a bad guy. In fact everyone's trying to be good – and to be *seen* to be doing good. But from genocidal master plans to marital bickering, we all do

Self-justification is a dreadful and universal disease.

great wrong while desperate to be right. Self-justification is a dreadful and universal disease.

These first four characteristics of Adam's race seem to follow a predictable pattern. It's possible to *explain* how suspicion leads to selfishness and how selfishness breeds slavery and self-justification. But the fifth characteristic is not explicable in the same way. It seems to come out of nowhere. I was tempted to call it 'self-sabotage' but I think 'stuff-ups' might be a better description.

5. STUFF-UPS

When God confronts the couple he asks a question every reader wants to ask: 'What is this you have done?'[14] It seems so incredible that Adam and Eve could have blown it so catastrophically. If even *God* has to ask, we get the sense of how baffling the fall really is. Think of it: Adam stood in paradise with the world at his feet. Everything was his for the asking, but instead he grasps eagerly at tragedy. The self-destruct button was well labelled yet Adam slams it with glee in a fit of madness we'd all find incredible except that we recognise it so well. This is what *we* do, isn't it?

I'll speak for myself, but I'm sure you can relate. I sabotage my own happiness continually. I sabotage my own success too. I manage to sabotage it better than anyone else. In my life no-one has stood in my way more than me. I am my own worst enemy. And then, out of the blue, I will turn on others as their enemy. And usually those others are the people I love the most. I can unleash shocking cruelty on the people I adore. In those moments I can't say, 'I don't know what came over me.' Nothing came over me. It all came *out* of me. It came out of somewhere very deep and dark and old.

Perhaps even now you are thinking of *that thing* which you can't believe you did. I get flashbacks of those moments at odd points in the day –

standing at the washing up, queuing for groceries, or last thing at night. They're baffling, maddening stuff-ups, and I can't undo them. The greatest moral teachers in the world have felt this. The Apostle Paul wrote half the New Testament and he confesses at one point: 'I do not do the good I want to do, but the evil I do not want to do – this I keep on doing.'[15]

I am my own worst enemy.

I don't want to be like this. I want to change. I want to 'turn over a new leaf' and make better choices. But this mad selfishness dominates me. These insidious slaveries shackle me. My implacable self-justification blinds me. And these stuff-ups just burst out of me – unwanted and unmanageable.

This is what the Bible means when it speaks of 'sin'. It's not about 'naughty but nice' indulgences or cheating on your diet. It's not even about bad behaviour – not deep down. 'Sin' speaks of something within me that goes much deeper than behaviour. It's deeper than bad choices. It runs to the core of my humanity. And it separates me from God.

6. SEPARATION

Genesis 3 concludes with these tragic words:

> To Adam God said, 'Because you listened to your wife and ate fruit from the tree about which I commanded you, 'You must not eat from it,'
>
> 'Cursed is the ground because of you;
> through painful toil you will eat food from it
> all the days of your life.
> It will produce thorns and thistles for you,
> and you will eat the plants of the field.
> By the sweat of your brow
> you will eat your food
> until you return to the ground,
> since from it you were taken;
> for dust you are

> and to dust you will return.'
>
> ... So the Lord God banished him from the Garden of Eden to work the ground from which he had been taken. After he drove the man out, he placed on the east side of the Garden of Eden cherubim and a flaming sword flashing back and forth to guard the way to the tree of life.[16]

We were made for God – made to share intimately in his life and love – but Genesis 3 ends with Adam cut off from God, dying and driven out of his presence. It is almost impossible for us to grasp the magnitude of this fall because we have never known the heights which Adam enjoyed. We have all been born 'east of Eden'. For us, separation from God is the very atmosphere of our lives.

Comedian Spike Milligan was once asked if he ever prayed. 'I do pray, desperately, all the time,' he answered. 'I just have no idea who I'm praying to.' That's a near-perfect description of our spiritual condition. Do we pray? Sometimes, perhaps. Do we actually feel spiritually connected? No, not really.

It actually sounds unnatural for people to claim a spiritual connection with God. Imagine that a friend confesses to you, 'I have a profound one-ness with God – God's life courses through me, my life courses through God. We are intimately and eternally *one*.' Are you inclined to take them seriously? Instinctively we would question their mental health. It sounds mad to be united to God.

And yet, if the Bible is true, then 'we live and move and have our being' in God.[17] He is the very environment of our lives. Shouldn't we, therefore, know God? Shouldn't we feel a connection? But we don't. We feel separated, estranged, disconnected.

Understandably people raise this separation as proof against the Bible. People say, 'If God is real, why don't I see him / feel him / know him?' Yet, properly understood, this separation is exactly what the Bible teaches. Just as I was born in Australia, far from the mother country, you and I were born into this world far from God. Our spiritual disconnection does not disprove but rather confirms the Bible's story.

Our spiritual disconnection does not disprove but rather confirms the Bible's story.

Wherever humans are found, they have spirituality but not certainty. Some might hunger for God but we don't naturally *have* him. And in those who even bother to speak of 'God', the profusion of deities and dogmas is testimony to our spiritual confusion. We don't know God – not naturally; not intimately.

For Adam, separation came last. For us, separation is the *first* fact of our existence, and it leads to all the others – to suspicion, selfishness, slavery, self-justification and stuff-ups. But wherever we have lived and whenever we were born, the human race has, universally, betrayed these faults. The character flaws of Adam have become the family traits of his offspring.

I wonder what you make of Genesis chapter 3. As modern people we can find it hard to 'get' such ancient stories. But actually it's the story that's meant to 'get' us. It's supposed to grab our attention and say, 'Look! What he did, *you* do!' Or, to put it the other way: 'You're always doing what he did!' In other words, the Adam story tells us that we all share a family likeness – an ugly family likeness and an even uglier family inheritance.

Our inheritance: death

God had warned Adam, 'when you eat [of the forbidden fruit] you will certainly die.'[18] Perhaps this sounds like an over-reaction on God's part. The equation 'sin = death' sounds a little over the top, perhaps. Actually, according to the Bible, 'sin = death' is a simple restatement of the terms. If God is our Life Source (and he is), and if sin is turning from our Life Source (and it is), then the equation 'sin = death' is an inescapable fact of existence. This isn't about facing up to a harsh standard of divine justice. Far deeper, it's about facing up to reality. Rejecting God means rejecting life – nothing could be more straightforward.

But at this point someone will highlight that Adam and Eve do *not* die as soon as they eat the forbidden fruit. At least they don't look dead. But that's the thing: there's death and there's death.

In December many will go into a forest and – in the name of Christmas joy – hack to death a perfectly thriving pine tree. The minute the tree is 'cut off', it's dead. It doesn't look dead. It looks alive and verdant. Nonetheless it *is* dead, it is perishing and within a few weeks it will be landfill. In the meantime we dress it up in fancy decorations, we surround it with family, food and festivities, and for a while it looks and smells wonderful. But there is no life in it and the clock is ticking.

Ever since Genesis chapter 3 we have been spiritually severed from God and now we are perishing.

According to the Bible, this is the state of the human family tree. Ever since Genesis chapter 3 we have been spiritually severed from God and now we are perishing. We don't have spiritual life within ourselves, we are cut off and our physical decay is one more symptom of our spiritual disconnection.

We don't *look* dead, of course, just as the Christmas tree doesn't *look* dead. We can dress ourselves up in decorations – our goodness and achievements can be, at times, breathtaking. We can surround ourselves with family, food and festivities. But we all experience decay – of the physical *and* the moral sort. At the end of it all, we too will be landfill.

There's death and there's death. Spiritually, says the Bible, we're dead already. Physically we're just catching up with reality. As my lifetime's supply of heartbeats deplete one by one, I'm living out the death I was born into.

As strange as these ideas might sound, we use this kind of language all the time: 'She came alive when the music played.' 'He was dead inside.' 'It was like being born again.' 'Life' and 'death' are far more than biological terms. Genesis is teaching what we feel intuitively – that there's more to life than a functioning brainstem and there's a death that's deeper than a cardiac flat line. Beyond our physical existence there's a death to be feared and a life to be sought. Therefore, just because we're alive, does not mean we're *alive*.

Life is something that must come to us from beyond. In ourselves we are disconnected. To return to the Christmas tree analogy, the trunk has been severed and the branches are now perishing. We are born cut off from true life in God, and our physical and moral decay is a symptom.

Are you saying what I think you're saying?

Perhaps your ears are pricking up at the moment. You're wondering, 'Is this that crazy old doctrine called "original sin"?' That depends what you mean. People have often heard third-hand reports of 'original sin' and imagine it to teach that children are monstrous little devils until their sins are washed away in baptism, or some other medieval nonsense. Let me assure you, it's not that. I'll explain it by way of illustration.

I am Australian by birth. I sat no entrance exam, passed no test, performed no deed and paid no price. It was not an achievement, it was not a choice, it was not a reward and it was not a punishment *(no snide remarks!)*. In short it had nothing to do with *me*. I am part of a family that just *is* Australian and that's where I find my national identity – not in me but in my family connections.

In the same way I was born disconnected from God. I didn't fail a test.

There was no test. It was never about my behaviour. I am part of a family that just *is* separated from God.

Let it be said straight away that this separation is far from the end of the story. God does not intend for anyone to remain in separation. But this is where our own personal stories begin: just as I was born far from the mother country, we all begin life away from the Father's house.

In a sense this is just the spiritual side of a truth we all know physically. Every child is born needy. By nature we must receive life from beyond us – oxygen, food, water and shelter. We're not born self-sufficient. Sustenance must come from outside or we perish.

'Original sin' says the same thing, only spiritually speaking. I'm not born with spiritual life in myself. I'm born disconnected and I must receive true life from beyond me. Jesus calls himself things like the Bread of Life or the Source of Living Water.[19] He is our spiritual sustenance from beyond. So none of this is teaching divine neglect; it's just about our human need.

The atheist Christopher Hitchens once characterised original sin like this: 'Created sick – commanded to be well.'[20] Actually it's much more like: 'Born hungry – offered food.' It's the teaching that I'm every bit as spiritually dependent as I am physically dependent.

Of course this grates against our pride. We want to be spiritually self-sufficient. In many ways we wish there were qualifications for a connection to God. We feel pretty sure we could meet them (if we really applied ourselves). But the story of Adam says, 'Too late! Your behaviour can't undo your family identity. Your actions can't change your being. You're going to have to bank on God's mercy not your efforts.'

Often we imagine God as some kind of Heavenly Schoolmaster grading our efforts. Actually the teaching of 'original sin' makes us rethink that completely. He's not scrutinising a range of promising (and not so promising) candidates. Rather the God of 'original sin' is more like a long-suffering

God is more like a long-suffering Father whose children have run away. And it is he who will seek them out and bring them home.

Father whose children have run away. And it is *he* who will seek them out and bring them home.

In fact let me develop the illustration I've been using throughout this chapter. Remember how Ann Forbes was transported for her crime and I was born as a foreigner to the mother country. That might sound seriously unfair *if* it was my job to get back to England. But, in the Bible, that's not how the story goes. The truth of TWO is that the King (Christ) wants to emigrate! The King has *always* determined to be with his exiles. The place he puts us is the place he will make his home. Therefore, even as those born far from the King, we are precisely where he is going to meet us.

The Bread of Life comes to us in our hunger; the Source of Living Waters comes to us in our thirst; the Life-Giver comes to us in our perishing; the Lord of Forgiveness comes to us in our sin; the God of Connection comes to us in our exile. All that we require are our needs and, in Adam, our needs are precisely what we're born with. Original sin enfranchises the world.

It's happening

In the last few pages I've dropped a couple of bombshells. Shocking truth number one is: we're disconnected from God and therefore spiritually dead. Number two is: we're *born* that way. This is far from the full picture but it is part of the biblical picture of reality. I wonder what you're thinking at the moment.

There's more to be said in chapter 6 but perhaps you're thinking, 'This can't be *true*.' Or perhaps you're thinking, 'This can't be *fair*.' Before you make up your mind, I urge you to consider whether it's *happening*. It seems to me that the world around us bears the imprint of the Adam story. Something has happened to the world, and something has happened to us. Those six features of Adam's story – the suspicion, selfishness, slavery, self-justification, stuff-ups and separation – dominate our lives. In fact there is no corner of the world free from these effects. My contention is that our lives are *like* Adam's story because our lives are *shaped* by Adam's story. It's worth considering.

Perhaps you began this chapter thinking that you cannot relate to an ancient story about a garden paradise. But as we have gone on I hope there's another sense in which you have found it profoundly familiar. When I consider these six features of Adam's fall I confess I can relate to them all too well. The Bible says we can relate because we're related. These are the family traits of our common humanity and our family inheritance is stark and unenviable. Cut off from God, our inheritance is death – personal, spiritual and cosmic.

The end is now!

If there's one thing that unites Hollywood films and religious fundamentalists it's an obsession with the end of the world. Often we're told that the earth will soon meet its doom and we should all be afraid – very afraid.

According to the Bible, though, there's a significant sense in which the end has already come. It came at the beginning. The catastrophic blow has been dealt. The future does not hang in the balance; judgement is pronounced. We're not on a precipice; we've already fallen. That's the biblical picture, and it's painted on a cosmic canvas.

In Genesis chapter 3 we see an unravelling of the natural order.[21] Human relationships are cursed. The battle of the sexes begins. Family, work and even the physical world is infected with disorder, decay and death. The Lord God says to the couple, 'Cursed is the ground because of you.'[22] Even the natural order is disrupted. In the words of Paul in the New Testament:

When humanity fell, the cosmos tumbled with it. Peace was shattered. All hell broke loose.

'creation was subjected to frustration'.[23] The natural order is 'groaning'; it's as though the world is 'in the pains of childbirth'.[24] How can such physical consequences flow from a spiritual disorder?

The Bible answers that Adam stood in a unique relationship to the world and a unique relationship to God. He was God's representative and earth's ruler. The God-human relationship was the axis on which the world turned. When humanity was at peace with God, all was right with the world. When humanity fell, the cosmos tumbled with it. Peace was shattered. All hell broke loose.

This means that there is darkness and chaos *out there* in the world, but there is also darkness and chaos *in here* in my heart. And the two are bound up together. They share the same origin. It's a hell of a problem.

The pit

At some point we need to talk about this. I think now's the time. Let's speak of hell. (For more on the subject see chapter 9.)

Raising hell is either terrific fun (in the sense of throwing TVs out of hotel windows) or dreadfully sobering. I'm afraid this is the sobering kind. But I should say straight away that I'm not really changing the subject in this section. We've already been talking about hell throughout the chapter – just by different names: separation, disconnection, spiritual death. As we have said, we are decaying branches in a tree that's cut off. We are, therefore, perishing. This is a physical but also a spiritual truth.

We're perishing *physically* and one day we will be dead *decisively*. But we're also disconnected *spiritually* and, if nothing happens, one day we'll be disconnected *decisively*. The Bible says all of us continue beyond our physical death. But if our spiritual estrangement is not dealt with, then that spiritual death will keep going. This is what the Bible means by hell.

Jesus continually describes it in terms of disconnection. He speaks of being 'lost'.[25] He talks about an outer darkness.[26] He tells stories of being shut out of the feast – where there is weeping and wailing and the angry gnashing of teeth.[27] Unlike the unbiblical portraits of medieval art, Jesus does not paint pictures of devils with pitchforks poking the damned. In Jesus' teaching the evil powers are not the jailers; they are the inmates. In a very real sense hell is not *for people*; it is 'for the devil and his angels'.[28] And yet, tragically, humans do end up there – caught up in an unnatural and enslaving evil.

God's intention for humanity is the enjoyment of his light forever. Yet there is a sphere of darkness – a place that stands against God, against his reconciling love, against his light and life. This is the outer darkness. Here separation – and all that flows from it – runs its full course.

In his starkest parable on the subject, Jesus speaks of a man who is full of suspicion, selfishness and self-justification.[29] In the story he dies and Jesus describes his life after death as a continuation of that very same suspicion, selfishness and self-justification. The man has not changed a bit, he is simply confirmed in that separation that marked his life. And Jesus speaks in unflinching terms of the desperate thirst and burning torment of separation from God.

Such descriptions are fearful. Yet one of the most confronting aspects of hell is that it isn't merely a future reality, *there and then*. According to the Bible, hell has its beginning in the *here and now*. As Jesus says in John chapter 3, the world is 'condemned already'.[30] God has already pronounced an angry and irreversible 'No' against the way of Adam. When the life of the THREE meets the darkness of our rebellion, there is anger – a righteous outrage that is born of love.

Perhaps you're thinking, 'Anger and love? Aren't they opposites?' Not at all. We know this even in a human context. When those that we love are harmed, we will feel a righteous anger. When the love is deep and the harm is great, our anger burns all the hotter. On the other hand if someone has no emotional reaction to evil, we generally label them a sociopath!

Of course when we get angry, we're generally quite terrible at handling it in appropriate ways. But even in our fallen humanity we see that love and anger are not opposed. Righteous anger can and will arise precisely because we love. How much more will it arise in the God of love who knows the depths of our evil and intends such heights for our world?

God is love. And therefore, in response to a hell-bent world, God is angry. This anger 'remains' on the world in its rebellion, even now.[31] This means that our best handle on hell is not medieval art or horror films. Our clearest picture of hell is disconnected life in the here and now. If we want to know what hell is like, we just need to look at the distorted relationships that flow from our separation and suspicion. Where selfishness runs riot, where addictions enslave or where evil is perpetrated and then justified as good, there we see snapshots of hell. And, chillingly, we see it in ourselves.

God is love. And therefore, in response to a hell-bent world, God is angry.

If we've ever used harsh words or stirred up gossip, we've felt the powers of hell – that's what the New Testament book of James says. James speaks of our tongues as fires.[32] Through our words we ignite devastating blazes in our lives and the lives of others. And what's the source of this burning? It 'is itself set on fire by hell'.[33] Hell is not just below us – it is within us and it comes out of us. You and I have felt hell-fire – in the searing words of others and in our own rash words.

There is much that is hellish in life and much that is hellish in us. Each instance is a massive warning about where disconnected living takes us. These hellish experiences are screaming at us not to follow through on the perishing way of Adam – because God has a very different destiny in mind for us.

Repeatedly God assures us that he wants no-one to perish.[34] His desire is for all to enter the light. You see the Light *shines*; the Light does not darken. To be sure, there is a realm of darkness, estranged from the Light. But God does not darken the darkness. He shines. He wants us all to have true spiritual life. That's why his will was always to send his Son as a second Adam. Jesus entered our hell so we could have his heaven.

INTERVAL

Congratulations, you've made it halfway through the grand tour! Thanks for sticking with it!

We haven't yet finished this chapter, but I realise things have gotten pretty heavy in the last few pages so I wanted to offer a refreshments break and a bit of encouragement. Be assured, you've now come through the hardest part of the tour. If you imagine a giant 'U' shape, we are now at the bottom and the only way is up!

Perhaps this is the time to stretch your legs, put on the kettle and have a think about your reaction to the book so far. In particular, ask yourself:

- What do I make of 'the Jesus-story'? Do I warm to him?
- What do I make of 'the Jesus-God'? Could *this* God be the one?
- What do I make of 'the Adam-story'? Do I see myself in it?

When you're ready, we'll rejoin the tour and find out how 'the Jesus-story' answers 'the Adam-story'.

All set? Let's return to TWO ...

Joining us in the pit

In one episode of *The West Wing*[35] Leo tells Josh a story that sounds like it's straight from the Bible:

> This guy's walking down the street when he falls in a hole. The walls are so steep he can't get out.
>
> A doctor passes by and the guy shouts up, 'Hey, you. Can you help me out?' The doctor writes a prescription, throws it down in the hole and moves on.
>
> Then a priest comes along and the guy shouts up, 'Father, I'm down in this hole. Can you help me out?' The priest writes out a prayer, throws it down in the hole and moves on.
>
> Then a friend walks by. 'Hey, Joe, it's me. Can you help me out?' And the friend jumps in the hole.
>
> Our guy says, 'Are you stupid? Now we're both down here.'
>
> The friend says, 'Yeah, but I've been down here before and I know the way out.'

It's a beautiful portrait of friendship and Aaron Sorkin, the writer, is either consciously or unconsciously echoing a story that's been told for 2000 years. Jesus spoke about a Good Samaritan who came across a helpless victim.[36] While the religious and cultural leaders of the day passed by, this beautiful stranger gets his hands dirty. To put it in the terms of *The West Wing* story, he jumps in the hole to be with the man and to lift him out.

Here is the beating heart of Christianity: The Son of God sees our fallen state and he does not pass by. He does not simply send instructions from on high. He does not yell down advice or provide incentives to climb. He does not try to convince us that the pit is 'all in our mind' or that 'it ain't so bad really'. No, he jumps into the pit to be with us, to fight for us and to lift us out. In short, Jesus is the God who befriends us.

Last chapter we said that Jesus joins us in our failures so that we can join him in his family. In this chapter we can develop that idea a little further: Jesus is the Son of God who became the second Adam. This suffering world cries out for an answer. Christians believe that Jesus *is* the answer. Every longing we have for a triumph over evil, every yearning we feel for a defeat of the darkness, every hope we hold out for a life beyond death is found in Jesus.

Because of TWO, Christians are both realists and optimists. We are realists in that we face the depths of our problems in Adam – we know there is no earthly hope for this world. But we're also optimists because we have caught sight of someone – a second Adam. In the midst of this dying world, we have seen someone who can turn it around.

So then, Jesus is our friend, who joins us in the pit. He joins us as our representative, to take hold of Adam's world and put it right. As we'll see, he comes alongside us to live the life we should live, die the death we deserve to die and then rise to a future beyond our wildest dreams.

The life we should have lived

'Can we play through?' said the two golfers behind us. We were on a stag do, hacking our way around a beautiful course.

'Sure,' we said, stepping aside.

They lined up their shots from the white tees, a good 40 yards behind us. No practice swing, no chat, no fuss – ping – the ball flew clear over our heads down the middle of the fairway. 'Thanks lads,' they said, and marched past our slack-jawed wonder.

'So that's how it's done!' we exclaimed. 'Who are those guys?'

'Pros,' came the answer. Within minutes they had birdied the hole and left us for dust.

In chapter 2 we caught a glimpse of the life of Jesus. Perhaps you were tempted to say, 'So that's how it's done!' And maybe, seeing the incredible life of Jesus, you've asked the question, 'Who *is* that man?' Chapter 3 gave part of the answer. He's the eternal Son of God, filled with the Spirit. Jesus is what true divinity looks like.

Jesus is not just what true divinity looks like. He is also what true humanity looks like.

But in this chapter we are learning something more. Jesus doesn't just 'play through', leaving us to marvel at his brilliance. Actually Jesus joins our team. He volunteers to play with us and for us, so that everything he does counts on our scorecard. Jesus is not just what true divinity looks like. He is also what true humanity looks like.

Bumbling around a golf course with my mates, I thought I knew what golf looked like. But when I saw the professionals, I realised I'd only ever seen 'happy hacking'. It's the same with humanity. Before we saw Jesus, we thought we knew what true humanity looked like. But seeing Jesus we come face to face with a man who is truly alive because he is profoundly connected to God. Jesus is everything we were meant to be.

Let's look at Jesus' true humanity through the six lenses we used with Adam:

1. SUSPICION?

Jesus implicitly trusts his 'Father' for everything, even through the starkest trials and temptations.[37] As he hung on the cross, his enemies scorned him: 'He trusts in God!' they spat.[38] In truth those words were the most fitting eulogy – here, finally, was a man of faith.

2. SELFISHNESS?

If anyone had a right to be served it was the Son of God. Yet far from claiming his rights, he abandoned them all, plunging headlong into utter self-giving on the cross. Jesus did not just give *things*; time and again the Bible says he gave *himself*. What he taught he also practised: he found his life by giving it away.[39]

3. SLAVERY?

Never has a man walked the earth with such liberty, poise and confidence as Jesus. *Because* he gave himself away, he seemed completely in possession of himself. In the words of The Blues Brothers, he was on a mission from God. No-one could cow him, corrupt him, seduce him or deflect him. Freedom was the very atmosphere of his life.

4. SELF-JUSTIFICATION?

The night before his death, Jesus stood trial before multiple courts. He was tortured, mocked, spat at and falsely accused for hours. He was undergoing the greatest miscarriage of justice conceivable and he was silent before his accusers. Jesus entrusted himself completely to his Father's care, never justifying himself but waiting for God's vindication. Self-justification is so hard-wired into us, it's difficult to imagine a human being without it. But with Jesus we see the most appealing picture. Here is someone with nothing to hide and nothing to prove.

5. STUFF-UPS?

'Nobody's perfect,' we say. Of course we don't say it as a lament – only as an excuse. But Jesus walked around claiming to be perfect. That sets a high bar for a public figure to live up to! Yet Jesus would challenge even his enemies to dish the dirt on him if there was anything amiss in his life.[40] No-one ever could. Even at the end his prosecutors could not make their charges stick.[41] Year in, year out, Jesus lived the good life that we cannot live for five minutes – a life in perfect connection with God.

6. SEPARATION?

Jesus is the unique Son of God, always full of the Holy Spirit. He is continually praying, continually quoting the word of God and continually calling God his Father – he uses that intimate title nearly 200 times in the Gospels. He is 'in' the Father and the Father is 'in' him.[42] Here is a man unlike any the world has seen – a man in perfect union with God.

Examining Jesus' life, we might be tempted to say, 'He puts us to shame.' In one sense that's true but, wonderfully, there's a deeper reality: he lives this perfect life *for us*. Like the golfer playing on our team, he takes responsibility for the life we ought to live. He also takes responsibility for the death we ought to die.

The death we should have died

Occasionally scandals will rock a government department. Someone has made a blunder and the public are 'baying for blood'. In these situations it's not unheard of for the minister or the head of the department to 'carry the can'. Even if they weren't directly involved in the failure, they recognise that it happened 'on their watch'. They take responsibility for the failure and resign. Of course later we may learn that they were given a massive redundancy package and we retract all our praise, but for a few days at least we admire them.

The Son of God was not responsible for our mess, but he took responsibility.

Taking responsibility is a noble thing to do. Even if the leader did not make the mistake, we respect those who make themselves accountable for what happens under them. In a sense this is what Jesus came to do. The Son of God was not responsible for our mess, but he *took* responsibility. He came to take charge of the situation and – though it was not his fault – to shoulder the blame.

Constantly Jesus spoke of the necessity of his death. '... the Son of Man must suffer many things and be rejected by the elders, chief priests and teachers of the law, and ... he must be killed and after three days rise again.'[43] His death would not cut short his mission – his death *was* his mission.

The whole family of Adam is disconnected from God. We are perishing and our lives produce all kinds of suspicion, selfishness, slavery, self-justification and stuff-ups. We are heading for spiritual and eternal death, and essentially Jesus says, 'No! I will take responsibility. I will take your sins to myself, I will even take your spiritual death to myself.'

As Jesus died, a fearful darkness fell.[44] Why? Because he's entering the outer darkness and experiencing it in full. He thirsts and cries out in agony. He bellows, 'My God, my God, why have you forsaken me?'[45] This is the ultimate spiritual separation. Jesus is suffering hell and he's doing it for us. As one Bible writer says:

> 'Christ ... suffered once for sins, the righteous for the unrighteous, to bring you to God.'[46]

Life beyond death

Imagine, once again, you've fallen in a pit. (I know, you really must watch where you're going.) Your friend stands at the top and declares, 'I'm here to rescue you,' and jumps in. This is wonderfully encouraging except that the fall kills him instantly. Now you are doubly dismayed. You've lost your friend *and* you've lost your hope. This would be something like our own situation if Jesus remained in the tomb. But the Bible insists that Jesus rose. In chapter 6 we will explore some of the reasons why Christians believe this:

- The prophecies foretold it.
- Jesus constantly predicted it.
- The tomb was empty.
- Hundreds of people met him after death in various situations.

- The Christian movement was established on its basis in the very city where they claimed he had risen.
- The body was never found.
- The disciples kept testifying to the resurrection even on pain of death.
- The Jesus movement itself experienced an incredible resurrection – out of utter hopelessness came the most extraordinary life and growth.

Jesus' resurrection seems by far the best explanation for the facts. On the other hand, conspiracy theories that seek alternative explanations turn out to be far more fanciful than the Bible. Whatever you think about Jesus' resurrection, understand that Christians believe in it, not as a flight from reason but precisely because we take the evidence seriously.

If you're sceptical, let me assure you there is every reason to believe that Jesus rose from the dead (more on that in chapter 6). But let's now ask the 'so what?' question. What is the meaning of Jesus' resurrection? Our central verse for this chapter gives the answer:

> 'For since death came through a man, the resurrection of the dead comes also through a man. For as in Adam all die, so in Christ all will be made alive.'[47]

By his death Jesus takes responsibility for our failures. In his resurrection he pioneers a whole new kind of life. Where Adam's fall gave death the last word, Jesus' resurrection gives life the final say.

Like a needle that pierces through the black shroud of death, Jesus entered into the hell of our disconnection and then burst out the other side. His intention is to pull the world through that same journey – through death and disconnection but then into feasting joy. Jesus, the second Adam, did not simply rise for his own sake. As a representative, he came through death so he could give us his victory.

In the six weeks following Jesus' resurrection, he appeared to hundreds of people giving them foretastes of the future. Every appearance showed us a snapshot of the life he offers beyond death. There were joy-filled reunions,[48] peace and awe,[49] plenty of meals,[50] fascinating conversations.[51] There were country walks,[52] fishing with friends,[53] barbecues on the beach[54] and Jesus at the centre of it all. That's the life, isn't it? That's eternal life, according to Jesus.

Isaac Azimov once said, 'Whatever the tortures of hell, I think the boredom of heaven would be even worse.' But Azimov can't have been thinking of *this*. With Jesus we have an earthy, fully human hope. It's not about disembodied bliss in the seventh dimension; it's about this world renewed. As the second Adam, Jesus has taken hold of this world in all its physicality and he intends to raise it up just as he was raised on Easter Sunday. What happened to Jesus – death then resurrection – is the plan for all his people and for all creation when he returns: 'For as in Adam all die, so in Christ all will be made alive.'

This is the future which Jesus offers. Therefore everything depends on being connected to Jesus. Nothing could be more important than being 'in Christ' as this verse describes. Our next chapter is all about that connection.

Watch this video: *three-two-one.org/World*

Optional reading: John chapters 9–12

- How is opinion about Jesus polarising? Why are there such extreme reactions?
- How does Jesus speak of his own identity?
- What does Jesus teach about his death and resurrection?
- What would it be like to follow Jesus do you think?

• COMING UP IN CHAPTER 5 •

We have been discussing some very big ideas in this book: the life and impact of Jesus, the nature of God and the salvation of the world. In this next chapter we bring it home. Now it's about *you*.

Where do *you* fit into all this talk about God and the world? The answer comes with the truth of ONE: you are one with Adam. Be one with Jesus.

5

ONE: YOU ARE **ONE** WITH ADAM – BE **ONE** WITH JESUS

We are Mo Farah lifting the 10,000 metres gold ... we are Sir Chris Hoy ... We are Nicola Adams ...

—*Carol Ann Duffy's poem 'Translating the British, 2012'*

I am in my Father, and you are in me, and I am in you.

—*Jesus, John 14:20*

Champions

'Who do you support?' they ask. 'In the football, who's your team?'

'Umm,' I hesitate. I've been here before. 'Well I'm Australian but I lived in Highbury for a while so I suppose I follow Arsenal. At a distance. Sort of.'

'Arsenal?! We STUFFED you on Saturday!' they beam.

'You did?' I look at their shirt. Yep, it's a dead ringer for the shirts worn by eleven men who, last weekend, bettered another eleven men neither of us have met. But that's not the way it's ever phrased. It's always 'We beat you.' When our champions win, *we* win.

At that point I want to protest: 'Who's *we*? I know where you were last Saturday. You were glued to the telly, part-man, part-sofa, bellowing advice at the greatest athletes in the world. I'm not sure shrieking "Referee!!" every 90 seconds helped the cause. But if you want to claim victory in the name of your champions, who am I to sneeze on your custard?'

By the way I'm not a complete spoilsport – only when my team loses. When they win, the word 'we' rushes back into my vocabulary. *The team* loses but *we* win! Funny that.

During the London Olympics the Poet Laureate, Carol Ann Duffy, wrote the poem above to capture the nation's feelings about Team GB. Apparently 'We are Mo Farah lifting the 10,000 metres gold.' Yet none of us have made the sacrifices such athletes have made. And if you asked *us* to compete, we wouldn't have a hope. (Speaking for myself, the most aerobic workout of my day is brushing my teeth.) But when Mo Farah wins, the nation celebrates – of course it does. He is Britain's champion and his victory is their victory.

Perhaps the epitome of 'faith in our champions' is seen in the football transfer market. Here managers, coaches and scouts sift the world's greatest leagues for that one miracle maker. Pundits speculate, fortunes are spent, millions of fans hold their breath and it's all founded on the myth of the one man.

The myth of the one man goes something like this. Somewhere, out there, is a player of such extraordinary talent that no price is too absurd, for – so the legend goes – if we have *him*, then everything will change. He will galvanise the team. He will win every game. He will turn our fortunes around. This man is out there and we must have him.

Of course it's a myth, but imagine it was true. Imagine your team actually found 'the one man' and, in spite of the naysayers, you'd always believed in him. He'd always been your guy. As the season unfolds, he scores the winner in every game, propelling the team up the league, through the cup and all the way to Wembley. There you are at the FA Cup final. His last-minute double strike snatches victory from the jaws of defeat. The noise is deafening as he runs over to your end of the ground, arms outstretched. He's mouthing the words 'For you ... It's for you.' There you are amidst the deafening roar. How do you feel?

Remember that you have not expended a calorie of effort in this victory. In spite of your high-quality coaching from the stands, none of it has affected the outcome. Nonetheless, how do you feel? 'Over the moon' is the usual expression. But that doesn't capture it. We're ecstatic – beside ourselves with joy. We jump, we shout, we sing, we hug complete strangers just because they too share a connection with the one man. Victory, camaraderie, euphoria – this is how Christians feel about Jesus.

Jesus is the one man who changes everything. A Christian is someone who believes in Jesus, our Champion. He wins and we celebrate because we are connected – we are ONE. That's what this chapter is about.

What is a Christian?

Let me use the champions analogy to describe where we've got to in the book. After studying the chapter on TWO it should be clear that we are members of a failing club – Team Adam. The club is on the brink of bankruptcy and relegation. But right from Genesis chapter 3 stories about 'the one man' had been circulating. He would join the club and defeat our enemy in a fight to the death.[1] Throughout the Old Testament hype surrounding 'the one man' built to epic proportions. Then one day, as John was baptising in the Jordan River, we got to see our man.

The baptism was his official 'signing' for the club. This was the ceremony where he wore our colours – identifying with Team Adam publicly and irreversibly. The rest of the Gospels reveal his 'wonder season'. He took on the forces that constantly defeat us: temptation, sin, evil, disease and death. These powers always get the better of us, but not Jesus. He 'played a blinder', living up to all the hype.

Then, at the end of his life, we see how deeply our Champion identifies with us. On the cross he took responsibility for everything that belongs to us – even our sins and the godforsaken death they deserve. As he died, the crowd fell silent, wondering if the hype was misplaced. Yet, just when they thought it was all over, Jesus scored a decisive winner against the ultimate 'baddy'.

'The last enemy to be destroyed is death,' wrote the Apostle Paul.[2] In billions of matches, death has never lost a battle. Without exception it sucks us down into the grave. But Jesus ran headlong into that pit and smashed a hole right through it. On Easter Sunday he burst through to the far side as the ultimate victor. Then, like the triumphant footballer running to his supporters, Jesus has his arms outstretched to the world and he cries, 'For you! This is for you!'

A Christian is someone who has found themselves swept up in the story. We have recognised our place in Team Adam. We have owned our failures and faced the certainty of defeat. But, more than this, we have seen Jesus. We have heard his claims to be the long-promised Champion. We have witnessed his life, his death and his resurrection. We are persuaded that he is who he says he is. And now the penny has dropped: if he is our Champion, then his victory is our victory. We know we look like 'a bunch of losers' and we know we've contributed nothing to the victory. Nonetheless we sing like we've won because, *in Jesus*, we have.

'In Jesus'

I just used a Christian-y phrase there: 'in Jesus'. That's deliberate. I think it's probably the most important two-word phrase in the Bible. If you want to answer the question 'What is a Christian?', this is a phrase you cannot avoid. The Bible uses 'in Christ' over 150 times. A Christian is *in Christ* (or *in Jesus*, or *in him*).[3] Sometimes the Bible uses other words like 'united with Jesus'[4] or 'hidden with Christ'.[5] These are all describing the same kind of intimate connection. A Christian is not simply 'under' the authority of Jesus. They are not just 'with' the Son of God in spirit. The Christian is 'in' Christ. And you cannot get closer than 'in'.

Rory Shiner, in his book *One Forever*,[6] describes our one-ness with Jesus using the analogy of plane travel. If you want to get to Australia then finding a flight to Sydney is a good idea. But it would be a strange traveller who goes to Heathrow, finds the relevant 747 and then sprints down the runway, hoping to follow after its general direction. Neither does the traveller watch the plane, awestruck, from the lounge and seek inspiration for their own powers of flight. No, if the traveller wants to get to Sydney, there's one relationship they must have to the plane. They need to be *in* it. If they are *in* the plane then everything that's happening to the plane will happen to the traveller.

This is our connection to Jesus. He is not merely our example to follow. He is not just our inspiration to admire. He is our champion and we are in him. The Christian life is not, foundationally, about copying Jesus' actions (though that becomes our great joy). It's not, at heart, about admiring Jesus from a distance (though we certainly do admire him). Fundamentally Christianity is about being united to Jesus – sharing forever in all that he is and all that he has done. A Christian is ONE with God's Son.

Let's explore a couple of images the Bible uses for this one-ness.

Pictures of one-ness

The night before Jesus died, he told his friends, 'I am the vine; you are the branches. If you remain in me and I in you, you will bear much fruit.'[7] This is a beautifully organic picture of one-ness. Like branches grafted in to a thriving vine, the believer is vitally connected to Jesus.

We've already thought about our disconnection from God. In Adam we are like branches in a Christmas tree, cut off and perishing. We have no spiritual life in ourselves and, though we may decorate ourselves nicely and surround ourselves with family and festivities, our days are numbered.

Jesus says he is a flourishing tree. He is profoundly and eternally connected to God his Father with the nourishing sap of the Spirit flowing through him. But Jesus is not to be admired from afar. In essence, his offer to the world is this: 'Be grafted into me.' A Christian is someone who finds life in connection with Jesus.

Consider another picture of one-ness: marriage. When my wife and I were married, we said these vows to each other: 'All that I am I give to you, all that I have I share with you.' At that moment there were sniggers in the congregation. Our friends were laughing because they knew we had absolutely nothing to offer each other. Essentially we were pledging to unite our poverty. 'All that I am I give to you, all that I have I share with you' is a funny vow when you have nothing to give.

But think about the fairytale weddings. Think of the children's stories where the handsome prince marries the downtrodden pauper. In these tales the prince declares, 'All that I am I give to you, all that I have I share with you.' He gives her his riches and his inheritance, he shares his throne and he brings her into the highest family in the land. Instantly she is royalty because of the marriage.

Remember, though, it's a two-way thing. She says to him, 'All that I am I give to you, all that I have I share with you.' Whatever debts she has, they go to her prince and he absorbs them all. If there is disgrace attached to her family name, he covers over it with his name. Whatever shame she once had as a pauper is transformed in a moment. Now she is a princess. From that point onwards, she is rich, royal and respected in the highest courts of the land: all because she is ONE with her prince.

Such fairytales point us to a deeper truth. From the first book of the Bible till the last, the relationship of God to his people has been described as a marriage-like union. According to the Bible, there is a Prince who belongs to the ultimate Royal Family. This Prince has chosen to unite with paupers. We are not royalty by birth. We have all sorts of debts, many sins and much shame. Nevertheless, the Prince offers to be ONE with us.

Jesus calls himself the bridegroom[8] and the Bible commonly calls his people 'the bride'.[9] Christ's proposal is like any marriage proposal. Essentially he says, 'All that I am I give to you, all that I have I share with you.'

Speaking as a Christian I can say that all his goodness, his love, his riches, his cosmic inheritance, his family connections, his royal status – everything that he is now belongs to me. Best of all, he shares *himself*. That's the heart of marriage. We don't marry someone to get their things (hopefully!). We marry them to get *them*.

Christians don't receive Jesus in order to gain some heavenly goodies (like forgiveness, eternal life and spiritual feelings). No, we receive him in order to have *him*. And if we have Jesus, then he absorbs all our debts – at the cross he pays them off himself. Never again will we have to answer for our sins since Christ has taken responsibility for them all. More than this, he rises again beyond the reach of sin, death and judgement and he brings us into the ultimate Royal Family. Now his Father is our Father, his Spirit is our Spirit and we are forever ONE with the Son of God: 'for better, for worse, for richer, for poorer, in sickness and in health, to love and to cherish, till death ...', when we meet – face to face.

This is the heart of the Christian faith. Is this how you picture it? Many think of Christianity as a club for do-gooders, or a creed for conformists, or a hobby for the religious, or a fantasy for the gullible. It's easy to identify Christianity with a set of practices or beliefs or morals or institutions. But primarily it is one-ness with Jesus. Of course this works itself out in new practices, beliefs, behaviours and structures – all marriages bring such revolutions. But none of those externals lie at the heart of it. The heart of Christianity is Christ himself. And he is offered to you.

Welcome to the family

One night a spiritual enquirer came to Jesus.[10] His name was Nicodemus and he seemed to tick every box imaginable – socially, morally and religiously. He was a respected community leader and a renowned Bible scholar. If anyone had heaven 'in the bag', it was this man. Yet Jesus didn't care about any of his credentials. Instead he spoke these shocking words to him: 'Very truly I tell you, no one can see the kingdom of God unless they are born again.'[11]

This sends Nicodemus reeling but Jesus doesn't back down. He repeats his teaching: 'You must be born again.'[12]

Imagine Uncle Edward picking up the newborn baby and asking its mother, 'When was she born?' 'Two weeks ago.' 'Oh dear,' says Ed frowning, 'I reckon she needs to be born again.'

At this point Uncle Edward loses all his visiting rights. This is highly offensive. The proud parents will say, 'How dare you! What was wrong with her *first* birth?!' To demand a new birth is shocking. It's even more insulting when you're speaking of a grown man – especially one as good as Nicodemus. Why does even *Nicodemus* need a new birth?

Jesus gives a five-word answer that summarises our problem: 'Flesh gives birth to flesh.'[13] This is every genealogy ever written – flesh gives birth to more flesh. Jesus could have said, 'Adam gives birth to Adam' or 'Natural life gives birth to natural life'. The children of Adam might perform amazing deeds and achieve incredible feats – Nicodemus was certainly an impressive man. But nothing we do in life produces *God's* kind of life. We only reproduce *our* kind of life. It's just a law of nature. Cherry trees produce more cherry trees. Walruses produce more walruses. Earthlings produce more earthly life. But heaven's life is different. It comes to us from above.

That's why Jesus continues: 'Flesh gives birth to flesh, but the Spirit gives birth to spirit.' There is a *spiritual* life and it is above and beyond our flesh life. This life is a gift from above.

Jesus knows all about the life of the Spirit. He and his Father have enjoyed the life of the Spirit eternally. Now Jesus has come to share it with us. God's Son has joined our family so that we can join his. He has taken our flesh so that we can have his Spirit.

In the Bible's most famous verse, Jesus tells Nicodemus how we receive this gift from heaven: 'God so loved the world that he gave his one and only Son, that whoever believes in him shall not perish but have eternal life.'[14] Here is heaven's gift. God the Father gives his Son to the world and whoever receives this gift receives eternal life.

Notice how Jesus defines eternal life. It's not so much a length of time or a place far away. 'Eternal life' is the spiritual life Jesus has been talking about. 'Eternal life' means being ONE with Jesus, receiving his Spirit, coming in on his heavenly Family. This connected life stretches on forever but it begins now. Such life is what we were made for. And it is all a gift from God.

Receiving Jesus

In the verse above it says 'whoever *believes*' will 'have eternal life'. I wonder how you picture 'believing'? What does it mean to 'have faith'? ('Belief' and 'faith' are the same thing in the Bible).

A popular picture of faith is provided by Indiana Jones in *The Last Crusade*. Indy has to make 'the leap of faith'. He must step out into a void, not knowing whether anything will catch him. We watch as he nervously summons up the requisite 'belief' and then – boldly, blindly – he makes the leap. Is that what faith is?

No. 'Believing in Jesus' is not a bold leap in the dark. We are not capable of bold leaps towards Jesus. It's Jesus who has to cross the void towards us. The famous verse above says that Jesus is God's gift to us. Therefore what does it mean to 'believe in Jesus'? It means receiving the gift – receiving Jesus.

John chapter 1 puts it like this: 'Yet to all who did receive him [Jesus], to those who believed in his name, he gave the right to become children of God.'[15] The first two phrases here are parallel. 'Receiving Jesus' is the same as 'believing in his name'. There is a gift offered to the world: the Father gives his Son. A believer is someone who recognises the gift and says, 'Yes please.'

You might well ask, 'How can you *receive* a person?' Well think of a couple on their wedding day. They receive each other into their lives. They say 'Yes please' to the offer of the other person. From then on they live in a united relationship of love and trust.

Receiving Jesus is the same. The Father offers us his Son and, if we receive him, then from that moment on we are united to Jesus. As those who are ONE with the Son of God, we enter his Family. We are adopted by the Father, united to the Son, and filled with the Holy Spirit. All this comes through faith because faith is receiving Jesus.

So when someone asks, 'What must I do to become a Christian?', there's a deep sense in which the answer is 'Nothing!' There's nothing you must *do* to become a Christian. Think about the various pictures of the Christian life we have considered:

- With the champion analogy: you are a spectator; you can't win the victory yourself.
- With the tree analogy: you are a perishing branch; you can't revive yourself.
- With the marriage analogy: you don't bring riches into the union, only debts.
- With the birth analogy: someone else does all the hard work; birth just happens to you.

Someone might ask, 'What must I do to become a Christian?' Actually everything must be done for you. This is why Jesus came. And it's why God the Father freely gives him to the world. We cannot earn him, we cannot pay for him and we don't deserve him. But he is offered anyway. God's love is unconditional, but *because* he has such love, it calls for a response.

Do you want in?

We haven't yet finished the book. In fact we haven't yet finished this chapter, but I think it's probably time to tell you how you 'come in on Jesus'. Let me explain how you 'get connected' or, in other words, how you become a Christian. Given all that we have talked about, you can probably guess what I'm about to say: get married.

Jesus has declared his vows. Through his life, death and resurrection he has pledged himself to you. A Christian is someone who receives the offer of Christ. In doing so they are ONE with Jesus. This one-ness is an all-embracing relationship of love and trust. In one sense it is as simple as saying, 'I will.' But it's also as revolutionary as saying, 'I will.' As with any marriage, it is both simple and revolutionary all at once.

The day I married my wife, we made some promises that took about three minutes to declare. It was very straightforward. Through those same promises single Glen died and married Glen came to life. There was a death and

To receive Jesus means a death and a resurrection.

a resurrection as I entered the relationship. It's the same with becoming a Christian. To receive Jesus means a death and a resurrection. It's death to the old Adam life but at the same time it means a new life in Christ.

I'm not sure how you picture becoming a Christian. People talk of 'getting religion' (which sounds like a nasty tropical disease) or of 'turning over a new leaf'. Sometimes Christianity can sound like a new year's resolution to 'try harder from now on'. But it's nothing like that. A Christian is not someone who has summoned up the willpower to do better. We haven't decided we're going to 'kill off' our old selfish ways. In fact we have recognised that we can't make the changes we wish we could. Frankly we don't have it in us to be Christians. But that's why it's given to us in Jesus.

When I got married, I didn't change myself into a married man – the marriage did that for me. The fact of the one-ness put the old single Glen to death. It also brought into existence a new married Glen. It's the same with Jesus. You might think, 'I could never live the Christian life' – in many ways I hope you *do* realise your inadequacy. But you're not called to 'clean up your life' and act like a Christian from now on. You *are* called to enter this one-ness – and to let the one-ness change you.

In the next few pages I will paint a picture of life 'in Christ'. I want to show you what one-ness with Jesus looks like in the everyday. I do this so that no-one receives Jesus unaware of the implications. There's an old saying: 'Love is blind but marriage is the eye-opener'. I want your eyes to be wide open before you 'take the plunge'. So here is a sneak peek at the Christian life. Being a Christian means: new life in the midst of the old, a new family and a new conversation.

New life in the midst of the old

When the pauper marries the prince, some things happen right away but other changes are more gradual. At once she is royalty but will she necessarily feel it? She may feel lost in her new surroundings. She may struggle to meet her prince's eye. She may wrestle with old habits till her dying day. By status she is royal but it may take a long time for her conduct, her conversation and her confidence to catch up with reality.

Being a Christian is like this. We are instantly ONE with Jesus and share in all he has. At once we are members of his family, having Christ's love, his status, his future, his Spirit and his Father: '… in Christ Jesus you are all children of God through faith.'[16]

But at the same time we belong to our human family with its Adam-like traits. Perhaps you have heard the saying: 'The Spirit is willing, but the flesh is weak.'[17] Jesus coined the phrase but the Bible is constantly speaking of this dual reality.[18] From Adam I have an old, selfish nature – the flesh. From Jesus, I have a new life – the life of the Spirit. This dual reality is a fall-out from the TWO and the struggle will be with us till our dying day.

Let's first think of the old life. Christians can still *feel* **separated** from God. We can still be **suspicious** of God. We still struggle with **selfishness**, **slaveries**, **self-justification** and **stuff-ups**. Though we have the Spirit, the old life of the 'flesh' clings to us like skin to our bones and will do so till we die. But the Christian life is about reminding ourselves of another, stronger reality: we belong to Jesus.

In Jesus the **separation** problem is, in fact, gone. We are now reconnected to God. Now we look to Jesus and see that he loves us more than his own life. Therefore our natural **suspicion** is replaced by trust. When we rely on his love, we are released from ***selfishness*** and ***slavery***. We don't need to grasp at little gods because they cannot compete with what we have in Jesus. Our ***self-justification*** is also deflated. We don't need to prove ourselves. We know our failures but we can admit them, secure in the love of Jesus. And whatever **stuff-ups** burst out of us, we can know the forgiveness and restoration of Jesus.

There was an African bishop in the fifth century called Augustine. He remains one of the most profound and influential thinkers in all history but as a youth he was quite a ladies' man. One time, soon after his conversion to Christianity, a former lover came to flirt with him (some versions of the story say she was a prostitute). Augustine was not responding so she cried out, 'Augustine, Augustine, it is I!' He replied, 'Yes, but it is not I.' Augustine was a new man. And from his new identity he found the resources to say 'No' to the old life.

New life in the midst of the old will mean saying 'No' to the Adam-like life. But these 'No's do not limit us. Actually it's the old life that limited us. Jesus teaches us the way of freedom.

Perhaps you read chapter 2 about the life of Jesus and were impressed by the character of Christ. In the Gospels we see a life filled by God's Spirit and then poured out for the world; a life of utter self-giving and therefore self-possession. It was a life of total freedom because it was a life of pure service. It was life in connection with God and others. Wonderfully the Christian is invited into this life.

Jesus gives us his good life to live – a life that is free, fearless and fulfilled. This way of life is not the downside of Christianity. This is not the fine print of the Christian life, full of snags, traps and hidden costs. Here is wonderful news: the good life that you see in Jesus is now *yours* to live.

But you will notice there are no promises of earthly riches or easy living. In fact Jesus leads us *into* a suffering world to engage with it *more*, not less. While most people spend their lives keeping back, filling up and clinging on, Jesus teaches us to press in, pour out and give away. The way of Jesus is not a trouble-free existence – far from it. But Jesus does promise that, in giving ourselves away, we will truly *find* ourselves.[19] The way of Jesus is not about restricting or punishing us; in fact it is 'life ... to the full'.[20] Whatever we give up in the Christian life, Jesus promises it is only for the sake of our greater freedom and flourishing.[21] All that we lose is the Adam-life that was perishing anyway. All that we gain is Christ's life – the life of the future.

Hopefully this new life is attractive to you. Christians reckon if it was good enough for the Son of God, it's good enough for us. And when I say *us*, I should stress: the Christian life is meant to be lived *together* ...

A new family

The good life is not a solitary life. How could it be, given who God is?

With THREE we learnt that God is a family of love and we're invited. TWO told us that God's Son entered our family to bring us into his. Now with ONE we see that coming to Jesus means joining an ever-growing community. If we're connected to Christ, we don't simply have a new Father; we also have new brothers and sisters. One-ness with Jesus brings us into a one-ness with church.

I don't know how you think of church. I'm not talking about buildings or institutions; I'm talking about a family. Church is Christ's extended family and you can't really have Christ without his church. He is connected to his church like a groom to a bride, like a head to a body and like a vine to a branch.[22] This means that church is absolutely indispensable to a life with Christ. When Jesus calls us to his good life, his community is a vital part of it.

At this point it's understandable that people get nervous. After all, hasn't the church been guilty of some awful crimes? The Inquisitions or Crusades spring to mind. Or perhaps the child sex abuse scandals of more recent years. In chapter 10 we will think more on this, but, briefly, how should we consider these blights on the name of the church? Clearly such atrocities have been horrendously un-Christ-like. These evils are a total rejection of

Christ's good life. Whatever was declared at the time, it should be obvious that those deeds cannot claim to represent Jesus. Instead they make us cry out for a true community of love and justice, and down through the centuries – imperfectly and sporadically – there has been a body of people seeking to live out the way of Jesus.

The church is easily history's largest sociological movement, spanning every imaginable boundary – national, linguistic, cultural, economic, political and historical. Billions have been members, decisively shaping the world for millennia. But actually the place you'll encounter church is not in a historical survey or cultural analysis. When you encounter church in the flesh, you will meet with a very ordinary bunch of people – perhaps a St Swithun's, meeting in a centuries-old building. Or it could call itself Grace Community Church, meeting in a school hall. Maybe you'll meet in houses, maybe you'll gather on a weekday, the details aren't so important. What's vital is that you're connected to some other believers on a regular basis.

What happens at these gatherings? Well church family goes beyond its activities – it means a shared life together – but let me highlight some of the things you will encounter.

BAPTISM

The way into church family is baptism. This is like the wedding ceremony – it proclaims our one-ness with Jesus and our one-ness with his people. When Jesus was baptised, it signified his one-ness with us. When we get baptised, it declares our one-ness with Jesus. At the baptism of Jesus, the Father spoke out his eternal love. Our own baptism is like joining Jesus in the water and hearing God's welcome. If you haven't been baptised before and you want in on Jesus, speak to the church you have joined (or want to join).

THE LORD'S SUPPER

Another key church practice is called the Lord's Supper or Communion or the Eucharist – it goes by many names. The night before Jesus died he told his followers to remember him by eating bread and drinking wine together. This meal is a powerful proclamation of Jesus' death for us – his body torn apart like bread and his blood poured out like wine. Communion preaches to us that Jesus welcomes his family to eat with him, but it cost him everything to do so. He had to be broken and poured out so that we could feast. When churches eat this ceremonial meal together, they are centring themselves on the life-giving death of Jesus.

PREACHING

You may notice that I have described the rituals of baptism and communion as 'proclaiming' truths to us. This is central to church life – proclaiming Jesus. Sometimes this happens in ceremonies, always it happens in words. Preaching is therefore fundamental. In preaching we hear someone declare the good news of Jesus from the Bible. Like a good story-teller, they will recount the epic tale that makes sense of our lives. We hear of our failures in Adam and then our hearts are thrilled with news of Christ and his victory. We gather to hear this story time after time because we forget it, constantly.

SINGING AND PRAYER

In response to this good news, Christians sing and pray together. Like football fans, rejoicing in their champion, we open our mouths in praise. Sometimes we join in enthusiastically; sometimes we need to be carried by the prayers and praise of others. But in everything the good news of Jesus comes to us from outside of ourselves. We need this because we still struggle with our old Adam nature and we still feel the curse of this broken world. Our brothers and sisters in church are a vital encouragement as they tell us again the good news of Jesus and inspire us to look ahead to his coming again.

If you're going to be ONE with Jesus, you will need to find a church. Make sure it believes in God's THREE-ness and in Jesus' freeness. What I mean is this: make sure they believe the doctrine of the Trinity and make sure they believe that Jesus' new life is a *free* gift from the Father, not something we have to earn. Besides these two vital criteria, you will also want a church where they obviously love Jesus, love his word the Bible and love one another. Such churches do exist. Get in touch if you want recommendations. But don't go solo – seek out a church. The Christian life is a family affair.

A new conversation

Relationships thrive on communication: listening and talking. The Christian life is no different. Listening is all about the Bible. Talking is all about prayer.

THE BIBLE

Let's think about God's side of the conversation. In particular, let's examine the Bible's author, its message and its purpose.

i. Author

On a purely human level the Bible is a library of 66 books, written by 40 different authors over the course of about 1500 years. But the Bible makes a deeper claim for itself. It maintains that, behind and through the human authors, these words are also *God's* words. No-one thinks the Bible crash-landed on earth as a letter straight from heaven. And no-one thinks the human authors were robotic scribes for God. But in and through these very human words God is powerfully speaking. In particular the claim is this: God's Spirit has inspired the human authors to write of God's Son. Essentially the Father wants the world to meet his Son and so his Spirit has overseen the Bible as the authorised biography of Jesus. Ultimately the Bible's author is the THREE.

ii. Message

As a library of books the Bible includes all kinds of literature – poetry, history, genealogy, sermons, sayings, song lyrics, letters and more besides. What unites it all is the concern to tell of Christ. The Old Testament speaks of God's Son and his anticipated birth among us. The New Testament speaks of God's Son coming among us and the immediate aftermath. The Bible is all about Jesus but this message comes as a movement. First we are brought down, then we are raised up; first we hear of our need, then we hear of God's solution; first we see our problems in Adam, then we see our salvation in Christ. Ultimately the Bible's message is TWO.

iii. Purpose

The point of the Bible is not simply education, though there is much to learn. Its point is not simply entertainment, though its stories and songs are inspirational. Its point is not simply ethical improvement, though it has shaped the moral life of civilisations. The point of the Bible is to encounter Jesus.

In John chapter 5 Jesus accuses some serious Bible scholars of completely missing the point:

> You study the Scriptures diligently because you think that in them you have eternal life. These are the very Scriptures that testify about me, yet you refuse to come to me to have life.[23]

These Bible students thought the Bible contained eternal life *in its pages.* It doesn't. You cannot simply follow the Bible's instructions to get to heaven. Eternal life, as we have seen, is a connection with Jesus and it happens purely by faith. What is the place of the Bible then? The Bible makes the introduction. It 'testifies' about Jesus so that the reader sees Christ and 'comes to him'. Ultimately, then, the Bible's purpose is ONE-ness.

Don't be daunted by the size of the Bible. Ten minutes a day will get you through the whole thing in a year (for suggested reading, go here: *https://www.10ofthose.com/justlooking*). Don't be put off by the complexity either.

We are all learners, but if Jesus wants to connect with us, he will manage it no matter how shaky our understanding.

This brings us to the other side of this conversation.

PRAYER

'One day Jesus was praying in a certain place. When he finished, one of his disciples said to him, "Lord, teach us to pray."'[24] Here is the essence of prayer – the Son spending time with his Father. Jesus' followers were watching him and they liked what they saw. They were witnessing a conversation that had been going on from before the foundation of the world. They wanted in and, wonderfully, Jesus lets them. In effect he takes them by the hand and leads them into his own relationship with God. Forever Jesus had been calling out, 'My Father.' Now Jesus turns to his disciples and says: 'This, then, is how you should pray: *Our* Father.'[25]

Prayer is talking to our heavenly Father because Jesus has made us children. Christians often begin their prayers by addressing God as 'our Father'. We usually end our prayers by saying 'in the name of Jesus'. Those aren't magic words but they are a recognition of what prayer is. Prayer is talking to our Father because one ness with Jesus has brought us into the family.

It's fascinating to see Jesus' attitude to prayer in the Gospels. He never criticises anyone's prayers *except* those who prided themselves on a strong prayer life! Jesus berates those who make lengthy prayers in public and those who use impressive-sounding language, thinking God will hear them because of their many words.[26] He doesn't want us to be strong pray-ers but weak pray-ers, confident of a strong Father.

Again and again Jesus' advice is to come before his Father with confidence and humility. If confidence and humility sound like a strange combination, remember that's just what children exhibit. A child before her loving father is bold but she also knows she is a child. She doesn't depend on her own goodness but on her father's love. That is the attitude that will produce true prayer.

When we come before our Father as children, we say what children say – or at least, what they ought to say. We say 'I love you' because God has first loved us. We say 'thank you' for the good in our lives. We say 'sorry' for our sins. And we say 'please', bringing our needs before a generous God.

As you begin to pray, no doubt it will seem very strange. And no doubt prayer will, at times, baffle and elude you. That's the way for all Christians. But as you are involved in church life, you can learn how to pray as you participate in church services and as you hear others. As with the Bible, no-one is a master, everyone is a learner – and the goal is not so much *getting it right* as enjoying your one-ness. That's the point of this new conversation.

Count me in

So that's the Christian life. On one level it's an extraordinary life; on the other it is very ordinary indeed. It's about a new life in the midst of the old. It's about a new family – the church. It's about a new conversation – listening to God in the Bible and talking to God in prayer.

It's important to stress once again that none of this is the *price* of eternal life. Actually this is the *nature* of eternal life. This is the good life we were made for – life in connection with Jesus. It begins now and will stretch on beyond death and into eternity. Do you want this for yourself?

At this point in the book I'm guessing you might fall into one of three categories:

1. Perhaps you don't buy any of this and you're happy to pass. Thanks so much for journeying with us this far, perhaps the questions of the next section will be more your cup of tea.

2. Perhaps you aren't sure what to do with Jesus' offer. You may have

questions that you want answered. Of course we all have questions for God, but perhaps you feel your questions are so serious they prevent you from trusting Jesus right now. If that describes you, let me encourage you to read the final section of the book dealing with eight common objections to Christianity. See whether the Christian story brings satisfying answers in these areas. If so, you can always return to these pages to say, 'I'm in!'

3. Perhaps, though, you're in a third category. Maybe you're saying to yourself, 'Count me in! I don't know much and I still have questions but I like the look of Jesus. I trust him. I want in.' You're in this category if you can answer 'Yes' to the following questions:
    - Do you think Jesus is Lord? Do you think he's *it*? The true face of God? The Son of the Father?
    - Do you recognise your own Adam-like failures?
    - Are you sorry for your sins – that is your suspicion, selfishness, slavery, self-justification and stuff-ups?
    - Do you realise that you can't save yourself from this disconnected life?
    - Do you recognise that Jesus – his life, death and resurrection – is the answer to your disconnected life?
    - Do you trust him with your failures?
    - Do you trust him with your life?
    - Do you want to be ONE with him, bound together in love and trust forever?

If you have answered 'Yes' to these questions, then rejoice, because Jesus says, 'whoever comes to me I will never drive away'.[27] Welcome to the Christian life! You may want to begin it with a prayer. Perhaps words like these could get you going:

Dear Father,

Thank you for your love. Thank you for my life.

I admit there are things in me that refuse and spoil your love. Please forgive me for my selfishness and sin.

Thank you for sending Jesus to rescue me. Thank you that he has loved me to hell and back, paying for my sins and rising again.

I now receive Jesus into my life. I want to be ONE with him from now on. Please send your Holy Spirit into my life to bring me your love and presence. Help me to live out this new life with Jesus and his people.

In Jesus' name,

Amen.

Watch this video: *three-two-one.org/You*

Optional reading: John chapters 13–17

- What does Jesus say about the THREE, i.e. himself, his Father and the Holy Spirit? How do the THREE relate to each other? How do the THREE relate to the believer?
- What kind of pictures of the Christian life does Jesus paint?
- What is the importance of loving and belonging to other Christians?
- What struggles in life does Jesus warn us of? What helps does he promise in the midst of them?

• COMING UP IN NEXT SECTION •

This book began with the analogy of a house. Jesus has been our tour guide through the household of Christianity – he has shown us God, the world and ourselves. Now, as we conclude the tour, we are putting the kettle on and taking questions.

We had to wait before looking at these questions because it's Jesus, THREE, TWO and ONE that will answer them. But now that we've heard the Christian story, we mustn't flee from the questions it prompts. Christian faith has nothing to fear from close examination. Questions are an opportunity to explore the truth in fresh ways. That's what we will be doing as we seek to answer eight frequently asked questions.

Frequently Asked Questions

Let's begin this final section with two related truths:

1. Answered questions do not make you a Christian.
2. Christians continue to have unanswered questions.

I say this because I have met folks who get so caught up with *questions* that they've forgotten what Christianity is. A Christian is someone who trusts Jesus. As we've seen, it's like a marriage – a relationship of love and trust.

But it would be a very strange relationship if the way you got to know your partner was with a clipboard, a pen and a series of 17 questions, each more thorny than the last. That kind of relationship would not be particularly rich, or long!

How do you get to know a potential partner? You spend time with them, you hear their stories and you enter their world. Certainly you will ask questions along the way – you might ask a lot of questions – but questions aren't everything. At some point you say to yourself, 'I don't know everything about this person, but I know enough to trust them.' At that point you make a commitment. *Then* – on the inside of the relationship – the questions come thick and fast!

- 'How can you live like this?'
- 'Why would you do it like *that*?'
- 'Who raised you?'
- 'What is the deal with your family anyway?'

I exaggerate, slightly. But anyone in a long-term relationship will tell you that the really serious questions get asked once you're *inside* the relationship.

It's the same with Christianity. Christians have big questions for God – probably bigger questions than non-Christians do – after all we know more

The point is being able to trust Jesus – and to trust him with all the things we don't know.

of what to ask and the answers are more critical for us. But the bottom line is that, beyond our questions, we have seen the trustworthiness of Jesus. Therefore we trust him with what we don't know. We will never get to the stage of knowing everything – in fact that is not the point. The point is being able to trust Jesus – and to trust him with all the things we *don't* know.

I pray you'll learn more of Christ through these FAQs, but I pray also that, if you haven't, you may return to page 119 and begin that life with Jesus – not so as to end your questions, but so as to continue your questioning from the inside of the relationship.

With that in mind, let's now address our eight FAQs. As we do so, we will show how Jesus, THREE, TWO and ONE answer them for us ...

6

OK, BUT IS IT TRUE?

Is Christianity just a drug? Karl Marx said, 'Religion is the opium of the people' and many others have thought the same. Maybe it's about escaping reality into a quaint fairytale, full of sweet falsehoods: heaven and angels, and a God who will work it all out in the end. Do Christians believe because it's true or because we *want* it to be true?

It's a good question to ask because, wherever we stand on religious matters, our hearts tend to make up our minds for us. Even those who see themselves as extremely rational have a *love* for rationalism. Even the head-strong have been heart-led! We all live our lives according to larger stories that have captivated us. We want the stories to be true, therefore we have a lot invested in fitting the facts to the story. This is true whether we are Christians, Buddhists, atheists, or anything else.

Aldous Huxley was a great 20th-century intellectual and author of the novel *Brave New World*. Later in life he became interested in many spiritual ideas but his early life was devoted to 'the philosophy of meaninglessness' (his name for it). Looking back on his earlier beliefs Huxley saw what had moved him:

> I had motives for not wanting the world to have a meaning; consequently assumed that it had none, and was able without any difficulty to find satisfying reasons for this assumption.[1]

Do you see the order? He wanted the world to be a certain way, then he found his reasons. Huxley's just being honest. We all operate like this. Scientists call it 'confirmation bias'. The Bible calls it 'self-justification' – we're all susceptible. Therefore religious belief might well be your opium, but so too could atheism and so too could Marxism!

If this is the case, how can we be certain we're not self-deluded – that we're not feeding our fantasy drug habit and refusing to live in reality? Let's think about how Jesus answers that.

Jesus – the One from beyond

Let me give you an unhappy thought experiment – you may have heard it before, it's not original to me. Imagine you're kidnapped at gunpoint and herded into an unmarked white van with a bunch of other hostages. As it speeds off, you're all injected with a drug that makes you forget who you are, where you're from and what you've done. It 'wipes your hard drive', knocks you out cold and you wake up with hundreds of others in a giant warehouse. There are no windows, no doors, no entrances and no exits; it is just a room full of groggy, bewildered captives.

As you all come to, you try to make sense of your predicament: 'Who am I? Where have I come from? What's the meaning of all this? What is the nature of the room? Is there anything beyond this room?'

You can imagine that various theories arise among the hostages – some more plausible than others. You can also imagine the good sense of the pragmatists. They say, 'Forget about *what's beyond the room* – that's fruitless. Let's get on and make the best of the room we're in!'

That sounds like the most sensible approach to me. In the face of fanciful speculation about 'life beyond the room', I would probably side with the pragmatists. Until, that is, an almighty crash is heard. Bits of ceiling lie around on the floor and standing in the middle of the room is a man out of breath. 'I'm from the other side,' he insists. 'I'm here to rescue you.'

This changes everything. His claim might not be true – this may be an elaborate hoax. Perhaps this so-called rescuer is just another hostage suffering from 'cabin fever'. Those are options worth exploring but the fact of this man and the nature of his claims change the conversation. Before his arrival you may have had no interest in 'what's outside the room' but now this man is making it your business. The claims of the rescuer demand investigation.

So the questioning can begin: 'Are you really from beyond? Prove it. What can you do? Do you know how the room works? Do you know what's outside? What's the meaning of all this?' We may be profoundly sceptical about the man, but once he makes those claims, no-one in the room can feign disinterest.

Jesus, of course, is the rescuer in this illustration. He is a towering figure in world history – he stands in the middle of the room, so to speak. He also claims repeatedly, with an almost embarrassing intensity, to be from beyond. In Jesus you have a unique combination. There have been many great figures of history who have walked the earth. But if you asked them who they were, they would never claim deity – or if they did, they would lose their following immediately. On the other hand there are stories of 'the gods' walking planet earth, but when you press in for the details, you find that these 'appearances' never happened in real-world history. In the ancient religions and myths the gods walked the earth in 'dream time'. With Jesus you have something unique. Here is a man who very much belongs to our history yet also claims to belong to heaven.

What do we do with the man who claims to be from beyond? Famously the author and scholar C.S. Lewis said you can only do three things with him:

> You can shut him up for a fool, you can spit at him and kill him as a demon or you can fall at his feet and call him Lord and God.[2]

That might sound extreme, but Jesus' claims about himself force us to extremes. When he claims to be 'Lord and God' he's either a lunatic (self-deceived), a liar (deceiving others) or he's telling the truth – in which case he simply *is* the Lord. Therefore the question must be asked: 'Which is it?'

Shortly we will discuss a fourth possibility. A very small number of sceptics, swimming against a powerful tide of historical consensus, have asserted that Jesus was a legend. In other words they have claimed that the story of Jesus is itself a deception. We will see that this possibility is the most unlikely of all. But for now let's look at the person of Jesus. As we ask the question 'Is it true?' we are not left with guess work and wishful thinking. Because of Jesus our questions about 'life, the universe and everything' now have a concrete focus: 'Is Jesus of Nazareth trustworthy?'

If the answer is 'No', then forget Christianity. If Jesus is not who he claimed to be, then Christianity would be a fantasy drug habit and we all should kick it. But if the answer is 'Yes', then everything changes. It would mean that Jesus is Lord, the rescue is real and the Christian story is not merely beautiful, it's true.

THREE – the Sun that explains the sparkle

We have just quoted from C.S. Lewis. Here's another of his thoughts, engraved on his memorial stone in Westminster Abbey: 'I believe in Christianity as I believe the sun has risen. Not only because I can see it but because by it I can see everything else.'

Here's what he's saying: you can get to grips with the sun in two ways. You can look at it (carefully!) but you can also look at everything else in its light. Both kinds of looking establish the reality of the sun.

The same is true of Jesus (who, incidentally, claimed to be the light of the world).[3] We can look at Jesus – and reading John's Gospels is perhaps the best way of doing that – but we can also look at the rest of the world as Jesus sheds light on it. What do I mean by that?

When we look at the world, no matter what we believe, we tend to value goodness, truth, beauty and love. We value these things as though they are self-evidently better than evil, lies, ugliness and hate. In other words, we think of the world's most important features as those that go beyond physics, chemistry and biology. Whatever we believe about God, it's ideas, courage, causes, stories, passion and personal connection that matter to us. But why should that be? How come we value minds, music and mercy if the world is ultimately shaped by slime, struggle and selfishness?The problem is not solved by imagining any old god. If we think of a solitary deity underneath all things, we're still left with a loveless foundation for life. A God all by himself would not *fundamentally* be loving. Such a God would be powerful, immense and all-controlling. Yet since this God is, by definition, alone, love is not at the heart of all things.

But what if we turn to the God revealed by Jesus? He shows us a God who is a loving union of THREE. With this God, love can truly be said to be ultimate. Here we have a 'Sun' that accounts for the light that we prize. By this God we can see everything else.

TWO – the Sunday that changed the world

Christianity is unique among all world-views. If it turns out there was no real Buddha, Buddhism would survive. If there was no Muhammed, the pillars of Islam remain. If there was no Marx, Marxism would stand (under a different name, obviously). But if Jesus did not actually live, die and rise again, then Christianity crumbles. As Paul says in the New Testament: '... if Christ has not been raised, our preaching is useless and so is your faith.'[4]

Christianity is not really an ethical code or philosophical system. It claims to be a true story explaining the world. This story stands or falls upon certain events that either happened or didn't. In particular – here is the truth of TWO – Jesus came as the Second Adam, to live our life, die our death and rise again. If that didn't happen, then Christianity is not merely mistaken, it is a damnable lie. So what is the truth?

At this point some may want to raise the issue of Adam. Are we really to believe that there was a 'founding father' of the human race? Who believes in a single point of origin for humanity? Well among anthropologists debates continue between multiregional and single-origin theories of humanity. But the Christian story is not hostage to the latest theories about the origins of *homo sapiens*. I'm not trying to *first* convince you of Adam and *then* of Jesus. Actually it's the other way around. The way into the Christian story is Jesus. According to the Bible, he rose *and therefore reversed the fall of Adam.* That's the way you investigate the Christian story. Don't first ask, 'Did Adam fall?' First ask, 'Did Jesus rise?' If he did, then the Christian story is vindicated – Adam included. So did Jesus rise?

Let me offer you ten facts which are accepted by all but the most hardened sceptics:

- Jesus lived in first-century Israel and drew a substantial following.
- Jesus was known by both friends and foes as a wonder-worker.
- Jesus fulfilled hundreds of Old Testament prophecies – many of which would be out of his human control.
- Jesus was crucified under Pontius Pilate, the Roman governor of Palestine. He died and was buried.
- On the Sunday morning the tomb in which he was laid was empty.
- Jesus' followers had many and various experiences of seeing Jesus alive again (and eating with him and touching him).
- Jesus' unimpressive followers were transformed into courageous preachers who testified, at the risk (and later the cost) of their own lives, that Jesus rose from the dead.
- Within weeks the church exploded in the very city where Jesus was buried.
- No-one ever found Jesus' body, despite the authorities having every incentive to produce it.
- Christianity has been built on the claim of the resurrection and grown

to become the largest sociological phenomenon the world has ever seen. Today billions of people worship a man who was executed 2000 years ago as an uneducated, powerless criminal.

These are the facts and there really isn't much dispute about them, even among atheistic scholars.[5] The question then is how do we account for those facts?

Some theories have been proposed: Jesus didn't really die on the cross; Jesus' 'appearances' were all group hallucinations; the disciples stole the body and lied about it; and so forth. Each theory involves you in more absurdities than the Bible's own explanation: Jesus rose, just as he said he would. The funny thing is that if Jesus *didn't* rise, it becomes very difficult to account for the facts:

- If Jesus only passed out on the cross and resuscitated in the cool of the tomb, how did he overpower the Roman guard posted outside? How did he then – as a left-for-dead torture victim – reassure his disciples that he had gained an eternal victory over death?
- If Jesus' followers were hallucinating, this would be the only ever case of *group* hallucinations by hundreds of people in different locations over many weeks! Not only is this unheard of, it fails to account for the empty tomb.
- If the disciples stole the body and lied about it, how come no-one ever rumbled the conspiracy? And how come they bore up under torture and death, still defending this testimony? Can we really believe the ethical teaching of the New Testament is founded on a grotesque lie and cover-up?
- If Jesus didn't rise from the dead, how do we explain the person of Jesus? How do we explain his fulfilment of the ancient prophecies? And more than that, how do we explain his fulfilment of human hopes and desires across the world and down through the ages?

The reality of Jesus' resurrection actually fits best with what we know of him. And it fits best with what we know of history. If Jesus did not rise, how do we explain the extraordinary success of the church? Within a few centuries the empire that crucified Jesus was hailing him as Lord and God. Something happened to a bunch of unschooled fishermen that made them turn the world upside down. On one Sunday in the first century there was an undeniable release of energy, the shockwaves of which we are still feeling today. This is historical fact. Christians say, 'We can explain that release of energy. Jesus really rose.'

Many of course refuse to be persuaded, no matter what the evidence. They simply insist, 'Dead men don't rise.' This is true. But what if Jesus is more than a man? What if he is who he claimed to be? In that case it would be extraordinary if he *didn't* rise from the dead.

Hopefully it is clear that Christian faith is not a leap in the dark. Believing in the resurrection of Jesus is about facing the facts. Actually, doubting the resurrection is what involves you in the really fanciful 'leaps'.

So then Christian faith faces the facts. But the facts alone don't make you a Christian. *With* the facts we must go further than the facts. We must experience one-ness.

ONE – getting personal

As we've already seen, there were some on Easter Sunday who met the risen Jesus but the penny did not drop. One couple, for instance, talked for hours with Jesus as they walked along the Emmaus road.[6] But even in this situation Jesus does not throw off the cloak with an almighty, 'Surprise!' Even in his resurrection appearances Jesus prefers to reveal himself through the Bible and a meal. When they 'break bread' together, the penny drops:

> Then their eyes were opened and they recognised him, and he disappeared from their sight. They asked each other, 'Were not our hearts burning within us while he talked with us on the road and opened the Scriptures to us?'[7]

Easter faith did not come through an emotional experience, a scientific experiment or a philosophical argument. It came through a Bible study and a meal together. Notice what this couple are astonished by, even as they realise who they have met: they are amazed at how Jesus 'opened the Scriptures'. As the preacher Rico Tice says, 'The Bible was Jesus' way of meeting Jesus.' That was true even on Easter Sunday. It has remained the case for 2000 years. There have been 100,000 Sundays since that first Easter and Christians have continued to do the same thing: open the Scriptures and share a family meal together. In this context – Jesus' way of meeting Jesus – billions have encountered him.

Sometimes people say, 'If Jesus just appeared before me now, I'd believe.' But three things should be said to that. First, on Easter Sunday that simply wasn't the case. The facts alone did not convert them. Secondly, Jesus does not want people assenting to truth at a distance. He seeks to draw us into one-ness. Thirdly, if your faith is based on such a sighting, how long before you would start to doubt again? For me, I'd need another appearance every fortnight, just to reassure me I hadn't dreamt it. But Jesus' way of meeting Jesus involves the Scriptures, which I can turn to at any time, day or night. It also involves God's people – it is a relational kind of knowing, not a dispassionate deduction or a one-off experience.

If you want this one-ness for yourself, the Scriptures have four words of advice: 'faith comes from hearing'.[8] Surround yourself with God's people and listen to God's word. Find a church, hear God's word preached and read it for yourself. As you do so pray, 'God speak to me personally. Show me Jesus.' Faith comes in this context. As John Piper says, 'It's like seeing the sun and knowing that it is light, or tasting honey and knowing that it is sweet.'[9] Faith is hearing Jesus and knowing that he is Lord. Don't stop short of knowing Jesus in this way.

7

IS THE BIBLE TRUSTWORTHY?

THREE, TWO, ONE – the author, message and purpose of Scripture

We have already seen how the Bible relates to THREE, TWO and ONE.

The ultimate *author* of the Bible is the THREE. The Father has written a biography of his Son through the Holy Spirit – the Spirit inspiring human authors.

The ultimate *message* of Bible is TWO – telling the story of our fall in Adam and our redemption in Christ.

The ultimate *purpose* of the Bible is ONE-ness. The Scriptures are given to us not simply to know information but to know Jesus himself.

If that's what the Bible is, let's ask the question: 'Can we trust this source?' Let's seek briefly to answer some objections.

Is the whole thing a fabrication?

Earlier we mentioned the position that a tiny minority have held: that Jesus was a 'legend'. Such people are called 'mythicists', claiming that the Jesus of the Gospels was concocted by a group of disgruntled Jews and there was no such historical figure.

Professor Bart Ehrman, an ancient historian and vocal opponent of Christianity, is nonetheless withering in his criticisms of the mythicists: 'These [mythicist] views are so extreme and so unconvincing to 99.99 percent of the real experts."[1] Professor Ehrman goes on to give three major reasons. Firstly there are too many independent sources: the four Gospels, Paul, Peter, James – an embarrassment of riches for an ancient historian. Secondly those sources come far too early to have given time for myth-making. Thirdly the writings are too inconvenient for those who are supposed to have fabricated them. Their story of a crucified Messiah was a shocking and shameful message, and one which did not benefit the authors at all.

Ehrman concludes:

> One may well choose to resonate with the concerns of our modern and postmodern cultural despisers of established religion (or not). But surely the best way to promote any such agenda is not to deny what virtually every sane historian on the planet – Christian, Jewish, Muslim, pagan, agnostic, atheist, what have you – has come to conclude based on a range of compelling historical evidence.
>
> Whether we like it or not, Jesus certainly existed.[2]

Isn't the Bible full of contradictions?

When I studied philosophy at university, I would often consider the authors I read to be contradicting themselves. My tutors, though, would encourage me to think that perhaps history's greatest thinkers knew what they were talking about. Maybe little old Glen didn't quite understand the nuances involved. And maybe my cultural biases, coming hundreds of years after they wrote, were blinding me to their true meaning. Once I gave these dead guys the benefit of the doubt, I found that actually I was mistaken, not them. The same has been true of my Bible reading. Some things can seem contradictory, but when I have assumed that the authors knew what they were talking about (an assumption we ought to grant when reading *any* text), these so-called contradictions have not merely disappeared, they have been the pathway to a deeper understanding of Scripture.

If there are particular questions you have about reconciling certain Scriptures, I recommend carm.org/bible-difficulties. But for now let me turn the question around. Given that the Bible is a library of 66 books written by 40 authors over 15 centuries, the headline story is actually the incredible *unity* of the Bible. If you would like to pursue this further, perhaps study Walter Kaiser's book, *Messiah in the Old Testament*,[3] as he examines 60 of the Old Testament's hundreds of prophecies about Jesus. On Good Friday alone Jesus fulfilled 29 separate Old Testament predictions – many of which were completely beyond any human ability to orchestrate. Read Genesis chapter 22 verses 1–14 or Psalm 22 or Isaiah chapter 53 and then read about the cross in Matthew chapter 27 or John chapter 19 to see their fulfilment. The consistency question is not a weak point for the Bible; it is perhaps the strongest argument for its divine origin.

How can you take the Bible literally today?

What would it mean to take your daily newspaper 'literally'? It contains news reports, opinion pieces, interviews, photographs, sports reports, political cartoons, advertisements, personal ads, weather forecasts and the like. Will you take it all literally? Well hopefully you will read the editorial differently to the personal ads. In other words you will read these different kinds of literature in the way they were intended. In just this way the Bible consists of history, poetry, letters, song lyrics, sayings and sermons. You don't read poetry the same way you read a letter, nonetheless you can take each piece of writing seriously in accordance with its original intention. That's what Christians seek to do.

When it comes to the biographies of Jesus – the Gospels – these four books were intended to be read as history. Study the Gospel of Luke, for instance, and you will see that he is offering a 'carefully investigated', 'orderly account' based on the testimony of 'eye witnesses'.[4] He mentions scores of historical figures and places.[5] This is not 'once upon a time in a land far away'. Luke is doing everything in his power to convey to us that these events happened in real world history. At that point he's either telling the truth or he's concocting an elaborate and wicked hoax which then managed to fool those who actually lived through the events being narrated. Does that make sense? Read it for yourself and see if these writings have the ring of truth to them.

Do we really have what the writers originally wrote?

As a child I played a game we now call 'The Telephone Game'. The idea was for each child to whisper what they heard to the next child in the line until you end up with a sentence wildly different to the original. Perhaps, some argue, the Bible has been corrupted in just this way as it's been copied down through the centuries. None of the original manuscripts have survived, so how can we be sure we've got what was originally written?

Actually our modern Bibles are nothing like the end process of 'The Telephone Game'. The copyists were incredibly careful in their transcription – after all, they believed they were handling the word of God. What's more, the process of copying was not at all linear – it was more like a vast family tree of manuscripts with multiple lines of transmission. Today we have nearly 25,000 ancient manuscript copies of the New Testament – a number which dwarfs anything else in ancient literature. We can compare these copies, not merely with 'parent' copies up the line but with a multitude of 'cousins' and 'distant cousins' that have come down many different paths of transmission. Our modern Bibles are not based on a single chain of whispers but a chorus of strong voices. Today's translations make use of all the earliest and best manuscripts.

Unsurprisingly, given they were all hand copied, there are discrepancies in the manuscripts. But this is not like having 50 pieces missing from a 1000 piece jigsaw puzzle. Actually these errors injected into the system are like having 50 pieces *extra*. Today we have, as it were, 1050 pieces and in the vast majority of cases it is very straightforward to identify the odd ones out. The errors that 'don't fit' stick out like a sore thumb. In rare cases – involving perhaps a phrase, a word or just a letter – scholars are uncertain about the original text, but any decent modern translation (like the NIV or ESV) will flag up the alternate options in the footnotes. There is no great conspiracy or cover-up – in each of these rare instances you can see for yourself these minor differences and how little hangs on them.

Did the church suppress other books of the Bible?

If you came to my house and spied out my bookshelves, you'd notice many titles that represent my beliefs and interests but there'd be other books I'd forgotten I owned and some I'd be embarrassed to be seen dead with. In the last century there have been some ancient libraries unearthed that included biblical books but also other books which the church never recognised as part of the Bible. Why not?

Some will say that this was a great conspiracy of the church to suppress alternative Gospels like 'The Gospel of Thomas' or 'The Gospel of Judas'. In reality those so-called 'Gospels' are nothing like Matthew, Mark, Luke and John. They are merely collections of sayings written not by Christians but by religious groups piggybacking on the burgeoning success of the church. They were concocted at least a century after the original four (in most instances, many centuries after), in a language Jesus did not speak and proposing concepts of God, creation, salvation, the body and women that are utterly alien to the Bible (and to all sanity). If you want to see why the church always rejected them, just read them.

Britain's most famous preacher, Charles Spurgeon, used to liken the Bible to a lion. There is no need to defend a lion – you simply let it out and it will defend itself.[6] At the end of the day arguments won't defend the Bible; the Bible will defend the Bible. We can argue for the Bible's consistency and historicity, but only one thing can vindicate it as *God's* word: that is God speaking to you through it. Therefore I urge you to 'unleash the lion' – open it up and read for yourself.

8

HOW DOES A GOOD GOD FIT WITH EVIL AND SUFFERING?

I'll never forget the room called 'Exploiting the Corpses'. It's the one place at Auschwitz where they don't let you take photographs. Here two tonnes of human hair is displayed. This was one more way the Nazis used and abused their victims, selling on the hair for profit before gassing and burning these men, women and children by their millions.

In the face of such shocking evil, people ask the question, 'How can you believe in a good God?' Add to this disasters, depression, disease and death and who can deny that this is a broken world? So then how does God fit with such suffering? Surely he's not good or he's not powerful or he's not there. Which is it?

Jesus – the God revealed in suffering

The Christian does not begin their thinking with an abstract God; we begin with Jesus. A philosopher might imagine a 'perfect being' and dream up a thousand qualities which this perfect being must display. Certainly if that's the 'God' you imagine, then the existence of an imperfect world is difficult to reconcile. But what if *Jesus* reveals God to us?

Jesus is described in the Bible as 'a man of suffering, and familiar with pain'.[1] He speaks of his 'glory' as his sacrificial and bloody death.[2] Incredibly the place where God is known most clearly is at the cross where Jesus suffers in unimaginable agony. We might have thought that suffering rules out God but Jesus shows otherwise. There are certainly gods whose existence are called into question by the reality of suffering. But suffering cannot disprove the God of Jesus – the God of the cross.

THREE – the God who has a problem with evil

It's a good thing to have a problem with evil. Evil is evil. The real problem would be *not* having a problem with it.

Unfortunately many in the world 'solve' the problem of evil by making their peace with it. In the face of evil people tend to make two different conclusions about the nature of reality. Either they say it's karma or they say it's chaos.

Karma is the belief that 'what goes around, comes around' – if there is suffering, it must be, on some level, deserved. In this life or a former life you, or your ancestors, have brought this about. The trouble is if karma were true, there would be no unjust suffering. Everything would be as it should be and there would be nothing to be outraged about. Suffering would be unpleasant but not *wrong*.

The other natural response to suffering and evil is to believe in chaos. With chaos we say, 'It's a mad, mad, world,' and there's no rhyme nor reason to the suffering we see. That is certainly how it feels when tragedy strikes. But if we believe that chaos is the final truth then, once again, we have lost our right to call it 'evil'. If everything is random, nothing is 'wrong'. Certainly suffering is painful, it is unpleasant, it is grotesque, it is undesirable. But if chaos reigns, then there is simply no 'Why?' question to answer.

Yet we constantly ask the 'Why?' question because we feel the evil of evil. These things aren't simply painful; we feel that *they should not be.* With karma or with chaos we cannot say that, but with the God of THREE we have a standard of justice and beauty that exists before and above this fallen world. With the God of THREE Auschwitz is *not* a just punishment for the sufferers, nor is it simply 'one of those things'. It is an appalling violation of ultimate goodness.

Of course at this point we haven't 'solved' the problem of evil. Actually we have done something much more important – we have allowed evil to *be* a problem. But then you may well ask, 'If God has a *problem* with evil, why does it exist? Where does it come from?' That's where the truth of TWO comes in.

TWO – the nature of evil and our hope beyond it

I once debated a leading humanist about whether God was worthy of worship. His speech was taken up mainly with a discussion of parasites. Since there are so many deadly nasties in the world, how can anyone believe in a good God? My response was simply to dwell on those parasites. Parasites cause harm because they feed off a life-giving host. This is just like our experience of evil in general. Evil is a defection from the good. It is disease thwarting well-being, darkness thwarting light, death thwarting life. Evil is a parasitic thing – it comes along later and spoils an original goodness. That's our experience of evil and it is precisely the Bible's story.

In the Bible there was an original goodness that was spoiled when we turned from our true Life-Source. Evil is this parasitic defection from the good. And it's something that you and I are caught up in. We have been part of this turn from the light, which means we are part of the darkness too.

As the evil of the Nazis was told to us at Auschwitz, two thoughts continually came to mind: 'You bastards' and 'I'm sorry.' Over and over again those thoughts returned. There was the outrage of the pointed finger but also the remorse of the contrite heart. This is a common human experience in the face of evil: we feel its power but we also know ourselves – somehow – to be complicit in it. The story of Adam explains all this. You and I suffer evil, yes. We are certainly victims. But we are also perpetrators. You and I are part of the problem. If we take a long hard look at ourselves, we realise that the evil out there is also *in here*.

The good news is that there is a second Adam – Jesus Christ – who meets us at the deepest point of our suffering and evil. He went to the cross to endure the ultimate suffering for our evil and he has burst through to the other side. Uniquely Jesus offers a hope for this world beyond suffering.

Some religions speak of escaping this world to 'a better place'. Materialism sees suffering continuing and eventually overwhelming us. Only Christianity has hope for this world and this kind of human life. Jesus gives us a dazzling but still *earthy* hope because he has taken on our worst and risen again to God's best as a *human forevermore*. According to the Bible our ultimate future is this world renewed and raised up just like Jesus was raised from the tomb. If we want an answer to this suffering world, no-one else is offering lasting hope for planet earth. Only Jesus.

ONE – knowing comfort in our suffering

In John chapter 11 we read the story of Lazarus dying. Jesus hears about his friend's illness and he deliberately delays visiting the family until it is 'too late'. Only then does he reveal that nothing is 'too late' for the Lord of resurrection. The story ends on a high – Lazarus is raised from the dead – but at the beginning we have a loving Lord who allows death to overtake his dear friend. He allows terrible grief to engulf the family. He refuses to answer the family's prayers, so to speak, and the nightmare they've begged him to fix eventuates. Why?

Jesus says it's more glorious this way.[3] Jesus could keep on healing the sick – fixing up the old life of Adam – but he would only be postponing the inevitable. At what point should he allow death to take us? Aged 100? 120? 200? No, Jesus is not committed to repairing Adam's old world. He is committed to raising up his new world. It's more glorious this way – not simply to heal the illness but to turn the funeral into a homecoming. What

Jesus does for Lazarus is a picture of his plans for the world. He is not committed to repairing this fallen world, but to raising it from the dead.

Yet precisely because he is committed to *resurrection*, therefore we must face death. All of which means that illnesses will develop, families will be torn apart by grief and disasters will strike. None of this disproves God's love; it is simply a part of this fallen world. We try to prop up the old but God, in his love, does not. Sometimes he will heal, but his commitment is to allow the old to die to give rise to the new.

This means that our world is on a pathway – down then up – through suffering and then to joy. If that sounds familiar it's because all our stories about suffering have the same shape:

1. All is well.
2. Crisis hits.
3. A hero steps forward.
4. They are out of their depth.
5. There is weakness, fear and a fight to the death.
6. The hero wins through sacrifice.
7. Peace is restored, but now everyone is wiser for the struggle.

Our stories sound like this because we live within God's story. And this story has a shape to it: down and then up. We are going to suffer – there's no getting around it. If even God's Son suffers – in fact he suffers *the most* – why do we think we will escape?

Since this is the case, the real issue becomes *how* we suffer. The truth of ONE is that we can suffer *with* Jesus. Millions of Christians can testify that, in the midst of suffering, they have known his sustaining love in the most profound ways imaginable. Lazarus's sisters certainly found this in John chapter 11.

Before Lazarus is raised from the dead, both of his sisters – Martha and

Mary – come to Jesus in their grief. One after the other they level the same accusation: '... if you had been here, my brother would not have died.'[4] They seem angry with Jesus, but Jesus can handle that. With Martha he patiently teaches her about hope beyond death: 'I am the resurrection and the life.'[5] This is what Martha needs. But Mary seems in a different place with her grief. Where Martha needed truth, Mary needs tears and so we get the shortest verse in the Bible: 'Jesus wept.'[6] The Son of God weeps with Mary, even though her brother would be alive and well within minutes. Here is a compassionate Lord who knows how to walk with his people through suffering.

If you are suffering, you might be tempted to get rid of God. But if you do, you've still got the suffering only now you have lost the right to call evil 'evil'. Worst of all you've lost a Lord who loves you and can walk with you through it all. Speaking for myself, I have known the closest one-ness with Jesus *in* suffering. I recommend calling out to him. You can get angry at him – Martha and Mary did – but don't reject him. He has the truth, the tears and ultimately the triumph you need to see you through suffering and into resurrection joy.

9

HOW DOES A LOVING GOD FIT WITH JUDGEMENT?

3-2-1 begins with a God of love and it ends with a free offer to the world: be one with the Son of God. At the same time the Bible speaks of hell. What should we think?

As we begin on this topic it's important to note that our modern ideas of hell have been heavily influenced by medieval art and literature. Today our views of 'hell' are drawn less from Scripture and more from Dante's 'Inferno' and Hollywood horror films. We should be aware that the Bible is speaking of something quite different. Nevertheless the Bible *does* speak of hell. So how do we fit these truths together?

Jesus – God of love *and* God of judgement

Jesus spoke a lot about hell. He spoke of it more than any other figure in the Bible. He talked about unquenchable fire,[1] of 'eternal punishment',[2] of being shut out of the great banquet 'where there will be weeping and [the angry] gnashing of teeth'.[3]

He also talked about loving the whole world and not wanting any to perish.[4] He said he longed to gather the rebellious like a mother hen gathers her chicks.[5] At his death he even prayed for the forgiveness of his killers.[6] So which is it – a God of hell-fire or a God of love?

Jesus insists on both and so must we. That's because love and judgement are not opposites. In fact, as we'll see, judgement comes not in spite of love but because of it.

THREE – love comes first

In the beginning there was love – and only love. The Father was not sometimes blessing his Son and sometimes cursing him. In eternity past there was only a heaven of love. This means that whatever we say about hell, it cannot be the equal opposite of heaven. For infinite ages there was nothing of God's judgement, only his love. Love is original. Judgement comes as a response to that love being debased and spurned.

TWO – we've already fallen for it

Our turn from God – in other words the story of Adam – was a turn into hell. That is just the nature of the case. When you reject the God of love, life and light, you embrace disconnection, death and darkness.

This is the state we all find ourselves in: cut off from our life-source and perishing. Right now the race of Adam knows something of this tragic disconnection. Sometimes we even talk about 'hell on earth' or feeling 'cursed'. The Bible also speaks like that.[7] The race of Adam is perishing *now* – therefore we all know something of the disconnection, death and darkness of hell.

It's not simply that hell is 'down there, later on' (wherever 'down there' is). There is a darkness that we feel now – a darkness that threatens to engulf us forever if we don't get it sorted out. Therefore God shouts his warnings in Scripture and he shouts them in the world. Every taste we have had of 'hell on earth' has been a warning: effectively God is crying out, 'This is where your disconnection takes you. Stop! Come home.'

Because God is love, he is not dispassionate about our perishing state. Actually he is angry at us for our mistrust and rebellion. Every parent knows that rebellious children arouse anger, not in spite of their parental love, but precisely because they care so much. In the same way God does not merely watch us damn ourselves; he is angry about our preference for the darkness. And he warns us strongly. But, wonderfully, he does more than warn us. He does something about our predicament.

Christ does not say to the human race, 'You've made your bed, now lie in it.' As the Second Adam, he dives down into this pit of our own making. On the cross he takes our hell and then rises up again to give us his heaven. Whatever else we say about hell, we should remember that God the Son has entered it so that we never have to. He has met us in the midst of our disconnection and offers reconnection for free and forever. Anyone who wants Jesus can have him. Anyone who rejects Jesus has preferred the darkness to the light. They have made their response to eternal life, and judgement for them will be a case of 'Have it your way.'

As we speak about judgement, many people will want to question Christians about the specific details of certain cases. 'Will this particular person be sent to hell? What about this scenario?' As they do so, they're expecting the Christian to be the judge. But the Christian is not the judge – Jesus is. And he's a Judge who has taken the harshest sentence on himself so that no-one need suffer it. Christians do not claim to know the ins and outs of each judgement but we trust the Judge because on the cross he has proven himself trustworthy.

ONE – disconnection/reconnection

The question is often asked, 'How can Jesus be the only way to eternal life?' But according to Jesus, he *is* eternal life.[8] To be disconnected from God is hell. To be reconnected by the Son of God is heaven. Therefore it should be obvious why Jesus is the way to eternal life – he is the unique Son of God bringing us into the love of the THREE. If someone wants Jesus, they can have Jesus and eternal life is theirs. If someone does not want Jesus, then tragically they are rejecting eternal life itself.

Perhaps you are thinking, 'Who on earth would reject eternal life?' Actually millions do it every day. I've already mentioned the parable of the Prodigal Son,[9] which is a famous story Jesus told to show what this is like. It's about a loving father with two boys. The younger son is a bad egg. He runs off with the family money and squanders it in 'wild living'. The older son is a good boy. He stays at home and works on the farm.

One day the bad boy comes home and receives the most incredible welcome and forgiveness from his dad. There is a massive party, which Jesus describes as a picture of heaven. Here is where the story gets heavy. The older brother is furious at this free forgiveness and he refuses to join the party. The father comes out and basically pleads, 'My son, I still love you. Everything I have is yours. Please come in and join the joy.' Yet the older son stands on his rights and excludes himself from these family celebrations.

At the end of this story the older son is shut out of the feast in outer darkness with weeping and the angry gnashing of teeth. Jesus is describing here a snapshot of hell – or at least a man on the verge of it. But let's ask the question: 'Is this man hell-bound because he's too bad for heaven?' No. He's 'too good' for heaven – he considers himself too good to celebrate mercy for sinners. Let's ask another question: 'Is this man hell-bound because the father is so cruel?' No. The father is kind – far too kind for the older son's liking. Therefore he rejects the reconciliation and remains shut out.

This story ends with one son in the feast and one son in the outer darkness. But the father's love is not in question. The outer darkness does not prove the father to be unloving at all. It only proves the madness of those who reject his reconciliation. The outer darkness is a place where proud fools stubbornly stand against a Father's love.

Hell is not at odds with the love of God. We are at odds with the love of God. That's why there's a hell.

Where do you stand? As we feel our disconnection in the world, eternal life is offered in Jesus. The story of Luke chapter 15 is screaming at us: 'Be reconciled! Come home! Join the joy!' For 'The Lord ... is patient with you, not wanting anyone to perish, but everyone to come to repentance.'[10]

10

HOW CAN ANYONE JOIN THE CHURCH WITH ALL ITS HATE, ITS HISTORY AND ITS HYPOCRISY?

This objection is raised on two levels. Some speak of historic atrocities like religious wars, the Spanish Inquisition or child-abuse scandals. Others have personal experiences with Christians that have put them off Christianity. How should we respond?

Jesus – the enemy of hypocrisy

No-one hates hypocrisy more than Jesus. He coined the use of the word. Before Jesus the word just meant a masked actor. Jesus used the word to describe the religious authorities of his day: actors! The most upstanding members of the community: actors! The moral policeman of Israel: actors! Read Matthew 23 and hear for yourself his holy outrage at the hypocrites. Here are just two verses from his tirade:

> You are like whitewashed tombs, which look beautiful on the outside but on the inside are full of the bones of the dead and everything unclean. In the same way, on the outside you appear to people as righteous but on the inside you are full of hypocrisy and wickedness.[1]

If we hate hypocrisy, we are in good company – so does Jesus. And if we've been put off Christianity by Christians, that is a great pity and cause for real shame among the Christians involved. Yet whatever has repulsed you about those particular Christians, I trust those criticisms can't be levelled at Christ. Remember that he is the centre. Make sure you do business with him and not simply with those who misrepresent him.

THREE – the God of integrity

Twice in the quotation above Jesus mentions what's 'on the inside'. That should make us question 'Why do we care about a person's insides? Why do we care if a person's inner life does not match their outward appearance?'

There are plenty of religions that don't really care about a person's heart but only value their actions. On the other hand, from a secular point of view, a person's inner life is nobody's business but their own. Why get worked up about hypocrisy in the first place?

The Bible says it matters because of who God is. The God of THREE is a God of *love* who is interested in heart-to-hearts far more than he's interested in external behaviours. With *this* God, what's on the inside matters.

This is why Christians have always thought of hypocrisy as a bad thing. That's not to say we're free from it – not at all. As TWO will show, hypocrisy is a universal problem. But no Christian can ever make their peace with hypocrisy. We are called to follow Christ, which means hypocrisy, hate, revenge and war-mongering are out. Any time Christians have failed here (for example with the Crusades or, more recently, with child sex abuse scandals), it should be obvious that these people are acting *against* their Lord.[2]

But before we admit to our failures – which we will do in the next section – it's important to say a word about the tremendous good done in the name of Jesus. The church has been the champion of the greatest social improvements: the establishment of hospitals, hospices and schools; the scientific enterprise; and the campaign for equality and human rights, to name but a few. Substantiating those claims is impossible in the space available, but let me recommend a book like David Bentley Hart's *Atheist Delusions*[3] as an outline of the Christian revolution from the first century onwards. Belief in this God has been an incredible force for good in the world.

When atheists like Christopher Hitchens have claimed that 'religion poisons everything', it turns out to be a lazy caricature.[4] For Hitchens to make his case he had to place Stalin into the religious (and therefore evil) category and Martin Luther King Jr into the non-religious (and therefore benevolent) category. Such intellectual dishonesty is rife in these debates. It surfaces often as the charge that 'religion is the cause of all wars'. Actually religion has been at the root of about 7 per cent of all wars chronicled.[5] Just a glance at the last century will tell you that God is not the common denominator in war – man is. Our problem is not religion or irreligion – it's us.

TWO – the problem we all face

My name is Glen Scrivener and I'm a hypocrite. There, I said it. Actually it's kind of liberating, you should try it. It's exhausting trying to pretend that you're authentic and consistent in all your relationships. Frankly I can't keep up the 'no hypocrisy' mask. I'm coming clean. I'm a hypocrite. And I've got a funny feeling that you are too.

Ever since Adam and Eve sewed fig leaves together to cover their nakedness,[6] human beings have tried to hide their shame. It's almost involuntary – we are desperate to conceal our badness and to prove our goodness. Therefore we cover up. Wearing masks springs from our fear, pride, guilt, control, love of status, love of power and love of self. It's something we all struggle with. Therefore the question is not whether or not we are hypocritical; the question is what will we do with our hypocrisy? The question is not whether or not we will mess up in life and harm others; the question is what will we do with our sin?

ONE – healing for hypocrites

Jesus was once asked by the moral policemen of his day, 'Why do you eat and drink with tax collectors and sinners?'[7] Jesus hung out with the worst kind of people – and he still does. The Pharisees thought this was a terrible advertisement for the Jesus movement, and people today think the same. But Jesus replied, 'It is not the healthy who need a doctor, but those who are ill. I have not come to call the righteous, but sinners.'[8]

Jesus is a spiritual doctor and calls people to admit their sickness. He doesn't seem to mind if the world looks on and sees a bunch of 'tax collectors and sinners'. He is not interested in people 'keeping up appearances'. He wants us to come to him the way a patient comes to a doctor – not hiding our problems but admitting them.

Yet something wonderful happens as we expose ourselves like this. We realise that we are ONE with Jesus in spite of our sins and apart from any masks we might have worn. As we look bad in the presence of love, the experience is wonderfully transformative. It's perhaps counter-intuitive but the path to becoming better is confessing that we are worse. The way out of hypocrisy is to admit that we struggle. The journey to wellness is admitting that we're sick.

Of course this makes Christians vulnerable to accusations – more vulnerable than anyone else actually. After all we are open about our failures (or should be). What's more, we are called to deep relationships in the church which will expose our sins all the more. And we are called to such a high standard of behaviour – Christ's! – so of course we will disappoint people.

But when Christians fail, this does not disprove their Christianity since we do not claim moral superiority. Quite the opposite – we know that we are sick. On the other hand, if a person finds themselves unable to join a church because 'churches are full of ...', we start to sound like the Pharisees above. If someone cannot pull up a chair at Jesus' table alongside all the other 'sinners', at that point it's not the church that's being judgemental.

11

WHAT ABOUT OTHER FAITHS?

3-2-1 has been obsessed with Jesus of Nazareth. Perhaps that seems outrageously narrow when billions of people follow other religions? What's so special about Christianity?

Jesus – a unique starting point

Jesus is unique. No-one else has credibly claimed *both* to be the living God *and* to be a genuinely historical figure in our time and space. In some religions God stays far away. In other religions the gods come down, but not in genuine, real-world history. In other words no other gods have ever actually showed up. Only Jesus has come into our world as a God who can be examined.

When he did come down, he fulfilled hundreds of ancient prophecies, spoke like no-one ever has, healed the sick, raised the dead, ruled over nature, died on a cross and then rose from the dead three days later. All of this happened publicly and can be investigated historically. No other religion comes close to having this.

THREE – a unique God

The Christian God is unique. In some religions God is an individual defined by supremacy. In some religions there are many gods who often war with each other. In neither case is love ultimate. With the THREE you have a Father loving his Son in the joy of the Spirit. Only the Christian can truly say, 'God is love.'

TWO – a unique salvation

The Christian salvation is unique. In some religions there is a future hope of carnal delights but this future is other-worldly. In some religions the hope is to dissolve into the ocean of being. In neither case is there a hope for life as we know it. But with the Second Adam, Jesus Christ, we have a salvation that is worked in our humanity and for our world. Every other religion envisages the mess that we've made of this world being ignored while the faithful are taken *elsewhere*. Only the Christian believes in redemption – the transformation of *this* world. Only a Christian has a genuine, lasting hope for planet earth.

ONE – a unique spirituality

The Christian life is unique. In some religions the closest you can come to God is to be his slave. In other religions the best you can hope for is to be one *with the cosmos*. In neither case are you ONE with a personal god. But in Christianity the very essence of our relationship with God is a ONE-ness of love and trust. What's more, this relationship – being a love relationship – is enjoyed freely. Every other religion operates on the basis of conditional blessings – rewards are earned for good slaving or good karma. But because of ONE-ness with Jesus, Christians are pledged his committed love apart from any earning or efforts of our own.

All of this makes Christianity utterly unique. None of it makes Christianity true, necessarily. But it does set it apart from the pack and perhaps gives some incentives for investigating *Jesus*. If it turns out that Jesus is who he claims to be, then the search is over: you have found 'the One'. If he's not who he claims to be, then you can quickly rule out Christianity. Either way it's Jesus who can give us a way through the religious marketplace.

12

WHY ARE CHRISTIANS SO WEIRD ABOUT SEX AND SEXUALITY?

People have always found the Bible's view of sex shocking. In Old Testament times the surrounding cultures of Egypt and Assyria saw sex differently to the Israelites. Similarly in the first century, Greco-Roman views of sex were worlds apart from those of the New Testament. The Bible has always set out a radically different vision for sex.

This difference has been difficult to see when, for more than a millennia, Christendom has legislated the sexual morality of the wider culture. What was counter-cultural in the Bible became law in the west. Now that we are post-Christendom (something that many Christians as well as non-Christians are happy about), we are realising once again a truth that is obvious within the Bible: Christians are different – in fact, they are meant to be.

Once we learn to accept this difference, hopefully we can drop the rhetoric of outrage on all sides. It would be nice if Christians stopped being outraged that the world doesn't share its views on sex anymore. It would also be nice if non-Christians stopped being outraged that the Christian vision of sex dares to be different. Hopefully, as all sides realise that this difference is here to stay, we can handle it with maturity.

Let's explore the difference and how Christians got their strange view of sex in the first place.

Jesus – a welcome for all

Jesus never flinched from anyone – no matter their background, no matter their sin. There was no such thing as a social pariah to Jesus. Luke chapter 7 tells the story of a prostitute gatecrashing a dinner party in order to embrace Jesus.[1] While all the religious authorities – the Pharisees – wanted her out, Jesus receives her, calls her devotion 'beautiful' and speaks peace to her. The religious policemen wanted to exclude her, making her sexual sin the defining fact of her existence. Instead Jesus welcomes her, saying all is forgiven.

The whole world is welcome at Jesus' table, no matter their sexual history, sexual desires or sexual activity. Unfortunately Christians have often operated more like the Pharisees in this story than like Jesus. Often the church has wanted to check people's credentials at the door before allowing access to Christ. Perhaps you have had first-hand experience of modern-day Pharisees. Perhaps there have been those who have sought to condemn and exclude you because of your sexual history or desires. Tragically such Pharisees often claim to act 'in Jesus' name'. If you have experienced pharisaical Christians, we can only apologise, repent and urge you to look once again to Jesus himself – he is the centre of it all. Read of Christ in the Gospels and ask yourself, 'Am I welcome at his table?' The answer of the Gospels is: 'Yes, you are welcome.' Your old life can never disbar you. Yet as you come to Jesus, he gives you a new life.

We have seen already the good life which Jesus offers us. It's about receiving God's love and pouring it out for the world. This will involve such radical acts as loving our enemies, forgiving our persecutors and giving away our money and possessions. It also, as we will see, involves chastity outside marriage and faithfulness within it. The radical nature of following Jesus includes the bedroom. Therefore the prostitute leaves Christ's presence as a new woman, but for that very reason she cannot go back to the brothel. She has come to Christ as she is, but she does not remain that way. Whatever our history and whatever our situation, the same will be true for us.

Let's think about why Christians think the way they do about sex. It all begins with the nature of God.

THREE – the foundation for gender

'Let us make mankind in our image,' say the THREE.[2] And so God creates these lookalikes and specifically he makes them 'male and female'.[3] The THREE create a reflection of their life in the world. They make a loving union of distinct persons: a male and a female who are meant to be fruitful and multiply and create a third –children.[4] When Christians look at men, women and children united in love, they see a picture of God – a very imperfect picture, but a picture nonetheless.

In the New Testament the Apostle Paul looked at the way husbands and wives related and likened it to the way the Father and the Son relate.[5] In both cases there is absolute equality but not interchangeability. When you look at the Father and the Son, there is a flow to their life together and you cannot simply swap the members around as though their particular role was irrelevant.

It's the same with gender. Men and women are utterly equal but not interchangeable. There is a male-ness to men and a female-ness to women, and when they enter into a certain kind of one-ness (that is marriage), they are meant to flow in a certain way. We will revisit this truth when we come to ONE but for now let's grab hold of the gender point: gender is not a surface-level aspect of our humanity. Gender is not like a set of clothes that we can discard or change because 'the real me' is somewhere underneath. Our gender is part and parcel of our personal identity.

This is not to say that we find it easy to accept our genders as male and female. I often struggle with what it means 'to be a man' and worry whether I am one – whatever one is. It's actually rare to meet people who find their gender identity straightforward. That has a lot to do with TWO.

TWO – no-one is 'straight'

There's a popular YouTube video where members of the public are asked, 'Do you think being gay is a choice?' Most answer, 'Yes.' The interviewer then asks, 'And when did you choose to be straight?' It stumps them all. Then they admit, 'I guess I didn't choose to be straight.' The interviewer follows up, 'Don't you think it's the same for gay people?' 'I suppose so,' comes the sheepish reply. It makes a powerful point. I wonder how you would have answered those questions.

Here's my response: who says I'm straight? I'm not 'straight'. My sexual history and desires are as crooked as the next guy's. It's true that I never *chose* my sexual desires. Desire is a hugely complicated thing. I therefore agree that I didn't *simply decide* upon my sexuality. But allow me to exercise my power of choice in one thing: I choose *not* to be 'straight'. I choose to come out as a 'sexual sinner'. In Adam that's what I am.

I asked earlier whether you thought you were welcome at Jesus' table. Let me tell you the one category of person who is not welcome with Jesus: the righteous. In Mark chapter 2 Jesus describes himself as the spiritual doctor for the sick.[6] Therefore he is not for the 'sexually righteous' but only for those who know themselves to be sinners.

Sometimes people ask, 'Can I come to Jesus if I'm gay?' With Mark chapter 2 in mind I reply, 'The real problem is coming to Jesus as "straight".' Ever since Adam we've been crooked. Every area of our lives has been twisted, including our sexuality.

It is very unfortunate that we tend to categorise people as 'straight' and then, alternatively, as lesbian, gay, bisexual, transgender, questioning, intersex, and so on – as though there is a group whose sexual desires are pure and then there's 'the rest'. These divisions are a modern, western fascination unknown to the rest of the world (and to the rest of history). The Bible has no interest whatsoever in our 'orientation'. Certainly Jesus never preached heterosexual *orientation*. He never taught his disciples to desire the opposite sex *en masse*, nor did he encourage anyone to identify themselves by their sexual preferences. Heterosexuality is not the point. And my orientation is not my identity.

All of us have twisted desires and we are called to come to Christ with them – not as 'straight' or 'gay' but as 'sinners'. As soon as we do that, we are relinquishing control of our own identities. We are saying, 'I won't let my life in Adam define me; I will let Jesus define me.' You see the woman in Luke chapter 7 came to Christ as a prostitute but she left as a daughter. Her life in Adam could not prevent her from coming to Jesus, but her life in Christ sent her out as a new woman.

In the same way everyone who wants to be a Christian will feel the tension between Adam and Christ. The prostitute will have to say 'No' to her old ways, but so will I, and so will you. Christ's new life will challenge our attitude to a thousand things – like money, work, rest, family and forgiveness but also sex. Everyone will struggle. That's why we need ONE-ness with Jesus.

ONE – the foundation for marriage

If THREE gave us our foundation for gender, ONE gives us our foundation for sex and marriage. Throughout the Bible the phrase 'one flesh' describes both sex and marriage.[7] That's because, for a Christian, the two belong together. Sex is the physical expression of the marriage union – it's an enjoyment of the one-ness that marriage is.

As we have already seen, the one-ness of marriage pictures a greater oneness: our union with Jesus. Jesus shares his life, his future and his blessings with us for free and forever. With Jesus we don't just get his things, we get him. In the same way the Christian believes that our earthly 'one flesh' relationships should be committed, faithful, life-sharing unions in which we give ourselves to our partner. For this reason Christians don't believe in sleeping around, we don't believe in cheating on our partner and we don't believe in sex before marriage. The 'one flesh' act belongs in the 'one flesh' relationship. And our 'one flesh' relationships should reflect the faithful, exclusive, permanent love of Jesus.

Christians also believe that this one-ness should be between a man and a woman. In Matthew chapter 19 Jesus quotes the early chapters of Genesis to make the point:

> ... at the beginning the Creator 'made them male and female,' and said, 'For this reason a man will leave his father and mother and be united to his wife, and the two will become one flesh'.[8]

Our genders are not created by ourselves but by God. Gender is a deep aspect of our identity, not a disposable outfit we tailor to taste. But it's not just our own gender that matters – Jesus says our partner's gender also matters. In our 'one flesh' relationship we are not called to another version of ourselves but to our 'opposite number'. For the Christian, marriage is a *flow* between two interlocking partners: a man and a woman. In this way, Christians believe that marriages reflect to the world the ultimate romance story: the love of Jesus for those who are different to him – us.

Such views might not be popular today in the west but if Jesus is right about sex and relationships some wonderful things follow. If Jesus is right, then our gender *means* something, the gender of our partner *means* something, our bodies *mean* something, sex *means* something and marriage *means* something. If Jesus is right, it means that sex is not just procreation or recreation but a sacred union of *lives* as well as bodies. If Jesus is right, then sex is a physical declaration of life-long faithfulness and love – more than this, it is an expression of a heavenly romance here on earth. This is a high view of sex, a strange view of sex but also a beautiful view of sex.

Maybe you don't yet think Jesus is Lord. If that's the case, we don't expect you to buy his sexual ethic. But maybe you don't think Jesus is Lord *because* you don't like his vision for sex. If so, let me encourage you to put first things first. If Jesus rose from the dead, then his words are true no matter what we feel about them. And if he is the Lord, then he knows what's good for us too.

Perhaps, though, you are attracted to Jesus but you don't think you could manage the life he speaks of. On one level I want to say, 'Join the club.' ONE-ness with Jesus does not just 'cramp our style'; it means death to our old lives. For some following Jesus costs them their job or their wealth, their family or their reputation. Who knows how things may pan out for you but conceivably following Jesus may cost you a sex life. That is a daunting prospect – especially in a world that says sexual expression is the very pinnacle of life. I won't pretend that these are small things; they aren't. But I will assure you that there is something better than sex. There is a ONE-ness with Jesus that far surpasses the 'one flesh' of this passing age. What's more, the ONE-ness we enjoy *together* in the church family is certainly able to sustain us with or without 'one flesh' relationships. It comes down to trust. When Jesus says his way means 'life ... to the full',[9] do we believe him?

Christ's message to the world is to come to him – not as heterosexual, homosexual or bisexual, but simply as a sinner. Jesus is not anti-anyone, so long as we are not pro-ourselves. At his table we all have a place equal to every other sinner. Though we fail to live his life in a thousand ways, Jesus knows how to lead us, step by step, into greater and greater freedom from sexual slaveries as well as from the other *really* dangerous sins – like greed, unforgiveness and moral self-righteousness!

13
AREN'T BELIEVERS ANTI-SCIENCE?

It's common to pit science and faith against one another as mortal enemies and then to argue about who 'wins'. Actually, as we'll see, science and faith are not foes at all. When viewed rightly, they are the greatest of friends.

Science and Christianity – friends not foes

Imagine the scene: a lab technician hands a botanical specimen to a scientist called Rachel. She takes it away and runs a series of tests to discover its biological and chemical make-up, how it was grown, the pesticides used, and so on. After many months of hard work she even manages to sequence the genome of the plant – a first for this species. She thanks the lab technician for giving her the specimen. 'Specimen?' he asks. 'Don't you get it, Rachel? It was the 14th of February. I gave you a rose!'

There was more to the rose than its genetic make-up. That 'something more' did not exist in a magical realm of fairies and pixie dust. But this 'something more' could not be captured by scientific analysis. It wouldn't matter how many tests Rachel ran, the romantic meaning of the 'specimen' would always escape her. So we see that the scientist requires more than her science in order to understand her world.

For the Christian the whole world is like that rose. We can analyse its chemical and biological make-up, and that will prove a fascinating and profoundly helpful study. But there are realms of meaning that cannot be grasped by the scientific method. That isn't to downplay science; it's just to face the nature of reality. On one level the world is physical and open to the physical sciences. On another it is a communication – a gift that's telling us about someone who loves us. To understand *that* aspect of the world requires a different kind of study.

Here we're talking about science and faith operating at different levels of explanation. The rose is *both* a plant *and* a romantic gesture, and it takes different kinds of investigation to grasp it in its fullness. Unfortunately some people look at science and faith as an either/or choice – you either embrace science or faith.

Recently I watched a video where a prominent atheist said, 'The only way of finding out true facts about reality is through the scientific endeavour.'[1] To me that's like Rachel insisting, 'The *only* way to truly know this rose is to map its genome.' It's a ridiculously narrow thing to say, but people forward such views because they have bought into a model of conflict – they think in terms of 'science *versus* faith'. The great scientists of the past certainly never thought their science was in conflict with their faith.

When Johannes Kepler discovered the laws of planetary motion in the early 17th century, he did not lose his strong Christian faith. Instead he spoke of the privilege of 'thinking God's thoughts after Him'. That has been the mindset of so many giants in the history of science: Copernicus, Galileo, Newton, Faraday and, in our own day, Christians like Francis Collins, leader of the Human Genome Project. They have not imagined a single level of meaning to the world with 'a God of the gaps' shrinking ever smaller as science progresses. They have believed in 'the God of the whole' – a God both in and beyond scientific enquiry. They considered themselves to be thinking God's thoughts after him – to be exploring his love gift, as it were. Therefore their Christian faith did not take them away from the laboratory but propelled them into it.

THREE, TWO and ONE – the foundation of science

Modern science depends on three things which we often take for granted:

1. Laws *up above*, which are coherent, consistent and comprehensible.
2. A world *out there*, which is real and open to investigation.
3. Minds *in here*, which are rational and dependable.

The fact we have these three elements ought to make us think:

- Why are laws *up above* consistent across time and space? Why is the world a cosmos and not a chaos?
- Why do we trust our senses about the world *out there*? Many peoples have thought of the world as an illusion – why don't we?
- Why do we trust our minds *in here*? Why should the brains of *homo sapiens* be of any use in comprehending the mysteries of the universe?

The fact of these three elements is amazing enough. What is really incredible is how these three elements line up together – they triangulate, if you like. There seem to be laws 'written' in the 'language' of mathematics – a language obeyed by nature and understood by my puny mind. Therefore when I use my mind, I can hypothesise about possible laws to explain the world. I can then test my hypotheses and discover that my predictions *in here* about the laws *up above* really do match the world *out there*. That's science. It's wonderful. And it depends on this miracle of triangulation. Albert Einstein put it this way: 'The eternal mystery of the world is its comprehensibility ... The fact that it is comprehensible is a miracle.'[2]

Science rests on a 'miracle' – so said Einstein. This is a deeply uncomfortable situation for a scientific community. Quite rightly scientists are not content with mystery, they want explanations. Thankfully the Christian can step forward with help. We say, 'Don't accept an unexplained miracle – dig deeper! Figure out *why* the miracle holds.'

You see the miracle is not really so inexplicable. Not once you know 3-2-1.

THREE: there is a God of order and truth. The Father, Son and Spirit have always enjoyed a rational, harmonious life and they have made a world that reflects that harmony.

TWO: the Son of God entered our world, anchoring himself to our kind of life. We can trust the reality of the world because God has pledged himself to it forever. Jesus – the Word of God – holds the laws *up above* together with the world *out there.*

ONE: the Son of God became one with us at every level, our mind included. What's more, Jesus wants us to be one with him and to share in *his* kind of life. Therefore Christians are optimistic about human abilities to grasp the mysteries of the universe. We are intended for the life of God, therefore our minds *in here* have the ability to grasp the things *up above*.

The Christian knows why science works. THREE, TWO and ONE ensure that natural laws, the world and our minds match up. The Christian story therefore gives the strongest possible foundation for the scientific enterprise. This is why modern science grew out of Christian contexts.

Without the Bible's story, science would never really have gotten off the ground. Throughout history there have been incredibly intelligent peoples, but they haven't given us science as we know it today. The ancient Greeks produced wonderful mathematics, logic and philosophy but not science. That's because, while they believed in reason, they did not believe in test- ing hypotheses with real-world data. They believed in laws *up above* but not so much in the world *out there*.

Coming from the opposite direction, the ancient Chinese produced incredible technology – spectacles, printing, gun powder – but nothing like a scientific method. They believed in a world *out there* but not so much in dependable laws *up above*.

Science has arisen only in cultures that have believed the *Bible's* view of God, the world and ourselves. Far from being anti-science, Christianity has generated science and remains the firmest foundation for the scientific endeavour.

What about evolution?

Christians take a huge variety of different positions on evolution. Is there any way of distilling a Christian answer from so many different viewpoints? Let me have a go.

I have never met a Christian who did not believe that evolution happens. Whatever else creationists believe, they happily acknowledge that natural selection occurs and causes great changes within species. For example, they accept that tabbies and tigers have a common ancestor and Darwin's finches evolved different-sized beaks on the Galapagos Islands. On the other hand I have never met a Christian evolutionist who thinks natural selection explains *everything* about our origins.

So if we ask about 'the Christian view on evolution' perhaps we can put it this way: everyone agrees that natural selection happens but everyone questions its ability to explain the whole show. It's a bit like the old saying: a hammer is a wonderful tool, but if all you have is a hammer, everything starts to look like a nail. Natural selection has great explanatory power, but if you try to explain everything by it, you come unstuck.

For the sake of argument, though, let's imagine that random mutations and natural selection account for all the varieties of life on planet earth. This only explains the origin of the *species*. That's as far as Darwin can take you. He cannot explain the origin of *life* itself (he must assume the origin of life). He cannot tell you the origin of the *cosmos*. And he cannot tell you the origin of *consciousness*. Those three origins questions are far more pressing, yet natural selection is no help for any of them.

And even if science discovered a credible mechanism for explaining these origins in the future, it would only be a *mechanism*. Mechanisms do not disprove makers – how could they? Figuring out the inner workings of a car engine does not abolish the need for a designer. Furthermore, mechanisms don't give you *meaning*. After all, the genetic code of the rose does not tell you that it's a love gift. So you see, mechanisms – like natural selection – are wonderful to study. But mechanisms don't rule out the Maker, nor do they answer our questions about meaning.

Doing good science

Recently I watched a documentary about the Large Hadron Collider. Brian Cox was explaining why physicists were spending so much time and money on these experiments:

> Physics is stuck and the only thing left to do is recreate the universe as it was a fraction of a second after the big bang. That's what the Large Hadron Collider is designed to do – to smash bits of matter together at energies never before achieved so that we can stare at the face of creation ...

The language here is fascinating. Cox excites us about the scientific quest by promising us a 'face' to creation. Of course 'face' says communicative, it says conscious, it says personality. No wonder Cox wants to reach for this kind of language. We all long to see personal reality at the heart of all things. The only trouble is that materialism can't give us a face actually. All it can give us are more particles.

Is there a way to see the 'face of creation'? There is, and it's a *scientific* method too. You see science works by investigating things according to their nature. You don't do astronomy with a microscope – you investigate according to the nature of what you're studying. So then, how should we investigate the very heart of reality?

If you think the universe is, fundamentally, just material, then smashing particles will be your method. But if you are really searching for a 'face' at the bottom of it all, then your methods should be adapted accordingly.

Smashing particles will never give you a 'face' but the Christian claim is this: the Face behind it all has shown up personally in history. Therefore, in order to do good science, we must use appropriate methods. We should study the words that predicted him (the Old Testament) and the words that testified to his coming (the New Testament). And since he is personal, it would make sense to call out personally to him – praying he would reveal himself. If we're really after creation's 'face', then this would be the most appropriate kind of study. That's not to detract from the wonders of particle physics, it's only to recognise its limits.

Exploring the material universe is awe-inspiring and Christians should be the first to enter the lab to study more of God's world. But smashing particles will not reveal to you a Person. If you want to go beyond the mechanisms to the *Maker* and to the *meaning* – if you want to understand the love gift – then *do good science*. Investigate the Person behind it all. Keep reading of Jesus and cry out, 'Show me your face.'

Optional reading: John chapters 18–21

- How does Jesus approach his own death?
- Given what you've read in John's Gospel, what do you think is the significance of Jesus' death?
- How does Jesus reveal himself once he has risen from the dead? What is he communicating to his followers?
- Chapter 20 verse 31 says that John's Gospel was 'written so that you might believe'. Do you believe? What has been your response to Jesus?

NOTES

1. Welcome

[1]This wording is taken from the King James Version of the Bible.

2. JESUS: The Way into the Story

[1]Matthew 2:1–12; Luke 2:8–18.

[2]Matthew 2:13–18.

[3]Luke 4:16–21.

[4]Matthew 3:1–12.

[5]Matthew 3:13–17.

[6]Luke 4:18–19, paraphrased.

[7]Luke 4:20–21, paraphrased.

[8]Luke 4:22–27.

[9]Luke 4:28–30.

[10]Luke 5:1–11.

[11]Luke 5:12–16.

[12]Luke 5:17–26.

[13]Luke 5:20.

[14]Luke 5:21, paraphrased.

[15]Luke 5:23, paraphrased.

[16]Luke 5:27–28.

[17]Luke 5:29–32, paraphrased.

[18]See Luke 7:34, paraphrased.

[19]Luke 7:36–50.

[20]Luke 15:2.

[21]Luke 7:34.

[22]Matthew 7:6.

[23]Matthew 7:15.

[24]Matthew 7:26–27.

[25]Matthew 16:6.

[26]Matthew 7:3–5.

[27]Matthew 23:27–28.

[28]Matthew 23:24.

[29]Matthew 6:2, 5, 16; 7:16.

[30]Luke 10:25–37.

[31]Luke 15:11–32.

[32]Matthew 23:25, 33, paraphrased.

[33]John 10:11; Luke 5:31; Mark 10:45; John 6:35 and 7:37; Luke 7:34.

[34]Matthew 22:21 and 26:52; John 8:7.

[35]Matthew 12:19, quoting Isaiah 42:2.

[36]Matthew 20:25–28.

[37]Matthew 12:20, quoting Isaiah 42:3, paraphrased.

[38]Mark 5:21–34.

[39]Malachi 4:2, as translated in the NIV of 1984.

[40]Mark 5:31.

[41]Mark 5:34.

[42]Mark 5:35–43.

[43]Mark 5:35.

[44]Mark 5:36, paraphrased.

[45]Mark 5:40–43, paraphrased.

[46]John 6:35; 8:12; 10:11; 14:6.

[47]Matthew 25:31–46 and 23:37; John 8:56–58.

[48]John 14:8–10, paraphrased.

[49]John 17:5.

[50]John 17:24.

[51]John 3:35, 5:22.

[52]John 5:19; 15:15.

[53]John 14:8; Matthew 10:40.

[54] John 6:38.

[55]Mark 8:27, paraphrased.

[56]Mark 3:21.

[57]Mark 3:22.

[58]John 10:11; Matthew 14:33; John 11:43; Luke 5:20; Matthew 28:20.

[59]Luke 6:37.

[60]Matthew 18:21.

[61]Matthew 18:22.

[62]Matthew 6:25–34, paraphrased.

[63]Matthew 6:25–34 and Luke 12:22–34, paraphrased.

[64]Mark 12:28–34, paraphrased.

[65]Matthew 5:43–48, paraphrased.

[66]Matthew 5:38–42, paraphrased.

[67]Mark 10:42–45 and Luke 14:7–14, paraphrased.

[68]Matthew 6:19–24 and Luke 12:13–15, 32–34, paraphrased.

[69]Matthew 10:39, paraphrased.

[70]Matthew 7:17–20.

[71]Mark 7:20–23.

[72]Matthew 7:11.

[73]Luke 12:49–59, paraphrased.

[74]Mark 13:1–8, paraphrased.

[75]Mark 10:38–39; 14:36.

[76]John 16:21; Matthew 8:11; 19:28.

[77]Matthew 13:42–43.

[78]Luke 12:50.

[79]John 2:19–21.

[80]Mark 14:36.

[81]John 1:29.

[82]John 12:31–32, paraphrased.

[83]John 12:27.

[84]Luke 13:33.

[85]Mark 8:31–32; 9:30–31; 10:32–34.

[86]John 13:1–17.

[87]John 13: 6, 8, 9, paraphrased.

[88]John 5:19, paraphrased.

[89]Matthew 26:17–29, paraphrased.

[90]Matthew 26:36–46, paraphrased; see also Mark 14:32–42 and Luke 22:39–46.

[91]Luke 22:54–62.

[92]Luke 22:47–53.

[93]Luke 22:48, paraphrased.

[94]Matthew 26:57 – 27:31 and John 1:19 – 19:16.

[95]John 18:34; Mark 15:2; Matthew 26:63–64.

[96]Mark 14:61–62.

[97]Matthew 26:67–68; 27:27–31.

[98]Luke 22:63–64.

[99]Isaiah 53:3–7.

[100]Luke 23:26–31.

[101]Luke 23:32–34.

[102]Deuteronomy 21:23.

[103]Matthew 27:42.

[104]Luke 23:34, 43; John 19:26–27; Mark 15:34; John 19:28; Luke 23:46; John 19:30.

[105]John 19:31–37.

[106]John 19:38–42; Matthew 27:57–61.

[107]John 20:1–18.

[108]John 20:13.

[109]Luke 24:13–35.

[110]Luke 24:17.

[111]Luke 24:26–27, paraphrased.

[112]John 20:19–23.

[113]John 20:19.

[114]John 20:24–29.

[115]John 21:1–19.

[116]Matthew 28:16–20 and Acts 1:1–8, paraphrased.

[117]Acts 2.

[118]Matthew 16:18, KJV.

[119]Philip Schaff, *The Person of Christ* (New York: American Tract Society, 1913).

[120]Romans 10:9; 1 Corinthians 12:3; Philippians 2:11.

3. THREE: God Is A Loving Union Of Three

[1]From an interview with *The Wall Street Journal*: http://blogs.wsj.com/speakeasy/2010/12/19/a-holiday-message-from-ricky-gervais-why-im-an-atheist

[2]From a lecture by Tom Wright on 'Jesus and the Identity of God', http://ntwrightpage.com/Wright_JIG.htm

[3]Stephen Hawking, *A Brief History of Time* (Bantam Books, 1988).

[4]Deuteronomy 33:27.

[5]Luke 3:21–22.

[6]John 17:24.

[7]'A personal god was nothing more than an exalted father-figure: desire for such a deity sprang from infantile yearnings for a powerful, protective

father.' Sigmund Freud, *The History of God.*

[8]See, for example, Laurence Krauss's popular book *A Universe from Nothing* (Simon & Schuster), where he writes, 'By nothing, I do not mean *nothing*' (p. 58), 'Nothing is something' (p. 141ff) and 'Nothing is unstable' (p. 153ff).

[9]From a debate with Peter Hitchens at Fountain St Church, Grand Rapids, on 3 April 2008: https://www.youtube.com/watch?v=nXwrZjh7pVU

[10]Isaiah 57:15, NKJV. Copyright © 1982 by Thomas Nelson, Inc. Used by permission. All rights reserved.

[11]Mark 10:45.

[12]John 14:10.

[13]1 John 4:8.

[14]Friedrich Nietzsche, *Thus Spoke Zarathustra* (1880s).

[15]The Greek word is *perichoresis*, if you care about such things.

4. TWO: The World Is Shaped by Two Representatives

[1]Genesis 1:28; 2:19–20.

[2]Genesis 2:21–25.

[3]'This is now bone of my bones and flesh of my flesh; she shall be called "woman", for she was taken out of man' (Genesis 2:23).

[4]Genesis 2:25.

[5]Revelation 12:9.

[6]See Ezekiel 28:12–17.

[7]Genesis 3:1.

[8]Genesis 2:16.

[9]Genesis 2:17.

[10]Genesis 3:5.

[11]Genesis 3:6.

[12]Genesis 3:7–8.

[13]Genesis 3:11–13.

[14]Genesis 3:13.

[15]Romans 7:19.

[16]Genesis 3:17–19, 23–24.

[17]Acts 17:28.

[18]Genesis 2:17.

[19]John 6:35; 7:37–39.

[20]Christopher Hitchens, *Letters to a Young Contrarian* (Basic Books, 2001).

[21]Genesis 3:16–24.

[22]Genesis 3:17.

[23]Romans 8:20.

[24]Romans 8:21–22.

[25]See Luke 15 or Luke 19:10.

[26]Matthew 8:12.

[27]Matthew 22:13.

[28]Matthew 25:41.

[29]Luke 16:19–31.

[30]John 3:18.

[31]John 3:36.

[32]James 3:5.

[33]James 3:6.

[34]Ezekiel 18:23, 30–32; 33:11; Matthew 23:37; John 3:16–18; Acts 17:30; Romans 11:32; 1 Timothy 2:3–6; Hebrews 2:9; 2 Peter 3:9.

[35]'Noel' (Episode 10, Season 2 of *The West Wing*).

[36]Luke 10:25–37.

[37]The famous temptations in the wilderness were a test of *faith*. Jesus was the one man to pass with flying colours. See Matthew 4:1–11.

[38]Matthew 27:43.

[39]Matthew 10:39.

[40]John 8:46.

[41]Matthew 26:59f; Luke 23:14f; John 18:38.

[42]John 14:11.

[43]Mark 8:31; see also Mark 9:31; Mark 10:33–34.

[44]Mark 15:33.

[45]Matthew 27:46.

[46]1 Peter 3:18.

[47]1 Corinthians 15:21–22.

[48]John 20:11–18.

[49]John 20:19–29.

[50]Acts 1:1–5.

[51]Luke 24:34–49.

[52]Luke 24:13–35.

[53]John 21:1–9.

[54]John 21:10–14.

5. ONE: You Are One with Adam – Be One with Jesus

[1]In Genesis 3:15 the LORD God promises a miraculous child. This Saviour would be born of a woman – one of us – and he would crush Satan's head, though he'd be struck in the process. This was the first of *many* promises in the Old Testament, building faith and expectation for Christ.

[2]1 Corinthians 15:26.

[3]For example the phrase is used nine times in Ephesians 1:3–14.

[4]Romans 6:5.

[5]Colossians 3:3.

[6]Rory Shiner, *One Forever* (Matthias Media, 2013).

[7]John 15:5.

[8]Luke 5:34–35.

[9]This is pictured in Ephesians 5:21–33; also see Revelation 19:7.

[10]John 3:1–21.

[11]John 3:3.

[12]John 3:7.

[13]John 3:6.

[14]John 3:16.

[15]John 1:12.

[16]Galatians 3:26.

[17]Matthew 26:41.

[18]See Galatians 5:16–26 or Romans 7 – 8.

[19]Matthew 16:25.

[20]John 10:10.

[21]Mark 10:29–30.

[22]Ephesians 5:21–33; John 15:1–8.

[23]John 5:39–40.

[24]Luke 11:1.

[25]Matthew 6:9.

[26]Matthew 6:5–7.

[27]John 6:37.

6. OK, But Is It True?

[1]Aldous Huxley, *Ends and Means,* pp. 270 ff.

[2]C.S. Lewis, *Mere Christianity* (Collins, 1952).

[3]John 8:12.

[4]1 Corinthians 15:14.

[5]Of course it's always possible to doubt historical assertions – we will consider such doubters with our next question. But at some point a person's scepticism becomes more incredible than simple trust in the eye-witness testimony. People are free to disbelieve the testimony of Matthew, Mark, Luke and John, but against that hefty weight of evidence (not to mention a dozen further sources that mention Jesus and the early Christians) they had better have an even more plausible counter-theory. Personally I have never come across one.

[6]Luke 24:13–35.

[7]Luke 24:31–32.

[8]Romans 10:17.

[9]John Piper, *Seeing and Savoring Jesus Christ* (Crossway Books, 2001).

7. Is the Bible Trustworthy?

[1]Taken from an article in the *Huffington Post*: http://www.huffingtonpost.com/bart-d-ehrman/did-jesus-exist_b_1349544.html

[2]http://www.huffingtonpost.com/bart-d-ehrman/did-jesus-exist_b_1349544.html

[3]Walter C. Kaiser, Jr, *The Messiah in the Old Testament* (Zondervan, 1995).

[4]Luke 1:1–4.

[5]See for example Luke 2:1–4 and 3:1–2, 23–38.

[6]From a sermon titled 'Christ and His Co-workers', given in 1886.

8. How Does a Good God Fit with Evil and Suffering?

[1]Isaiah 53:3.

[2]John 12:27–33.

[3]John 11:4.

[4]John 11:21, 32.

[5]John 11:25.

[6]John 11:35.

9. How Does a Loving God Fit with Judgement?

[1]Mark 9:48.

[2]Matthew 25:46.

[3]Matthew 8:12.

[4]John 3:15–18.

[5]Matthew 23:37.

[6]Luke 23:34.

[7]John 3:18, 36; Romans 1:18; James 3:6.

[8]John 17:3.

[9]Luke 15:11–32.

[10]2 Peter 3:9.

10. How Can Anyone Join the Church with All Its Hate, Its History and Its Hypocrisy?

[1]Matthew 23:27–28.

[2]Matthew 5:38–48; 26:52–54; John 18:36; Matthew 18:6.

[3]David Benley Hart, *Atheist Delusions* (Yale University Press, 2010).

[4]This was the American subtitle of Hitchens' book *God Is Not Great* (Atlantic Books, 2007).

[5]http://carm.org/religion-cause-war

[6]Genesis 3:7.

[7]Luke 5:30.

[8]Mark 2:17.

12. Why Are Christians So Weird about Sex and Sexuality?

[1]Luke 7:36–50.

[2]Genesis 1:26.

[3]Genesis 1:27.

[4]Genesis 1:28.

[5]1 Corinthians 11:3.

[6]Mark 2:17.

[7]Genesis 2:24; Matthew 19:5; 1 Corinthians 6:16; Ephesians 5:31.

[8]Matthew 19:4–6.

[9]John 10:10.

13. Aren't Believers Anti-Science?

[1]Andrew Copson, Chief Executive of the British Humanist Association, from *An Introduction to Humanism*, https://www.youtube.com/watch?v=DZN8Ne1nmr4

[2]Quoted in *Einstein: His Life and Universe* by Walter Isaacson.

Yuto Tsukuda

It's...volume 3. I have already received a lot of support from many people, and their help is what got me this far. I hope for your continued support in the future as well. Yeah! For reals.

Shun Saeki

Eek! That's scary! Who would have thought my angelic, adorable ferret could make such a demonic face? Still...that's just another endearing side of my little angel!

About the authors

Yuto Tsukuda won the 34th Jump Juniketsu Newcomers' Manga Award for his one-shot story *Kiba ni Naru*. He made his *Weekly Shonen Jump* debut in 2010 with the series *Shonen Shikku*. His follow-up series, *Food Wars!: Shokugeki no Soma*, is his first English-language release.

Shun Saeki made his *Jump NEXT!* debut in 2011 with the one-shot story *Kimi to Watashi no Renai Soudan. Food Wars!: Shokugeki no Soma* is his first *Shonen Jump* series.

Volume 3
Shonen Jump Manga Edition
Story by Yuto Tsukuda, Art by Shun Saeki

Translation: Adrienne Beck
Touch-Up Art & Lettering: NRP Studios
Design: Izumi Evers
Editor: Jennifer LeBlanc

Printed in the U.S.A.

Published by VIZ Media, LLC
P.O. Box 77010
San Francisco, CA 94107

10 9 8 7 6 5 4 3 2 1
First printing, December 2014

RATED T+ FOR OLDER TEEN

PARENTAL ADVISORY
FOOD WARS! is rated T+ for Older Teen and is recommended for ages 16 and up. This volume contains sexual situations/humor.

ratings.viz.com

Food Wars!
SHOKUGEKI NO SOMA
3
THE PERFECT RECETTE
ORIGINAL CREATOR:
YUTO TSUKUDA
ARTIST:
SHUN SAEKI
CONTRIBUTOR:
YUKI MORISAKI

CHARACTERS
SOMA YUKIHIRA First Year High School
Helping out at his family's restaurant since he was little, Soma trained as a chef with the goal of someday surpassing his father. Out of junior high, he's suddenly sent off to culinary school. He's skilled, but sometimes invents questionable new recipes.
ERINA NAKIRI First Year High School
Granddaughter of Senzaemon Nakiri, dean of the Totsuki Institute, she has a sense of taste so refined, famous restaurants across the nation come to her to taste test their dishes. She's a member of Totsuki's Council of Ten Masters, the institute's highest decision-making student body.
STORY
Soma grew up cooking in his family's restaurant, Yukihira. But one day his father enrolled him in Japan's premier culinary school, the Totsuki Institute. There he meets and befriends the residents of the Polaris Dormitory and wins his first shokugeki cooking battle. Now Soma faces the first hellish challenge the Totsuki Institute places in front of all first-year students, the cooking camp! What trials will await him there?

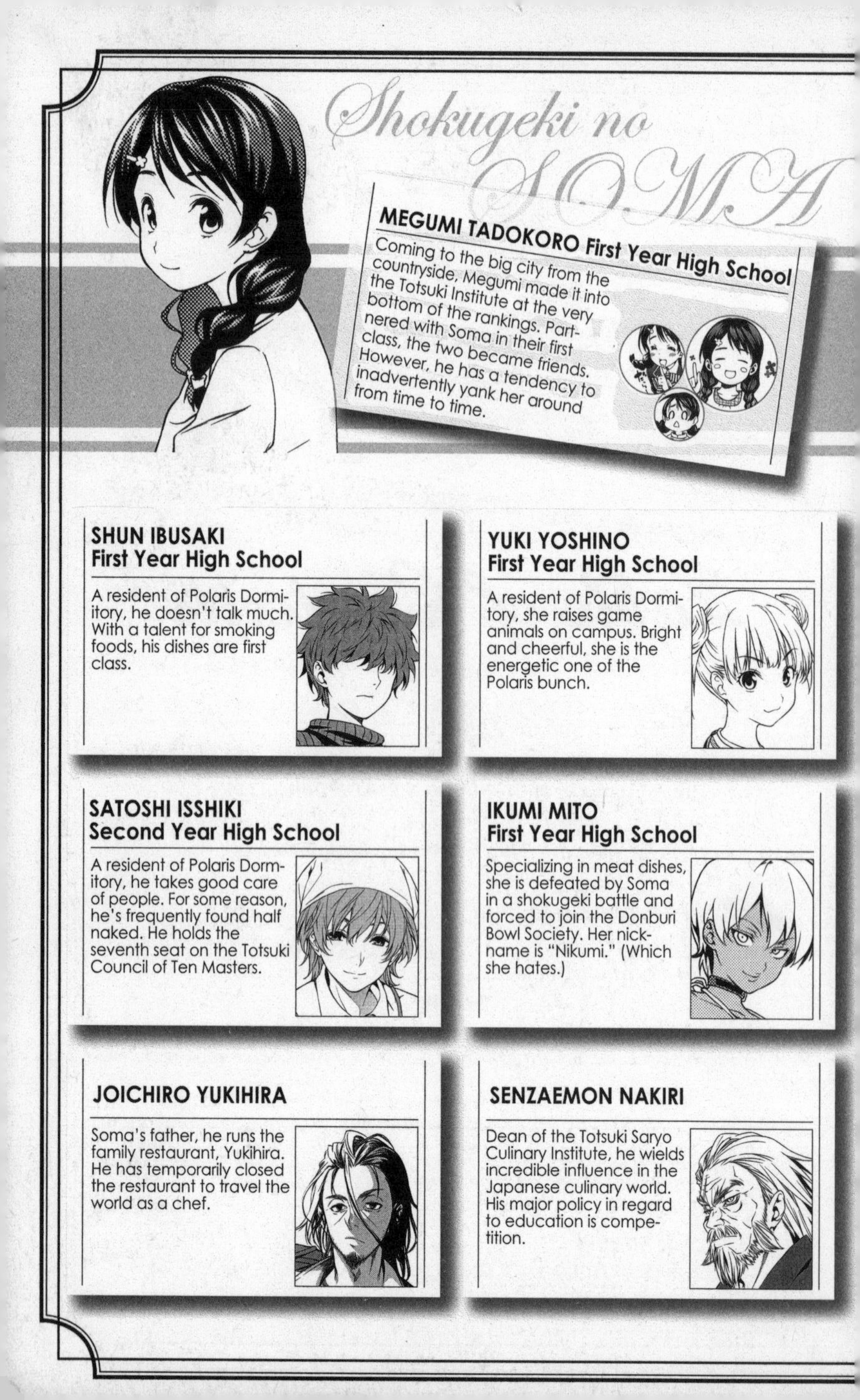
Shokugeki no SOMA
MEGUMI TADOKORO First Year High School
Coming to the big city from the countryside, Megumi made it into the Totsuki Institute at the very bottom of the rankings. Partnered with Soma in their first class, the two became friends. However, he has a tendency to inadvertently yank her around from time to time.
SHUN IBUSAKI
First Year High School
A resident of Polaris Dormitory, he doesn't talk much. With a talent for smoking foods, his dishes are first class.
YUKI YOSHINO
First Year High School
A resident of Polaris Dormitory, she raises game animals on campus. Bright and cheerful, she is the energetic one of the Polaris bunch.
SATOSHI ISSHIKI
Second Year High School
A resident of Polaris Dormitory, he takes good care of people. For some reason, he's frequently found half naked. He holds the seventh seat on the Totsuki Council of Ten Masters.
IKUMI MITO
First Year High School
Specializing in meat dishes, she is defeated by Soma in a shokugeki battle and forced to join the Donburi Bowl Society. Her nickname is "Nikumi." (Which she hates.)
JOICHIRO YUKIHIRA
Soma's father, he runs the family restaurant, Yukihira. He has temporarily closed the restaurant to travel the world as a chef.
SENZAEMON NAKIRI
Dean of the Totsuki Saryo Culinary Institute, he wields incredible influence in the Japanese culinary world. His major policy in regard to education is competition.

Food Wars! SHOKUGEKI NO SOMA

3

Table of Contents

15 FRICTION AND THE ELITE

...
WHOA!
D
UN
IT'S HUGE!

ON THE EDGE OF A CERTAIN PROVINCE...
...OVERLOOKING LAKE ASHI AND MT. FUJI, IN AN AREA RENOWNED FOR ITS LUXURY HOMES AND RETREATS...
...THE FIRST-YEAR STUDENTS OF THE TOTSUKI INSTITUTE HAD REACHED THEIR DESTINATION.

A TOTSUKI RESORT
Totsuki
JUST WHAT YOU'D EXPECT FROM A SCHOOL FOR THE RICH.
THEY'VE EVEN GOT THEIR OWN LUXURY HOTEL.
THIS ISN'T THE ONLY ONE. *ALL* THE HOTELS AND INNS NEAR HERE ARE OWNED BY TOTSUKI.
HUH. Y'KNOW, THERE ISN'T MUCH THAT COULD SURPRISE ME ANYMORE.
THEY RUN ABOUT A DOZEN HOTELS UNDER THE "TOTSUKI RESORT" BRAND.
MANY INSTITUTE GRADS WIND UP WORKING FOR ONE OF THEM.
SINCE THIS IS THE TIME OF YEAR THEY STOP ACCEPTING GUESTS, THEY USE THE HOTEL FOR THIS CAMP.
I HEAR A ONE-NIGHT STAY STARTS AROUND 80,000 YEN.
EIGHTY THOUSAND YEN FOR ONE PERSON TO STAY ONE NIGHT?!
THAT'S ENOUGH TO PAY A MONTH'S RENT FOR MOST PEOPLE!
AND WE REALLY GET TO STAY HERE? OOOH, I CAN'T WAIT!
ONLY IF YOU PASS TODAY'S ASSIGN-MENT.

BOO!
HMPH! QUIT BEING A BUZZKILL, IBUSAKI.
I'M A REALIST.
C'MON, THE ASSEM-BLY'S STARTING.
YAMMER
YAMMER
YAMMER
TOTSUKI RESORT HOTEL
TOTSUKI VILLA
GRAND BALLROOM
FREEZE
...

MURMUR
MURMUR
I DON'T LIKE THIS SILENCE.
YOU'D NEVER GUESS THERE ARE ALMOST A THOUSAND STUDENTS CRAMMED INTO THIS ROOM!
WHAT'S ABOUT TO BEGIN...
...IS THE TRAINING CAMP FROM HELL!
MUTTER
MUTTER
OF ALL THE STUDENTS IN THIS ROOM, HOW MANY WILL STILL BE HERE WHEN IT'S OVER?
HM?
OH! HEY, NIKUMI!
?!
JOLT

IT'S BEEN A WHILE!
HOW YA DOIN'?
Y-YUKIHIRA!
WHRL
AREN'T YOU AT ALL NERVOUS?!
H-HEY! DON'T SAY THAT NICKNAME OUT LOUD!
HUH? I THOUGHT YOU WERE OKAY WITH IT, NIKUMI.
I AM NOT OKAY WITH IT!
YAMMER
LOOK, IT'S THAT TRANSFER STUDENT.
SOMA YUKIHIRA.
PSST
PSST
PSST
WATCH YOUR BACK, YUKI-HIRA.
HUH? WHAT FOR-
YAMMER
YAMMER
GOOD MORNING, EVERYONE.

MAY I HAVE YOUR ATTENTION, PLEASE?
I WILL NOW PRESENT TO YOU AN OVERVIEW OF THIS COOKING CAMP.
TODAY MARKS THE BEGINNING OF THE TOTSUKI INSTITUTE FRIENDSHIP AND TEAM-BUILDING COOKING CAMP.
IT WILL LAST FOR SIX DAYS AND FIVE NIGHTS.
EACH DAY YOU WILL BE GIVEN AN ASSIGNMENT THAT IN SOME WAY RELATES TO THE CULINARY ARTS.
THESE ASSIGNMENTS DIFFER EVERY YEAR.
Friendship & Team-bu
Cooking Camp
Training Course Pamphlet
Let's build happy, lifelong memories!
Be careful not to forget your
Name:
Totsuki Saryo Culinary Institute
ON THIS FIRST DAY, THE 980 STUDENTS PRESENT WILL BE DIVIDED INTO 20 GROUPS.
ONCE THIS PRESENTATION IS COMPLETED, YOU ARE EACH TO PROCEED TO YOUR DESIGNATED AREA AND JOIN YOUR GROUP.
EACH INSTRUCTOR WILL SET A BASELINE GRADE FOR EACH ASSIGNMENT. ANY STUDENT WHO DOES NOT MEET THAT GRADE WILL FAIL.
THERE ARE BUSES WAITING ON HAND TO SEND THESE STUDENTS BACK TO THE INSTITUTE IMMEDIATELY...
...WHERE THEY WILL BE FORMALLY EXPELLED.
SPEAKING OF YOUR INSTRUCTORS...
...WE HAVE INVITED GUEST TEACHERS TO JUDGE YOUR WORK.
GUESTS?
EACH HAS MADE TIME IN HIS OR HER BUSY SCHEDULE TO BE HERE TODAY.
PLEASE WELCOME THESE TOTSUKI INSTITUTE ALUMNI.
YAMMER

HERE, THEN, ARE THOSE CULINARY GENIUSES WHO BEAT THE SINGLE-DIGIT ODDS TO REACH GRADUATION!

HM?
SNIFF
YOU, THERE.
NINTH ROW FROM THE FRONT, THE BOY WITH THE SCAR ABOVE HIS EYE.
?
OH, SORRY. NOT YOU, THE ONE TO YOUR RIGHT.
YES, YOU.
YOU'RE EXPELLED.
YOU CAN GO HOME NOW.
?!
WHAT?!
YOUR HAIR-CARE PRODUCT HAS A CITRUSY SCENT TO IT.
TOK
TOK
THAT SMELL CAN OVERPOWER THE FRAGRANCE OF YOUR COOKING.
FASHION IS AN IMPORTANT INGREDIENT.
IF THE CHEF IS UNFASHIONABLE, THE DISHES ARE THAT MUCH LESS ATTRACTIVE.
SHINO'S
FRENCH RESTAURANT
CHEF KOJIRO SHINOMIYA

I SUGGEST YOU CHOOSE UNSCENTED HAIR-CARE PRODUCTS IN THE FUTURE.
W-WAIT! EX-PELLED?!
FOR THAT ONE LITTLE THING?!
GLARE
THAT "ONE LITTLE THING" IS ENOUGH TO LOSE YOU CUSTOMERS.
ARE YOU TRYING TO RUN MY RESTAURANT OUT OF BUSINESS?
YEEP!
GOOD-BYE, LITTLE STUDENT.
SLUMP
THAT'S CHEF SHINO-MIYA!
HE'S THE FIRST JAPANESE CHEF TO BE AWARDED FRANCE'S PLUSPOL AWARD!
LOOK OVER THERE!
RISTORANTE F
ITALIAN RESTAURANT
CHEF FUYUMI MIZUHARA
THERE'S F'S CHEF MIZUHARA...
...AND HINOWA'S HEAD CHEF, SEKIMORI!
GINZA HINOWA
SUSHI RESTAURANT
HEAD CHEF HITOSHI SEKIMORI

AMAZING! THEY'RE ALL SO FAMOUS, THEY'RE IN CULINARY MAGAZINES EVERY MONTH!
TEZORO
FRENCH AUBERGE
CHEF DONATO GOTODA
IT MAY BE THAT I WAS BORN TO MEET YOU HERE TODAY, MY SWEET.
WOULD YOU CARE TO JOIN ME AT MY AUBERGE SO WE MAY CHAT THE NIGHT AWAY?
EH? UMM... I-I...
AH, SUCH LOVELY, RUSTIC BEAUTY, LIKE THAT OF A SIMPLE WHITE CLOVER.
?
PLEASE LET GO OF HER HAND, CHEF GOTODA.
HINAKO.
I'M SO SORRY, DEAR. HE DIDN'T MEAN TO FRIGHTEN YOU.
PAT
HINAKO! PROFESSOR CHAPELLE IS GLARING AT YOU! GET ON THE STAGE!
PLEASE STOP BY MY RESTAURANT SOMEDAY. TEE HEE HEE!
BLUSH
BY THE WAY, YOU ARE VERY CUTE.
YOU'RE SO PRETTY, I COULD EAT YOU RIGHT UP.
?!
KIRINOYA
JAPANESE RESTAURANT
CHEF HINAKO INUI
STMP

DUN
TOTSUKI RESORT
HEAD CHEF AND COMPANY DIRECTOR
GIN DOJIMA
THAT'S THE MAN IN CHARGE OF ALL CHEFS WORKING IN THE TOTSUKI RESORT CHAIN OF RESTAURANTS!
HE'S RESPONSIBLE FOR AN ENTIRE CORNER OF THE TOTSUKI BRAND!
HE GRADUATED AT THE TOP OF HIS CLASS WITH A SCORE SO HIGH NO ONE HAS YET BEATEN IT!
BUT OUT OF ALL OF THAT, HE IS MOST FAMOUS FOR TURNING DOWN OVER 800 OFFERS FROM TOP RESTAURANTS JUST TO TAKE THE POSITION HE HOLDS NOW!
I...I CAN HARDLY BELIEVE I'M IN THEIR PRESENCE!

STANDING BEFORE US...
...ARE THE ELITE CHEFS WHO ARE THE DRIVING FORCE BEHIND JAPAN'S ENTIRE CULINARY WORLD!
SHFF
WEL-COME, EVERY-ONE...
...TO THE TOTSUKI RESORT HOTELS.

THE ALUMNI GATHERED HERE TODAY...
...ARE ALL HEAD CHEFS AND OWNERS OF THEIR OWN RESTAURANTS.
FOR THE SIX DAYS YOU ARE HERE, YOU WILL EACH BE TREATED AS ONE OF THEIR EMPLOYEES.
IN OTHER WORDS, THAT MEANS IF YOUR WORK ISN'T UP TO OUR STANDARDS...
SLASH
...YOU'RE FIRED.
AS YOU'VE ALREADY SEEN, THE INSTRUCTORS CAN EXPEL YOU AT ANY TIME FOR ANY REASON.
I WISH YOU ALL THE BEST OF LUCK.
THAT IS ALL.

EVERYONE, PROCEED TO YOUR GROUPS!
SEE YA!
LATER.
AH! LET'S ALL GET TOGETHER IN MARUI'S ROOM FOR CARDS LATER TONIGHT!
H-HEY! THERE'S NO REASON FOR YOU TO PICK MY ROOM THIS TIME!

OH, GOOD. EVERYONE IS HERE.
FOR MY ASSIGNMENT, I WILL HAVE EVERYONE GATHER IN PAIRS.

IN FACT, YOU CAN ALL PAIR UP IN THE GROUPS ASSIGNED TO YOU IN MR. CHAPELLE'S CLASS...
...THEN PROCEED TO THE COOKING STATIONS ASSIGNED TO YOU.
TP TP TP TP
SOMA! THANK GOODNESS I CAN PARTNER UP WITH YOU!
YEAH! LET'S KNOCK THIS OUTTA THE PARK.
YOU'RE SOMA YUKIHIRA, RIGHT?
HUH? YEAH.
WHAT'S UP-
STOMP

TWIST
STOMP
STOMP
STOMP
STOMP
STOMP
STILL GOING?
THEN IT'S SAFE TO SAY YOU'RE DOING IT ON PURPOSE, AM I RIGHT?
YEP.
I WAS HOPING I'D GO AGAINST YOU SOMETIME IN CAMP...
...BUT NEVER THOUGHT I'D GET MY CHANCE ON DAY ONE.

WE'RE GONNA STOMP YOU FLAT, YUKIHIRA!
JUST LIKE I DID TO YOUR SHOE.
OH, YEAH?
UM, E-EXCUSE ME? TH-THIS IS ALREADY A REALLY HARD CLASS...
I, UM... I DON'T THINK WE SHOULD BE FIGHTING ...
SO, UM... G-GUYS?

OKAY, I'M GONNA DO IT! I'M GONNA STOMP ON HIS FOOT!
MUMBLE
MUMBLE

16 A CONCERTO OF CREATIVITY AND CREATION

I FINALLY HAVE THE CHANCE TO STOMP YOU FLAT...
...SOMA YUKI-HIRA!
WELL, GOOD FOR YOU. CONGRATS.
I GET YOU'RE TRYING TO PICK A FIGHT, BUT YOU CAN GET OFF MY FOOT NOW.
ALL RIGHT, EVERY-ONE!
SHRIP
I WILL BE SITTING RIGHT HERE...
KRNCH
KRNCH
...SO IF YOU HAVE ANY QUESTIONS ABOUT TODAY'S ASSIGNMENT, FEEL FREE TO ASK.

UM, CHEF INUI?
YOU HAVEN'T EVEN TOLD US WHAT THE ASSIGN-MENT IS, YET.
OH? I HAVEN'T ?
HUP
GOODNESS, I GUESS I HAD BEST EXPLAIN IT, THEN!
...
MY ASSIGN-MENT...
SHFF
...IS TO USE THESE INGRE-DIENTS HERE...
...TO COOK A JAPANESE MAIN DISH. ANY DISH WILL BE FINE!
UM, CHEF?
THERE ISN'T ANY-THING THERE.
OH, YES THERE IS. THERE ARE LOTS OF THINGS!
BOUNTI-FUL NATURE, A BLUE RIVER...
IT'S A TREASURE TROVE OF WONDERFUL INGRE-DIENTS!
?!

THIS BUILDING AND PROPERTY HAVE LONG BEEN PRIVATELY HELD BY THE TOTSUKI INSTITUTE.
A FENCE MARKS ITS BOUND-ARIES.
IF YOU CROSS THAT FENCE, YOU FAIL.
THEY ARE HERE.
WOODS
WOODS
RIVER
TO PASS THIS ASSIGNMENT, YOU MUST FIND YOUR INGREDIENTS INSIDE THIS AREA ONLY, PREPARE THEM...
...AND PRESENT THEM TO ME IN A JAPANESE DISH THAT MEETS MY APPROVAL.
!!!
ANY SEASONINGS, OILS AND UTENSILS YOU MAY NEED ARE PROVIDED INSIDE THIS ROOM.
YOU MAY ALSO USE ANY OF THE FISHING RODS AND HUNTING EQUIPMENT LOCATED IN THE SHED.

YOU HAVE TWO HOURS.
READY? BEGIN.
CLAP
HUH? WAS THAT THE START?
SHE NEEDS TO SPEAK LOUDER!
YAMMER
FIRST, WE NEED TO RESEARCH WHAT FISH ARE IN THAT RIVER!
YAMMER
SWEET-FISH! GRILLED SWEETFISH WOULD WORK, WOULDN'T IT?
YAMMER
BUT ARE SWEETFISH IN SEASON NOW? I DON'T REMEMBER ...
WHATEVER! WE'VE ONLY GOT TWO HOURS!
SLAM
WE GOTTA HURRY!
DASH

LET'S MAKE A CONTEST OF IT, YUKIHIRA.
A CON-TEST?
DUN
YES. LET'S DECIDE WHICH OF US IS BETTER, ONCE AND FOR ALL!
CHEF INUI!
I WOULD LIKE TO HAND OVER THIS DECISION TO YOU.
YOUR IMPARTIAL JUDGMENT CAN PUT THIS MATTER TO REST...
...AND DECLARE FOR ALL WHICH ONE OF US MADE THE BETTER DISH!
HM? WHY WOULD I WANT TO DO THAT?
IT HAS NOTHING TO DO WITH MY ASSIGN-MENT...
...SO I'D RATHER NOT, THANKS ANYWAY.

UM... I-I SEE.
HUH? O-OH...
...
HEH HEH.
SO NOW WHAT?
SMIRK
YOUR ANTICS HAVE REALLY TURNED THIS AWKWARD, Y'KNOW.
BLUSH
...!
GWAH HA HA! THAT WAS SO LAME, BIG BRO! HA HA!
SH-SHUT UP! DON'T YOU START LAUGHING TOO!
"BIG BRO"? THEY'RE RE-LATED?
THEY DON'T LOOK ANY-THING ALIKE!
A-ANYWAY! I WILL NEVER LOSE TO YOU, YUKIHIRA!
ANYTHING YOU MAKE, I WILL MAKE BETTER!
YOU HEAR ME, YUKI-HIRA?!
OKAY, TIME TO GO, BRO.
DRAAAG
EESH. WHAT WAS THAT ABOUT?
S-SOMA, WE OUGHT TO HURRY TOO!

SHHHHH
DAMN IT, I CAN'T CATCH A THING!
QUIET DOWN, YOU IDIOT! YOU'RE SCARING THE FISH AWAY!
OKAY, WE GOT ONE. WE CAN USE IT TO MAKE A MEUNIÈRE AND-
HOW? WE DON'T HAVE ANY FLOUR.
SHOOT!
I TOLD YOU TO GO FIND BAMBOO SHOOTS OR SOMETHING OUT HERE!
I TRIED! I LOOKED EVERYWHERE, BUT I COULDN'T FIND A THING!
BAMBOO SHOOT
WHEN PEOPLE ARE THRUST INTO SUDDEN, UNFORESEEN SITUATIONS, THEIR FIELD OF VISION SHRINKS CONSIDERABLY.
Kaki
THEIR THOUGHTS SCATTER AND GO IN CIRCLES.
THEY DON'T THINK CHOICES OR ACTIONS THROUGH.
THIS ASSIGNMENT IS JUST A SMALL TEST.
SIP
ANY CHEF WHO FAILS SOMETHING THIS MINOR...
...HAS NO PLACE AT TOTSUKI.

SHHHHHH
FIDGET
PACE
PACE
FIDGET
OMIGOSH, WE HAVE TO HURRY AND START COOKING SOON!
SOMA, HAVE YOU DECIDED ON WHAT DISH WE'LL DO?
IF WE CATCH A CHAR OR A RAINBOW TROUT, WE COULD GRILL IT... OR SHOULD WE BOIL IT IN SOY SAUCE, INSTEAD?
OH! AND WHAT ABOUT THE GARNISH?
WE NEED TO FORAGE FOR VEGETABLES TOO!
*A GARNISH IS THE SIDE ITEM TO GO ALONG WITH THE MAIN DISH.
MAYBE, BUT DON'T YOU THINK EVERYBODY ELSE IS GONNA DO SOMETHING SIMILAR?
I WANNA TRY TO MIX IT UP A LITTLE.
THIS ISN'T THE TIME FOR THAT!
OUR BIGGEST WORRY IS FINISHING ANY DISH!
YEAH, THAT'S TRUE.
...USE THESE INGREDIENTS HERE...
HMM...

OH, THANK GOODNESS! WE CAUGHT A FISH!
YEAH. LET'S HEAD BACK TO THE KITCHEN...
BLINK
...AND PREPARE FOR "IMPARTIAL JUDGMENT."
SHUT UP, SHUT UP, SHUT UP!
HMPH! YOU TWO WENT FOR FISH AS WELL? SHEESH, EVERYBODY IS TODAY!
JUST BECAUSE THE DISH HAS TO BE JAPANESE DOESN'T MEAN IT MUST BE FISH.
HONESTLY, DOESN'T ANYONE HERE HAVE ANY CREATIVITY AT ALL?
WELL, DON'T YOU SOUND SMUG.
WHAT OH-SO-CREATIVE THING DID YOU FIND, HUH?
HEH HEH. YOU WANT TO KNOW?
I FOUND A DUCK!
DUN

WHAT?!
YAMMER
HE FOUND A DUCK?!
DAMN IT! THERE WAS MORE THAN JUST THE RIVER OUT THERE!
SHOO! OUTTA MY WAY.
AND NOT JUST ONE. THEY HAD CHICKENS AND RABBITS INSIDE THE AREA TOO.
I WAS TOTALLY SURPRISED NO ONE EVEN THOUGHT TO LOOK FOR THEM!
YEAH, MAYBE. BUT I DON'T KNOW HOW TO DRESS DUCKS OR RABBITS.
YOU TOO, YUKIHIRA.
GRAB
SOMA, WHAT'S WRONG?
...
ISAMI, BUTCHER AND TRIM THIS, WOULD YA?

GLEAM
ON IT!
OH, WOW! HE'S SLICING OFF THE BREAST AND THIGH MEAT WITH SUCH PRECISION!
SLICE SLICE
HE'S GOING SO FAST, BUT HE ISN'T NICKING THE BIRD'S INNARDS AT ALL!
WHAT DEFT WORK!
HM? DO YOU NEED SOME-THING?
O-OH! NO, I-I WAS JUST THINKING HOW GOOD YOU ARE AT THAT.
HEH HEH, YOU THINK SO? THANKS...
BUT MY BIG BROTHER IS THREE TIMES FASTER AT IT THAN I AM.

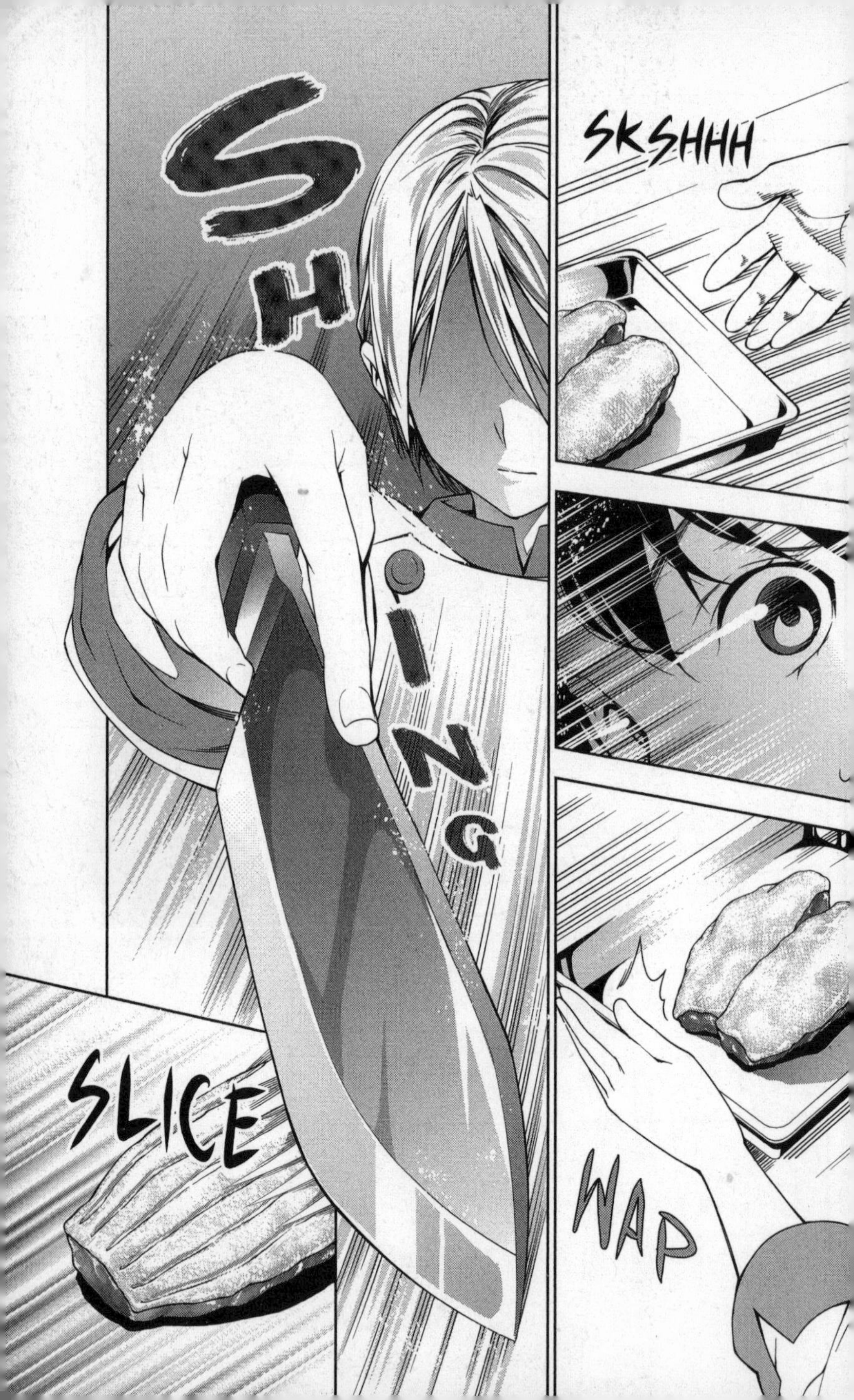
SKSHHH
WAP
SHING
SLICE

SWSH
SKRCH
SKRCH
WSH
DLOOP
SIZZZZZ

THERE'S NO DELAY, NO WASTED MOVEMENT.
EVERY MOTION FLOWS SEAMLESSLY FROM ONE INTO THE NEXT.
IT'S AMAZING! WHO IS HE?
YEAH, I'M NOT SURPRISED HE CAN DO THAT MUCH, AT LEAST.
WHAT?
HIS HANDS.
THOSE ARE THE HANDS OF SOMEONE WHO KNOWS THEIR WAY AROUND A REAL KITCHEN.

WSH
BAM
FORNO...
(OVEN)
ACCENDERE...
(ALIGHT)

BWOOSH
OOOOOOOO
OH, RIGHT. I HAVEN'T INTRODUCED MYSELF YET.
MY NAME IS TAKUMI ALDINI.
AND THIS IS MY YOUNGER TWIN BROTHER, ISAMI ALDINI.
WE WORK AT OUR FAMILY'S TRATTORIA BACK HOME IN ITALY.
TRAT-TORIA?
IT'S THE ITALIAN WORD FOR A LOWER-END EATERY THAT SERVES THE MASSES.

SHFF
I'M JUST LIKE YOU, YUKI-HIRA.
I, TOO...
...AM A CHEF WHO'S SPENT HIS LIFE PROTECTING THE FAMILY RESTAURANT.
Trattoria Aldini
TRATTORIA ALDINI.
Trattoria Aldini

WHAT WAS IT YOU SAID? YOU HAVE "NO INTENTION OF LOSING TO ANYONE WHO HASN'T COOKED FOR CUSTOMERS"?
HOW ABOUT YOU SAVE THAT LINE FOR *AFTER* YOU'VE BEATEN ME.
YUKIHIRA OR ALDINI...
I'LL PROVE TO YOU WHICH ONE IS BETTER!
HAH. SOUNDS LIKE FUN!
SWIP
SHFF
お食事処
ゆきひら
BRING IT ON!

RISTORANTE: HIGH-CLASS RESTAURANT
TRATTORIA: LOWER-TIER CAFETERIA
OSTERIA: BAR/TAVERN
BAR: BAR/CAFÉ
THERE ARE MANY DIFFERENT KINDS OF RESTAURANTS IN ITALY.
THESE ARE JUST SOME GENERAL CATEGORIES, BUT KEEP THEM IN MIND.

17 THE SPLENDOR THAT CLOAKS THE MOUNTAIN

THE WESTERN COAST OF CENTRAL ITALY...
FLORENCE, TUSCANY'S REGIONAL CAPITAL...
Trattoria Aldini
JAPAN?!
TAKUMI ALDINI (13 YEARS OLD)
UNCLE, I DON'T GET IT!
WHY DO I HAVE TO GO TO SOME STUPID COOKING SCHOOL, AND ONE ALL THE WAY IN JAPAN AT THAT?!
IT ISN'T JUST ANY SCHOOL, TAKUMI. IT'S WORLD FAMOUS.
GOING THERE CAN ONLY HELP YOU.
DON'T WORRY ABOUT THE SHOP.
YOU GO ON TO JAPAN AND HONE YOUR SKILLS AS MUCH AS YOU CAN.
YEAH
WHAT DO YOU THINK, ISAMI?
IF YOU'RE GONNA GO, BIG BRO, THEN I'LL GO TOO.

ISAMI AND I ARE HALF-JAPANESE TWINS. OUR DAD WAS JAPANESE, AND OUR MOM ITALIAN.
WE'VE BOTH BEEN HELPING OUT AT THE FAMILY TRATTORIA SINCE WE WERE FIVE.
Trattoria Aldini
BUT THANKS TO OUR JAPANESE UNCLE'S ADVICE...
...WE TRANSFERRED INTO THE TOTSUKI INSTITUTE IN OUR SECOND YEAR OF JUNIOR HIGH.
I'M GOING TO LEARN EVERYTHING I CAN FROM THIS PLACE BEFORE GOING HOME TO ITALY.
THEN I'M GOING TO CREATE A STYLE OF ITALIAN FOOD ONLY ALDINI'S COULD MAKE!
THERE'S NO WAY I'M GOING TO LOSE TO ANY OF THESE KIDS MY AGE.
I'VE ALREADY SPENT MY WHOLE LIFE WORKING IN A REAL KITCHEN!
I'VE GOT NO INTENTION OF LOSING TO A PACK OF NOOBS WHO'VE NEVER COOKED FOR CUSTOMERS BEFORE.
CLENCH
SO NOW THAT I'M IN...
...I'LL BE TAKING THE TOP SPOT.

YOU CALLED YOURSELF A PRO.
IN THAT CASE...
?!
WOW!
SHING
WHAT THE HECK IS THAT?!
...AS ONE PRO TO ANOTHER, I CAN'T LET YOU BEAT ME!

AHH, A MEZZALUNA.
MEANING "HALF-MOON" IN ITALIAN...
WAP
...IT'S A TWO-HANDED KNIFE USED IN MANY FACETS OF ITALIAN COOKING.
TIME TO BEGIN.
SKNCH
SKNCH
SKNCH
SKNCH
SKNCH
SKNCH
TRITARE!
(ITALIAN FOR "MINCING")
SKNCH
SKNCH

SKNCH
SKNCH
SKNCH
SKNCH
SKNCH
SKNCH
WHOA! HE MINCED THOSE VEGETABLES TO PASTE IN NO TIME!
HOW'D HE GET SO GOOD AT USING THAT WEIRD KNIFE?
SKNCH
SKNCH
GOOD! WE'LL USE THAT TIME TO FINISH THE SALSA!
SEVEN MINUTES UNTIL THE BREAST MEAT IS FINISHED ROASTING.
OKAY, BRO!
TRITARE WILL BE FINISHED IN DIECI CTEND...
ROGER. WASHING COMPLETE HERE.
TRE...
DUE...
UNO!
SKNCH
WSH
WHAP
WSH

SKNCH
SKNCH
SKNCH
SKNCH
SKNCH
SKNCH
SKNCH
SKNCH
WSH
DLOOP
SWIP
WSK
WSK
WSK

SPICY ROAST DUCK
~WITH GREEN SALSA~

BUON APPETITO!
CHOMP
THE GAMEY FLAVOR OF THE DUCK IS STRONG AND FRAGRANT...
CHEW
...!
SNIFF
THE MELDING OF REFRESHING SPICES WITH THE MASCULINE TASTE OF GAME MEAT CREATES A DEEP, BASS HARMONY THAT REVERBERATES ALL THE WAY TO THE STOMACH.
IT IS A VERITABLE DUCK ARIA!
AAH!
...
...AND THE POTENT SPICES CLEAR THE SINUSES WITH A FRESH BURST, REFINING THE MEAT'S FLAVOR EVEN FURTHER!
SPLSH

THIS IS ONE DUCK WHOSE SERENADE...
...I WOULD GLADLY GIVE IN TO!

HEY, WAIT! THAT GREEN SAUCE!
I KNOW WHAT THAT IS!
IT'S SALSA VERDE!
SALSA VERDE.
A SAUCE MADE PRIMARILY OF FINELY MINCED ITALIAN PARSLEY AND CURED ANCHOVIES*...
IT IS OFTEN A GARNISH FOR GRILLED MEAT OR VEGETABLE DISHES...
...AND IS CONSIDERED A STAPLE SAUCE IN ITALIAN CUISINE.
*CURED ANCHOVIES ARE ANCHOVIES PICKLED IN SALT AND FERMENTED.
WHAT WAS HE THINKING? THIS WAS SUPPOSED TO BE A JAPANESE DISH!
MAKING SOMETHING ITALIAN MEANS HE AUTOMATICALLY FAILS!
NO, HE DOES NOT.
THIS SALSA WASN'T MADE FROM CURED ANCHO-VIES.
INSTEAD, IT PRIMARILY USES URUKA, A SPECIFIC TYPE OF SHIOKARA SAUCE MADE FROM SWEETFISH.
?!
*SHIOKARA IS SALTED, FERMENTED FISH VISCERA.
URUKA TYPICALLY REQUIRES OVER A WEEK TO MAKE. HOWEVER, THIS IS AN "INSTANT" VERSION, IS IT NOT?
COR-RECT!
WASH SWEETFISH VISCERA AND BOIL THEM IN SAKÉ FOR TWO MINUTES.
THEN FLAVOR WITH SOY SAUCE, SALT AND MIRIN.
THE RESULT IS A QUICKLY MADE, YET STILL RICH AND APPROPRIATELY BITTER, URUKA.

INSTANT URUKA?!
I DIDN'T KNOW THAT WAS POSSIBLE!
EXACTLY. WITH INSTANT URUKA AS ITS BASE...
...I MADE A JAPANESE-STYLE SALSA VERDE!
THAT WASN'T THE ONLY PLACE HE WAS CREATIVE.
INSTEAD OF PARSLEY, HE MINCED JAPANESE PERILLA LEAVES AND GREEN ONION TO GIVE IT A BRIGHT GREEN COLOR AND REFRESHING KICK.
AND SINCE GARLIC IS HARDLY USED IN TRADITIONAL JAPANESE CUISINE, HE CHOSE YUZUKOSHO, A SEASONING MADE FROM CHILI PEPPERS, YUZU FRUIT PEELS AND SALT, TO GIVE IT A DISTINCTLY JAPANESE FLAVOR.
WHOA, JUST LISTENING TO WHAT'S IN IT MADE ME DROOL!
HE TOOK AN ITALIAN SAUCE AND RECREATED IT USING ONLY JAPANESE INGREDIENTS?
SO MANY INGREDIENTS! HOW COULD HE EVEN FIND ALL OF THEM IN THESE MOUNTAINS?
HE'S INCREDIBLE!
UNLIKE JAPAN, ITALY'S CUISINE HAS LONG CENTERED ON MEAT DISHES.
IN THEIR HOME PROVINCE OF TUSCANY, DUCK, RABBIT AND EVEN BOAR WOULD BE SERVED IN THE RIGHT SEASON.
I SUSPECT THAT IS HOW THEY LEARNED HOW TO BUTCHER AND DRESS A DUCK.

THE BREAST MEAT WAS GLAZED WITH A MIXTURE OF SOY SAUCE, JAPANESE MUSTARD, BLACK PEPPER AND HONEY TO GIVE IT A STRONG, SPICY FRAGRANCE...
THE PERFECT COMPLEMENT TO THE SAUCE.
DUCK AND SALSA VERDE.
THEY FOUND AND ENHANCED THE JAPANESE ESSENCE OF BOTH...
...TO CREATE AN IMPRESSIVE AND THOROUGHLY JAPANESE DISH!
TAKUMI ALDINI, ISAMI ALDINI... YOU PASS!
OOOOOOO
GRAZIE!
BUMP
THEY MADE CLEVER USE OF A RESTRICTED LIST OF HARD-TO-FIND INGREDIENTS...
...AND PUT TOGETHER A REALLY AMAZING DISH THAT NO ONE ELSE EVEN THOUGHT OF!

THAT'S JUST LIKE WHAT SOMA DOES...

HEH. IT LOOKS LIKE YOU'VE HARDLY MADE ANY PROGRESS AT ALL.
WHAT DID YOU DECIDE TO MAKE?
OH, THAT'S RIGHT. YOU TWO WERE CHALLENGING EACH OTHER.
IF I CAN EXPECT A DISH ON PAR WITH WHAT I JUST TASTED...
...THEN I SHALL GLADLY MAKE AN EXCEPTION AND JUDGE FOR YOU WHICH ONE IS TASTIER.
!!
DID YOU HEAR THAT, YUKIHIRA?
YEAH, LET'S DO THIS!
HEE HEE! WONDERFUL. NOW, WHOEVER LOSES MUST KOWTOW TO THE WINNER.
BWUH?
I SAID, WHOEVER LOSES MUST KOWTOW RIGHT IN FRONT OF THE WINNER...
...AND SHOUT "I AM A WORTHLESS LOSER" THREE TIMES.
IF YOU ARE PITTING YOUR FAMILY RESTAURANTS' REPUTATIONS AGAINST EACH OTHER, THE CONSEQUENCES SHOULD BE NO LESS SERIOUS.
TEE HEE HEE!
...
OH! BUT YOU WON'T HAVE TO KOWTOW TO ANYONE, MEGUMI TADOKORO. NO, NOT TO ANYONE...
WHAT LOVELY FINGERS YOU HAVE.
UMM...TH-THIS TEACHER IS STARTING TO SCARE ME!
SHUDDER
R-RIGHT! ANYWAY...

I DARE YOU TO MAKE A DISH BETTER THAN OURS, YUKIHIRA...
POINT
IF YOU EVEN CAN, THAT IS!
!
HE WENT INTO THIS WITHOUT ANY PRECONCEIVED NOTIONS...
...AND FOCUSED ON USING DUCK FOR HIS MAIN INGREDIENT.
THEN HE ROUNDED UP A WHOLE BUNCH OF COMPLEMENTARY INGREDIENTS TO MAKE IT REALLY STAND OUT.
THINK!
WITH WHAT I HAVE RIGHT HERE, RIGHT NOW...
...WHAT IS THE BEST POSSIBLE DISH I COULD MAKE?

...HAD CHICKENS AND RABBITS...
...USE THESE INGREDIENTS HERE...
!
...!
SMIRK

TADO-KORO!
HERE'S WHAT I WANT TO USE FOR THE GARNISH.
SCRIBBLE
SCRIBBLE
COULD YOU GO GET 'EM FOR ME?
SHFF
THINK YOU'LL BE ABLE TO FIND THEM ALL?
UM... YES! I THINK I CAN.
I USED TO GO FORAGING IN THE MOUNTAINS A LOT BACK HOME.
GREAT!
I'M COUNTING ON YOU, TADOKORO!
WHAT ARE YOU GOING TO DO, SOMA?
I'M GONNA GO BACK OUTSIDE. THERE'S ONE MORE THING I WANNA FIND.
AH! BUT FIRST...
CHEF INUI!
YOU SAID AS LONG AS IT'S HERE...
...WE CAN USE ANYTHING AT ALL, RIGHT?

?
YES.
YOU CAN USE ANYTHING FOUND WITHIN THE FENCED-IN AREA...
GLINT
THE ONE INGRE-DIENT...
...THAT IS THE KEY TO OUR DISH...
WSH
...IS THIS!
RSTL
WHAT?
EH?
B-BUT THAT'S-!

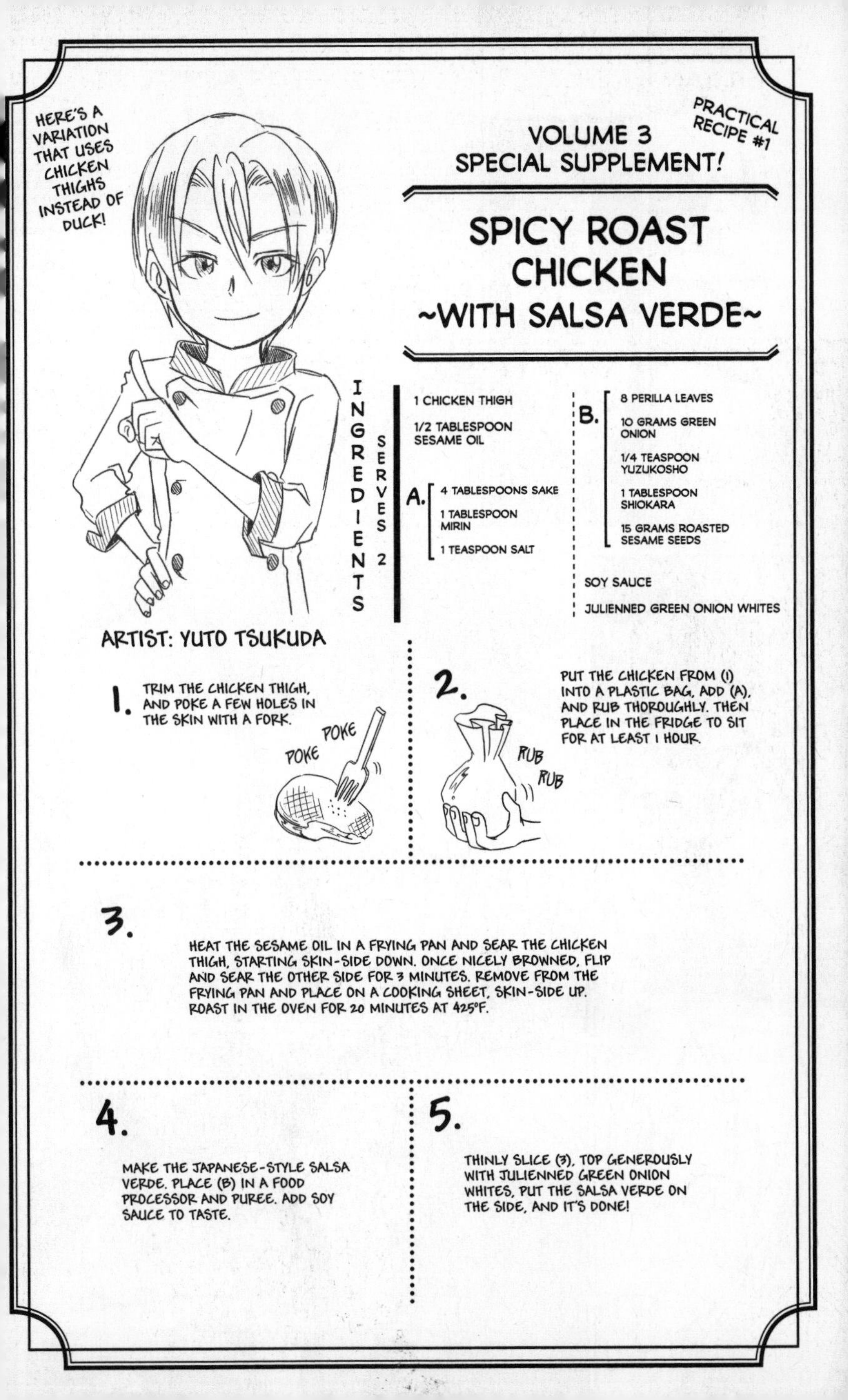

PRACTICAL RECIPE #1

VOLUME 3 SPECIAL SUPPLEMENT!

SPICY ROAST CHICKEN ~WITH SALSA VERDE~

INGREDIENTS SERVES 2

- 1 CHICKEN THIGH
- 1/2 TABLESPOON SESAME OIL

A.
- 4 TABLESPOONS SAKE
- 1 TABLESPOON MIRIN
- 1 TEASPOON SALT

B.
- 8 PERILLA LEAVES
- 10 GRAMS GREEN ONION
- 1/4 TEASPOON YUZUKOSHO
- 1 TABLESPOON SHIOKARA
- 15 GRAMS ROASTED SESAME SEEDS

- SOY SAUCE
- JULIENNED GREEN ONION WHITES

ARTIST: YUTO TSUKUDA

1. TRIM THE CHICKEN THIGH, AND POKE A FEW HOLES IN THE SKIN WITH A FORK.

2. PUT THE CHICKEN FROM (1) INTO A PLASTIC BAG, ADD (A), AND RUB THOROUGHLY. THEN PLACE IN THE FRIDGE TO SIT FOR AT LEAST 1 HOUR.

3. HEAT THE SESAME OIL IN A FRYING PAN AND SEAR THE CHICKEN THIGH, STARTING SKIN-SIDE DOWN. ONCE NICELY BROWNED, FLIP AND SEAR THE OTHER SIDE FOR 3 MINUTES. REMOVE FROM THE FRYING PAN AND PLACE ON A COOKING SHEET, SKIN-SIDE UP. ROAST IN THE OVEN FOR 20 MINUTES AT 425°F.

4. MAKE THE JAPANESE-STYLE SALSA VERDE. PLACE (B) IN A FOOD PROCESSOR AND PUREE. ADD SOY SAUCE TO TASTE.

5. THINLY SLICE (3), TOP GENEROUSLY WITH JULIENNED GREEN ONION WHITES, PUT THE SALSA VERDE ON THE SIDE, AND IT'S DONE!

18 THE SEED OF AN IDEA

NOW ALL THAT'S LEFT IS...

UM...

THERE! THAT'S ALL OF THEM.

NOW I HAVE TO HURRY BACK TO SOMA!

BUGOCK
YEOWCH!
OW, OW, OW!
STUPID FEATH-ER DUSTER!
BOCK
IF THERE ARE CHICKENS OUT HERE...
WSH
!
YOINK
BOCK
GOT ONE!
...THEN THERE ARE ALSO FRESHLY LAID CHICKEN EGGS!

TNK
THAT WASN'T TASTY AT ALL.
GULP
DOOM
DO IT AGAIN.
IT DOESN'T FEEL LIKE THERE'S ANY WAY WE CAN PASS THIS!
SO MANY PAIRS HAVE BEEN JUDGED, BUT BARELY A HANDFUL HAVE PASSED!

HINAKO INUI.
A MEMBER OF THE TOTSUKI INSTITUTE'S EIGHTIETH GRADUATING CLASS...
SHE WAS A FEARED CHEF KNOWN BY THE NICKNAME "THE EMPRESS OF MIST."
STILL, GOODNESS ME.
GRILLED FISH, GRILLED FISH, AND MORE GRILLED FISH. IT'S ALL BEGUN TO TASTE THE SAME TO ME.
SIGH
I FIND MYSELF WANTING A DISH WITH MORE BITE TO IT.
YEAH, YOU CAN WANT THAT ALL YOU'D LIKE...
...BUT WHAT ELSE DO YOU EXPECT US TO MAKE WITH NOTHING BUT WHAT'S OUT ON THOSE MOUNTAINS?!
NOW, NOW, DON'T GIVE UP! YOU CAN ALL TRY AS MANY TIMES AS YOU'D LIKE BEFORE TIME RUNS OUT.
HOW?! THERE'S HARDLY ANY TIME LEFT!
DAMN IT, WE'VE GOTTA TRY AGAIN!
GYAH
GYAH
BOY, I'M REALLY GLAD WE PASSED ALREADY, BRO.

FIDGET
FIDGET
TAP
TAP
TAP
TAP
SO HOW ABOUT YOU RELAX A LITTLE?
YUKIHIRA STILL HASN'T COME BACK!
DOESN'T HE REALIZE HE HAS LESS THAN TWENTY MINUTES LEFT?
BUT IF HE RUNS OUT OF TIME, THEN YOU WIN BY DEFAULT, RIGHT? WHAT'S WRONG WITH THAT?
WHAT I WANT IS A HEAD-TO-HEAD, ALL-OUT BATTLE! I WILL NOT ACCEPT ANY STUPID "VICTORY BY DEFAULT"!
AND WHY DID HE ASK ME TO HOLD THESE FOR HIM?
GLANCE
WHAT RECIPE DOES HE THINK HE CAN USE THESE THINGS IN, ANYWAY?
TMP
TMP
DUN
YUKI-HIRA!

YOU'RE LATE! YOU ONLY HAVE FIFTEEN MINUTES LEFT!
ARE YOU TRYING TO FAIL SO YOU CAN ESCAPE ME WITHOUT A FIGHT?!
SKRUNCH
BIG BRO, YOU'RE CRUSHING IT!
OOPS! S-SORRY!
I DIDN'T MEAN TO DO THAT, YUKIHIRA. HONEST!
DON'T WORRY ABOUT IT.
YOU SAVED ME SOME TIME, ACTUALLY. THANKS!
SHFF
...?
AND BESIDES, I'VE GOT A WHOLE FIFTEEN MINUTES TO WORK WITH.
WHAT?
IF I MADE OUR CUSTOMERS AT THE RESTAURANT WAIT THAT LONG...
...THEY'D ALL GO HOME!

WSA
LET'S GET STARTED, TADOKORO!
RIGHT!
SWISH
SWISH
FIRST, I HAVE TO PREPARE THE VEGETABLES...
...STARTING WITH PEELING THE TARANOME SHOOTS.
I HAVE TO BE REALLY, REALLY CAREFUL...
FFFD
WHEN YOU'RE DONE WITH THAT, COULD YOU SEPARATE THE EGG YOLKS?
OKAY!

RSTL
WHAT? DEEP-FRIED?
YEAH! LET'S DO DEEP-FRIED FISH FOR OUR DISH.
RSTL
RSTL
RSTL
BUT WE DON'T HAVE FLOUR, PANKO, OR ANYTHING WE CAN USE FOR THE BREADING.
ARE YOU THINKING OF DEEP-FRYING IT AS IS?
I THOUGHT FISH MEAT HAD TOO MUCH WATER IN IT FOR THAT TO WORK WELL...
YOU'RE RIGHT ON THAT PART, BUT THAT'S NOT A PROBLEM...
...BECAUSE WE ALREADY HAVE THE PERFECT BREADING!
YOU SAVED ME SOME TIME, ACTUALLY.
FISH.
EGGS.
CRACKERS.
NOW I GET IT!

YUKIHIRA IS GOING TO CRUSH THOSE CRACKERS...
...AND USE THEM AS BREADING FOR THE FISH!
WNCH
SLSSS

PLIP
FWSH
FWIP
SIZZZZZ

TA-DAH
OH MY, LOOK AT THIS!
MY KAKI NO TANE CRACKERS TURNED INTO A LOVELY BREADING!
GO ON, CHEF INUI.
DON'T LET IT GET COLD.
DIG IN!

CHEW
CHEW
KRRCH
KNCH
KNCH
KMUNCH
HAFF
HAFF
GULP
AAH ...
...!
WHAT A WONDERFUL CRUNCH!
SPARKLE
AND YET THE CHAR'S MEAT WAS STILL HOT AND DELICIOUSLY JUICY!
THE BREADING PERFECTLY CONTAINED INSIDE ITS PROTECTIVE SHELL THE SAVORY FLAVOR OF THE FISH!
THE KAKI NO TANE CRACKERS CAME ALREADY SEASONED...
...SO THE BREADING ITSELF HAD A SOLID, DELICIOUS TASTE.

THE KI NO ME MIXED WITH TAMAGO NO MOTO IS WONDERFULLY LIGHT AND FLUFFY!
AND THE DIPPING SAUCE IS PERFECT!
TAMAGO NO MOTO.
MAYONNAISE WITHOUT THE VINEGAR, IT IS SIMPLY EGG YOLKS AND VEGETABLE OIL WHISKED INTO A CREAMY CONSISTENCY.
IT'S OFTEN USED TO BRING INGREDIENTS TOGETHER OR TO ADD FLAVOR TO A DISH.
*KI NO ME: THE YOUNG LEAVES OF THE JAPANESE PEPPER PLANT. CLAPPING ONE IN YOUR PALM CRUSHES THE LEAF'S CELLS, RELEASING A DISTINCTIVE SCENT.
SOME SALT AND MINCED KI NO ME ADDS AN OVERALL REFRESHING TASTE TO THE FISH...
...ERASING ANY OILINESS AND GIVING IT A REFINED FLAVOR.
THAT WONDERFULLY SMOOTH CREAMINESS HIDING BETWEEN THE CRISPY CRUNCHINESS OF THE BREADING REALLY SPURS THE APPETITE!
THE BREADED AND DEEP-FRIED MOUNTAIN VEGETABLES ON THE SIDE CANNOT BE IGNORED, EITHER.
THEY PROVIDE AN EYE-PLEASING CONTRAST WHEN ARRANGED SIDE-BY-SIDE WITH THE DEEP-FRIED FISH.
SOMA, WHERE ON EARTH DID YOU GET THE IDEA FOR THIS?
IN JAPANESE COOKING, THERE'S A TYPE OF TEMPURA CALLED OKAKIAGE, RIGHT?

WHEN DEEP-FRYING THINGS, USE CRUSHED-UP OKAKI RICE CRACKERS INSTEAD OF PANKO TO GIVE THE DISH SOME UNIQUENESS AND KICK.
I MADE THIS AT HOME ONCE LONG AGO WITH MY DAD.
AND THAT GAVE YOU THE IDEA TO USE THE KAKI NO TANE CRACKERS IN PLACE OF THE OKAKI RICE CRACKERS?
YEP!
I CALL IT THE YUKIHIRA STYLE OKAKI-
TA-DAH
YUKIHIRA STYLE OKAKI-NO-TANE-AGE CHAR!
!
AH
kaki no tane
YOU JUST SLAPPED THE TWO NAMES TOGETHER!

ON ONE HAND, TAKUMI ALDINI MAINTAINED A BROAD VISION THAT DID NOT OVERLOOK POTENTIAL INGREDIENTS, SUCH AS THE DUCK.
ON THE OTHER, SOMA YUKIHIRA'S RARE ABILITY TO THINK OUTSIDE THE BOX...
...LED HIM TO CREATE A DISH THAT NO ONE ELSE EVEN EXPECTED!
KAKIUCI
Kaki no Tan
NEITHER WAS INTIMIDATED BY THE TIME CONSTRAINTS OR THE LIMITED INGREDI- ENTS.
THEY INSTEAD FOCUSED ON WHAT THEY COULD DO TO CREATE THEIR DISH.
THAT IS THE SPIRIT OF A TRUE PROFES- SIONAL!

HEE HEE! THIS IS HARDLY THE FIRST TIME I'VE GIVEN THIS ASSIGNMENT.
AND STUDENTS HAVE MADE DEEP-FRIED ITEMS BEFORE... WITHOUT BREADING.
BUT HE IS THE FIRST ONE TO FIND A WAY TO PRESENT TO ME FISH THAT IS BOTH BREADED AND DEEP-FRIED!
KRUNCH
HAFF
HAFF
THE CHAR, IN SEASON THIS SPRING...
...IS SNUGGLY WRAPPED IN A PROTECTIVE SHELL OF KAKI NO TANE CRACKER BREADING.
IT'S ALMOST LIKE...
...AN ELEGANT MERMAID SWIMMING THE SEAS...
...CAUGHT UP IN A WARM, PASSIONATE, ALL-ENCOMPASSING EMBRACE.
OH, NO!
HUG

I... I FEEL LIKE I'M DROWNING!
DROWNING IN MY LOVE OF CRACKERS!

SOMA YUKIHIRA. MEGUMI TADOKORO.
YOU PASS!
SMAK
HAPPY TO SERVE!

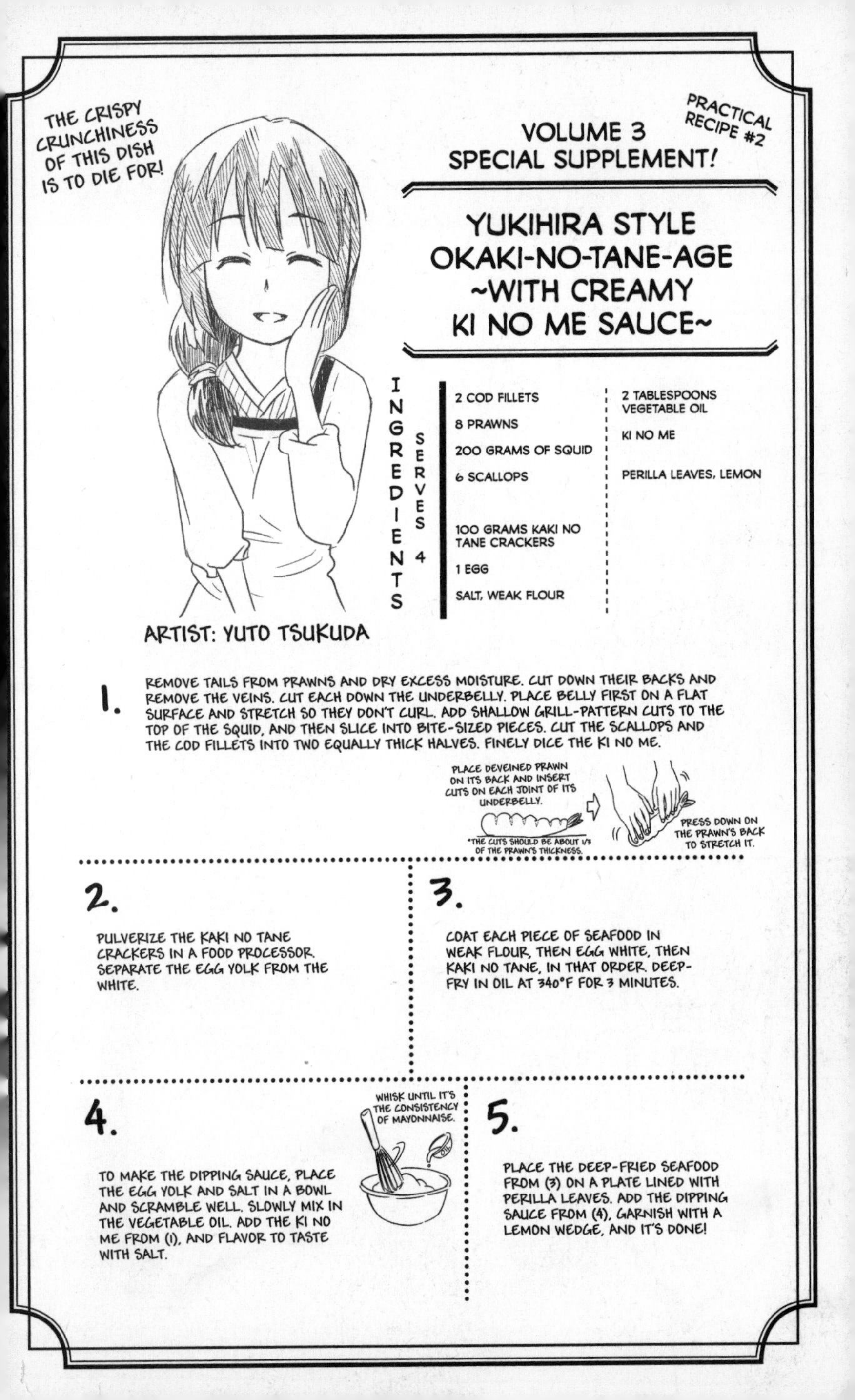
THE CRISPY CRUNCHINESS OF THIS DISH IS TO DIE FOR!
PRACTICAL RECIPE #2
VOLUME 3
SPECIAL SUPPLEMENT!
YUKIHIRA STYLE
OKAKI-NO-TANE-AGE
~WITH CREAMY
KI NO ME SAUCE~
INGREDIENTS
SERVES 4
2 COD FILLETS
8 PRAWNS
200 GRAMS OF SQUID
6 SCALLOPS
100 GRAMS KAKI NO TANE CRACKERS
1 EGG
SALT, WEAK FLOUR
2 TABLESPOONS VEGETABLE OIL
KI NO ME
PERILLA LEAVES, LEMON
ARTIST: YUTO TSUKUDA
1.
REMOVE TAILS FROM PRAWNS AND DRY EXCESS MOISTURE. CUT DOWN THEIR BACKS AND REMOVE THE VEINS. CUT EACH DOWN THE UNDERBELLY. PLACE BELLY FIRST ON A FLAT SURFACE AND STRETCH SO THEY DON'T CURL. ADD SHALLOW GRILL-PATTERN CUTS TO THE TOP OF THE SQUID, AND THEN SLICE INTO BITE-SIZED PIECES. CUT THE SCALLOPS AND THE COD FILLETS INTO TWO EQUALLY THICK HALVES. FINELY DICE THE KI NO ME.
PLACE DEVEINED PRAWN ON ITS BACK AND INSERT CUTS ON EACH JOINT OF ITS UNDERBELLY.
*THE CUTS SHOULD BE ABOUT 1/3 OF THE PRAWN'S THICKNESS.
PRESS DOWN ON THE PRAWN'S BACK TO STRETCH IT.
2.
PULVERIZE THE KAKI NO TANE CRACKERS IN A FOOD PROCESSOR. SEPARATE THE EGG YOLK FROM THE WHITE.
3.
COAT EACH PIECE OF SEAFOOD IN WEAK FLOUR, THEN EGG WHITE, THEN KAKI NO TANE, IN THAT ORDER. DEEP-FRY IN OIL AT 340°F FOR 3 MINUTES.
4.
WHISK UNTIL IT'S THE CONSISTENCY OF MAYONNAISE.
OIL
TO MAKE THE DIPPING SAUCE, PLACE THE EGG YOLK AND SALT IN A BOWL AND SCRAMBLE WELL. SLOWLY MIX IN THE VEGETABLE OIL. ADD THE KI NO ME FROM (1), AND FLAVOR TO TASTE WITH SALT.
5.
PLACE THE DEEP-FRIED SEAFOOD FROM (3) ON A PLATE LINED WITH PERILLA LEAVES. ADD THE DIPPING SAUCE FROM (4), GARNISH WITH A LEMON WEDGE, AND IT'S DONE!

CLAP
TIME'S UP!
DOOM
THIS CONCLUDES TODAY'S ASSIGNMENT.
19 SPARKING SOULS
WHEW, THAT WAS CLOSE! MADE IT JUST UNDER THE WIRE.
IT'S OVER.
NO!
CHEF INUI.
IF YOU WOULD PLEASE GIVE YOUR JUDGMENT ON OUR DISHES?
AS YOU WISH.
THE WINNER IS-

19
SPARKING SOULS

THE WINNER IS THE ONE WHO THOUGHT OF AN IDEA NO ONE ELSE DID...
...AND GAVE A DELECTABLE CRUNCH TO A TENDER FISH-
...!
NO, WAIT A MOMENT.
?!
OKAY, NOW I'VE MADE UP MY MIND.
THE WINNER IS THE ONE WHO KEPT AN OPEN MIND AND OPEN EYES, NOTICING DUCK AS A POSSIBILITY...
DISPLAYING SUPERIOR SKILL AT SELECTING INGREDIENTS-
...!
NO, HOLD ON...
SLUMP
WHAT THE HECK ARE THEY DOING?
A COMEDY SKIT?
RIIING
HMM?

BIP
GOODNESS, WHAT IS IT? I'M IN THE MIDDLE OF AN IMPORTANT DECISION–
WHAT THE HECK ARE YOU DOING, HINAKO?! IT'S PAST TIME FOR YOU TO BRING YOUR GROUP BACK HERE!
...!
AH
QUIT SCREWING AROUND AND GET MOVING, YOU IDIOT!
EEP!
I-I'M SO SORRY, CHEF SHINOMIYA!
EVERYONE, WE MUST ALL HURRY BACK TO THE HOTEL RIGHT NOW!
HUH?!
BUT WHAT ABOUT YOUR DECISION? WHO WON?!
OH, RIGHT!
MY OFFICIAL DECISION ...
...IS THAT THIS CHALLENGE IS A DRAW.

NOW EVERYONE, HURRY TO THE BUSES!
FILL THE SEATS FROM BACK TO FRONT!
ZOOOM
GONG
SHE TEASED AND TEASED AND THEN DECIDED NOT TO DECIDE AT ALL!
WELL, UH... YOU HEARD HER.
Y-YES, BUT WHO CAN ACCEPT THAT RESULT?!
THERE WILL BE A DAY OF RECKONING BETWEEN US, YUKIHIRA!
SURE, WHAT-EVER. BUT HOW DO YOU WANNA DO IT?
SHFF

A SHOKU-GEKI!
ONE DAY, I WILL CHAL-LENGE YOU!
DON'T TRY TO GET OUT OF IT.
ACCEPT IT LIKE A MAN.
ON THAT DAY, I WILL STOMP YOU FLAT!
LOOK FORWARD TO IT, YUKIHIRA. AND DO TRY TO GET BETTER.

UNTIL WE MEET AGAIN...
...SOMA YUKIHIRA!
PSHUUU
VRMMMMM
WELL, WELL.
HEY, THERE!
LOOKS LIKE WE "MEET AGAIN."
SMIRK
BLUSH
SHUT UP! DON'T TALK TO ME!

WHAT, AREN'T YOU GONNA STOMP ME FLAT NOW?
I SAID DON'T TALK TO ME!
THAT ASSIGNMENT MADE ME USE EVERY SKILL I HAD TO THE FULLEST.
WHEN I HIT ON THE IDEA OF USING DUCK, I THOUGHT I'D WON.
BUT HE SOMEHOW MANAGED TO MATCH ME.
DAMN IT! THE CHALLENGE ENDED IN A DRAW.
SO WHY DO I FEEL LIKE I'VE LOST?
THIS ISN'T THE END!
ONE DAY, I SWEAR I'LL...!
TAKUMI...
...FROM TRATTORIA ALDINI.
THERE'S SOMEONE ELSE MY AGE JUST AS GOOD AS I AM.

IF I'D STAYED HOLED UP IN YUKIHIRA...
...I'D NEVER HAVE FOUND THAT OUT.
VRMMMM
MEGUMI!
YUKIHIRA!
YOU MADE IT!
OOF! Y-YUKI! RYOKO!
WHERE IS EVERY-ONE ELSE?
IBUSAKI'S CHECKING ON THAT RIGHT NOW.
RIGHT. GOOD JOB.

IT'S CONFIRMED.
EVERYONE FROM POLARIS SURVIVED DAY ONE.
YEAH!
OH, THANK GOOD-NESS!
UH... DOES MARUI REALLY COUNT AS "SURVIVED"?
HE LOOKS DEAD TO ME.
HE SPENT FOREVER RUNNING AROUND IN THE MOUNTAINS, I HEAR.
AH. SOUNDS LIKE HIS ASSIGNMENT WAS A LOT LIKE OURS.
WHEW! TODAY WAS EXHAUST-ING.
YEAH. I'M SO BONE TIRED, I CAN HARDLY MOVE.
WHAT ARE YOU TALKING ABOUT? TIRED?! NOW IS WHEN THE FUN REALLY STARTS, LADIES!
DINNER AND A BATH, AND THEN OUR OWN GUEST ROOMS!
I'M SURE EACH AND EVERY ONE WILL BE LUXURIOUS, GORGEOUS AND UTTERLY DECADENT!
I INTEND TO FULLY ENJOY EVERY LAST SECOND OF THEM!

FLEX
?!

ONCE YOU'VE FINISHED PREPARING DINNER FOR THESE GENTLEMEN, YOUR TIME IS YOUR OWN.
FLEX
WHO ARE THEY?!
THEY'RE THE MEMBERS OF THE BICEP COLLEGE BODYBUILDING CLUB, PARTICIPATING IN THEIR OWN CAMP AT A NEARBY HOTEL.
WE HAVE ALSO INVITED THE COLLEGE'S AMERICAN FOOTBALL CLUB AND PROFESSIONAL WRESTLING CLUB.
SIZZZZZ
EACH STUDENT WILL PREPARE FIFTY SERVINGS.
~TODAY'S MENU~
STEAK DINNER SET
DOOM
WSH
FIFTY SERVINGS? STARTING NOW?!
THAT'S CRAZY!
QUESTION, SIR! WHAT ABOUT OUR DINNERS?
ONCE YOU'VE FINISHED FIFTY SERVINGS, YOU'RE RESPONSIBLE FOR MAKING YOUR OWN DINNER.
MAKING OUR OWN?!
BUT WHAT ABOUT THE DECADENT HOTEL DINNER?!
THERE WILL BE NONE OF THAT.

ALSO, PLEASE BE AWARE THAT EACH STUDENT WILL BE RESPONSIBLE FOR THEIR OWN BREAKFASTS AND DINNERS, NOT JUST TODAY, BUT EVERY DAY OF CAMP.
OH, THE POOR THING! I CAN HEAR THE SOUND OF YUKI'S HEART BREAKING...
KRAK
KRIK
KLIK
ONE LAST THING.
ANY STUDENT WHO HASN'T FINISHED ALL FIFTY SERVINGS INSIDE THE NEXT HOUR...
...WILL BE EXPELLED ON THE SPOT.
WAAAAAH
BEGIN!

HEY! DON'T CUT IN LINE!
YOU WERE TAKING TOO LONG! GET OUTTA THE WAY!
CHOMP
SKARF
GOBBLE
THIS, THAT AND THAT.
THE PORTIONS ARE TOO SMALL. DO IT AGAIN.
POINT
POINT
POINT
UGH! I STILL HAVE THIRTY SERVINGS TO GO. I CAN'T TAKE IT!
DRAG
I CAN BARELY LIFT MY ARMS ANY-MORE ...
TROMP
TROMP
HEY, MARUI! YOU OKAY?
SHAKE
SHAKE
AAAAH
THEY WERE RIGHT.
THIS CAMP IS HELL.

FOOD!
MEAT!
LIKE, HONEST TO GOODNESS HELL!
SOMA YUKIHIRA, FIFTY SERVINGS COMPLETED!
THAT WAS FAST!
HAPPY TO SERVE!
SWIP
DUN
DAMN IT, HE FINISHED FIRST!
BUT MINE TASTED BETTER THAN YOURS, YUKIHIRA! I THINK!
YOU, THERE! MORE COOKING, LESS TALKING!
45TH SERVING

SEE YOU UP IN YOUR ROOM, MARUI!
THE NIGHT'S STILL YOUNG!
HEY, FOUR-EYES! WHERE'S MY FOOD?!
WAAAAH
GYAAAAH
I REALLY WISH YOU'D NOT! I JUST WANT TO GO TO MY ROOM AND RIGHT TO BED!
YEEEEE!
MAN, YUKIHIRA IS TOUGH.
WELL, BEING DONE EARLY IS ALL WELL AND GOOD...
...BUT THAT MEANS I'VE GOT NOTHING TO DO.
WONDER WHAT'S ON TV...
ゆ
Grand Baths / Family Baths

Grand Baths / Family Ba
WHRL
I KNOW!
I'LL GET MY BATH FIRST!
WITH EVERYBODY DOWNSTAIRS, THE GRAND BATH COULD BE TOTALLY EMPTY!
PAFF
I'D BETTER HURRY AND GET MY TOWEL AND ROBE...
DASH
SKREECH
EEP!
WHOMP

OWW...

AH!

DA
DA-DA
DAAAH
PUFF
WHEEZE
YUKI HAS
LEVELED UP!

20 DECLARATION

YOU!
SOMA YUKI-HIRA!
20 DECLARATION

!
WSH
WHOA, SORRY! YOU OKAY, NAKIRI?
I COULDN'T STOP...
YOU DIDN'T TWIST YOUR ANKLE OR ANYTHING, DID YOU?
DON'T TOUCH ME! I CAN STAND ON MY OWN!
HOW CARELESS OF ME!
I LET MYSELF RELAX, THINKING I WAS ALONE.
UGH! WHY DID IT HAVE TO BE HIM I RAN INTO?!
HE... DIDN'T HEAR ME, DID HE?
SHFF
YOU CERTAINLY LOOK LIKE YOU'RE IN A GREAT MOOD, HUMMING AND SKIPPING LIKE THAT.
H-HUMMING? ME?! I-I HAVE NO IDEA WHAT YOU'RE TALKING ABOUT!
AUGH! HE HEARD ME!
BLUSH
I TOTALLY UNDERSTAND WHY YOU'D BE HAPPY, THOUGH. WHAT WITH GETTING TO STAY AT A FANCY HOT SPRINGS RESORT.
I BROUGHT SO MANY CARD GAMES ALONG, I DON'T KNOW WHERE TO START.
HEH HEH.
I-I AM NOT HAPPY! I'M NO FRIVOLOUS COMMONER, LIKE YOU!

HMPH
HONESTLY, THIS PIDDLING CAMP IS A WASTE OF MY TIME.
EVERYONE ELSE SEEMS TO THINK IT'S SOME SORT OF HELL...
...BUT TO ME IT IS NOTHING BUT BORING.
HAH.
COME TO THINK OF IT...
...I MAY BE ABLE TO AMUSE MYSELF WITH A LITTLE GUESSING GAME...
...ABOUT WHICH DAY OF CAMP YOU'LL BE EXPELLED.
THIS FROM THE GIRL WHO WAS HUMMING AND SKIPPING A MINUTE AGO.
...!
URK
MISS ERINA!
DMP DMP DMP DMP DMP
I'M SO SORRY, MISS!
IT TOOK LONGER THAN I'D THOUGHT.
DMP DMP DMP DMP

AUGH
?!
SOMA YUKIHIRA!
MISCREANT! WHAT ARE YOU DOING HERE?!
HUH? OH, WELL, SHE WAS DOWN ON HER KNEES-
WHAAAA?!
WILL YOU PLEASE NOT SAY THINGS THAT CAN BE TAKEN THE WRONG WAY?!
BESIDES, WHY ARE YOU STILL HERE? LEAVE IMMEDIATELY!
FLAIL FLAIL
A-ARE YOU SURE YOU'RE ALL RIGHT, MISS?
I'M FINE.
NOW HURRY UP AND TAKE YOUR BATH.
SHFF
YES, MISS. OH! I HAVE WONDERFUL NEWS!
I'VE CONFIRMED WITH THE FRONT DESK THAT THEY CAN LEND US A FEW THINGS.
THEY HAVE PLAYING CARDS AND AN UNO DECK!
HARUMPH
I WILL PLAY NO SUCH THINGS!
WHAT? BUT MISS, YOU ASKED ME TO GO-
I WILL TOUCH NO FRIVOLOUS, HAPPY, FUN GAMES!
UMM... IS SOMETHING WRONG, MISS?
HMPH
NOTHING!

SHEESH, WHAT'S WITH HER?
TWRL
TWRL
DRIVES ME NUTS.
MEN
OH, WELL.
TIME TO RELAX IN A NICE, HOT BATH!
SHOOP
FIRST ONE IN-!
KRIK

OOOOOOOOO
HM?
SO THE FIRST ONE DONE IS HERE ALREADY.
TOTSUKI RESORT
HEAD CHEF AND COMPANY DIRECTOR
GIN DOJIMA
MY APOLO-GIES.
I MAKE A HABIT OF DOING A LITTLE... *PHYSICAL MAINTENANCE* IN THE BATH.

IT WAS A RARE MOMENT FOR SOMA TO THINK...
HOLY CRAP, HE SCARES ME!
...WITH ALL SINCER-ITY.
BUT IT WAS ONLY FOR A SECOND.
AW, DARN! I WAS SO EXCITED THINKING THAT I'D GET TO BE THE FIRST ONE IN THE BATH.
HA HA HA! SORRY, SORRY.
YOU'RE THE FIRST OF THE STUDENTS, THOUGH. I HOPE THAT WILL SUFFICE.
YAMMER
YAMMER
THERE ARE SOME VERY GOOD STUDENTS IN THE INSTITUTE.
STILL... LAST YEAR, NOW THIS YEAR TOO.
LAST YEAR TOO?
YES. THE FIFTY-SERVINGS TRIAL TESTS THE ABILITY TO MANAGE MULTIPLE STOVES AT ONCE.
I HAD MADE IT MY HABIT TO FINISH MY BATH BEFORE THE FIRST STUDENTS FINISHED THE TRIAL AND CAME HERE.
BUT LAST YEAR, TOO, THERE WAS A STUDENT WHO FINISHED ALL FIFTY SERVINGS IN TIME TO CATCH ME.
THIS YEAR HE'S PART OF THE COUNCIL OF TEN MASTERS. SEVENTH SEAT, I BELIEVE.
OH, HEY! I KNOW HIM!

HE WAS A PRETTY WORTHWHILE FELLOW.
WOW. THAT'S ISSHIKI SENPAI, FOR SURE.
WAIT.
NOW THAT I THINK ABOUT IT...
...SHE WAS ALREADY DRESSED.
DOES THAT MEAN SHE FINISHED ALL FIFTY SERVINGS BEFORE ME?
ERINA NAKIRI? AH, THE DEAN'S GRAND-DAUGHTER.
I'VE HEARD THE RUMORS.

IT'S SAID THAT WHEN SHE WAS A BABY, SHE WAS GIVEN ONLY FORMULA MADE BY THE SENIOR TEACHERS OF THE INSTITUTE.
ANOTHER STORY HAS HER SUCCESSFULLY IDENTIFYING EIGHT DIFFERENT TYPES OF SALT WHILE BLINDFOLDED.
BUT SHE HAD THE SKILL TO BE THE YOUNGEST EVER...
...TO EARN A SEAT ON THE COUNCIL. THAT SPEAKS VOLUMES FOR HER TALENT.
YOU COULD GO ON UNTIL YOU'RE BLUE IN THE FACE ABOUT HOW SHE TRULY HAS THE DIVINE TONGUE.
AT THIS PACE ...
...SHE WILL BE THE GREATEST CHEF...
NO... THE GREATEST MONSTER THE INSTITUTE HAS EVER PRODUCED!
BUT AT THE MOMENT, SHE'S STILL ONLY A STUDENT.
A DEVIL'S JUNGLE, WHERE TALENT GATHERS AND ONLY THE STRONG SURVIVE ...
THAT IS THE TOTSUKI INSTITUTE.

HONE YOUR SKILLS TO RAZOR SHARPNESS, YOUNG MAN.
THIS IS A PROFOUND PLACE ON MANY LEVELS.
YES, SIR!
SHWAK
YUKIHIRA! THERE YOU ARE!
I MAY HAVE BEEN SLOWER THIS TIME, BUT-
ACK! CHEF DOJIMA!
HM? I'VE OVERSTAYED MY TIME. I SHOULD BE GOING.
KEEP IN MIND, THIS CAMP HAS ONLY JUST BEGUN.
DON'T FORGET TO TAKE GOOD CARE OF YOUR BODY.
SPLSH
GOOD LUCK TOMOR-ROW.
CLASP
YES, CHEF DOJIMA.
GAPE

Y-Y-YUKI-HIRA! DO YOU HAVE ANY IDEA WHO THAT IS?!
YEAH. CHEF DOJIMA.
YES... NO! THAT'S NOT WHAT I MEANT!
HOW COULD YOU SHAKE HIS HAND LIKE HE'S SOME NORMAL GUY?!
YUKIHIRA?
WHERE HAVE I HEARD THAT NAME?

SPARKLE
SPARKLE
SPARKLE
SPARKLE

Yoshino
OOOOOF!
COME ON, MEGUMI. JOIN US.
I-IT ALL SEEMS SO LUXURIOUS, I'M STILL NOT SURE I SHOULD TOUCH IT...
BOFF
FLOP FLOP
EHEH HEH HEH HEH HEH!
YUKI, I KNOW YOU'RE HAPPY...
...BUT THAT LAUGH IS SERIOUSLY CREEPY.
OH, MY. MARUI, YOU LOOK LIKE YOU'VE GOTTEN THINNER.
DO I? THEN I HOPE YOU'LL LISTEN TO THE POOR, THINNER ME...
HOW ABOUT WE ALL CALL IT A NIGHT AND REST UP FOR TOMORROW, STARTING N...
BLANCH
YO! WE'RE ALL HERE!
DUN
LET'S DO THIS!
AAAAAAH!

SEVERAL MINUTES LATER...
SCHNOOR
Z Z Z
Z Z Z
Z Z Z
SCHNOOR
Z Z Z
IT LOOKS LIKE THEIR EXHAUSTION HIT ALL AT ONCE.
LET'S LEAVE 'EM THERE UNTIL LIGHTS OUT.
AREN'T YOU SLEEPY YET, MEGUMI? YOU AREN'T USUALLY UP LATE.
MOST OF THE TIME YOU HEAD TO BED ON THE EARLY SIDE.
I KNOW. IT'S WEIRD. I'M SO TIRED, BUT MY EYES WANT TO STAY OPEN.

YEAH, WE DID SPEND PRETTY MUCH THE WHOLE DAY ON EDGE.
?
TRUE, BUT, UM, I DON'T THINK THAT'S ALL OF IT.
I'VE ALWAYS BEEN SO NERVOUS DURING CLASS THAT I'D MESS UP...
...AND WHEN I MESSED UP, I'D GET LOST AND START PANICKING.
BUT TODAY WHEN I BACKED SOMA UP I WAS ABLE TO DO EVERYTHING RIGHT.
SO IT FEELS LIKE...
...MAYBE I'VE GAINED A LITTLE CONFIDENCE IN MYSELF.
JUST A LITTLE. AND THAT'S EXCITING TO ME.

B-BUT, UM! A-ALL THE CREDIT GOES TO SOMA, NOW. I AIN'T THAT GOOD. IF HE HADN'T BEEN TELLIN' ME WHAT TA DO, I'DA BEEN LOST!
FLAIL
FLAIL
DON'T SELL YOUR-SELF SHORT.
I NEVER WOULD'VE GOTTEN THAT DISH TOGETHER IF YOU HADN'T FOUND ALL THOSE INGREDIENTS IN THE MOUNTAINS.
YOU DID A GREAT JOB WITH COOKING THEM UP TOO.
HE'S RIGHT. YOU CAN DO WHATEVER YOU PUT YOUR MIND TO.
HAVE SOME CONFIDENCE IN YOUR-SELF...
OKAY?
I WON'T GIVE UP.
I'M GOING TO KEEP TRYING MY HARDEST!
I WANT TO STAY WITH EVERYONE LONGER.
I WANT TO GET BETTER AT COOKING.

QUIVER
QUIVER
POINT

YOU'RE EXPELLED.

21 THE PERFECT RECETTE
DAY 2 9:00 A.M.
BONJOUR.
I'M SHINOMIYA, SEVENTY-NINTH GRADUATING CLASS.
HAS EVERYONE RECEIVED A COPY OF THE RECETTE (RECIPE)?
FOR MY ASSIGNMENT, YOU WILL PREPARE THE DISH I HAVE SPECIFIED.
AUGH! CHEF SHINOMIYA? THIS SUCKS!
I HEARD HE EXPELLED OVER THIRTY STUDENTS YESTERDAY!

AND FOR OUR ASSIGNMENT WE HAVE TO MAKE THE RECIPE HE PICKED?
FWAP
A FRENCH CUISINE STAPLE...
NINE-VEGETABLE TERRINE.
IT'S A LOVELY DISH THAT DISPLAYS COLORFUL VEGETABLES BEAUTIFULLY...
...BUT EACH OF THE NINE VEGETABLES USED REQUIRES DIFFERENT PREPARATION AND COOKING.
ALL OF THE VEGETABLES MUST BE KEPT IN BALANCE, WITH NONE DOMINATING OR FADING INTO THE BACKGROUND.
TO MANAGE ALL THAT AND KEEP IT TASTING WONDERFUL IS EXCEPTIONALLY DIFFICULT!
I CHOSE SOME VERY SIMPLE INGREDIENTS FOR THIS VERSION OF THE RECETTE, YOU KNOW.
WOULD YOU RATHER I HAD CHOSEN MORE DIFFICULT ONES?
WAGGLE
WAGGLE
DAMN IT!
I REALLY WANNA PUNCH HIM IN HIS SMUG MOUTH!
ANOTHER THING. THIS ASSIGN-MENT WILL NOT BE DONE IN PAIRS.
EACH STUDENT WILL PREPARE A TERRINE ON HIS OR HER OWN.
ADDITIONALLY, AIDING OTHERS OR PROVIDING ADVICE DURING PREPARATION IS FORBIDDEN.

CHOOSE YOUR INGREDIENTS CAREFULLY FROM THE STACKS PROVIDED AT THE BACK OF THE KITCHEN.
OH, AND BEFORE WE BEGIN, LET ME GIVE YOU A QUICK TIP...
IT'S WISE TO ASSUME EVERY STUDENT HERE IS YOUR ENEMY.
...?
YOU HAVE THREE HOURS.
READY?
BEGIN!

WHAP
OUT OF THE WAY!
WHMP
AH!
...!
OW! HEY! OUTTA MY WAY!
HELL NO! YOU MOVE!
THERE'S SUCH A NASTY GLEAM IN EVERYONE'S EYES!
THE PRESSURE IS EVEN WORSE THAN IT WAS YESTERDAY!
BUT...
SHFF
...I CAN'T AFFORD TO BE AFRAID.

I WON'T LET THEM BEAT ME!
HNNNNGH
STARE
THERE! THIS ONE.
SOME PEOPLE HAVE ALREADY BEGUN COOKING.
IT LOOKS LIKE GETTING SHOVED AROUND IN THAT SEA OF PEOPLE PUT ME PRETTY FAR BEHIND.
BUT ALL I HAVE LEFT IS TO PICK A HEAD OF CAULIFLOWER AND-
...?!

THIS ONE...
AND THIS ONE TOO...
OH, NO!
ALL OF THEM ARE OXIDIZING AND TURNING BROWN!
THERE AREN'T ANY GOOD ONES LEFT!
IF I TRY TO PREPARE THEM AS THEY ARE, THE OXIDATION WILL ONLY GET WORSE, RUINING THE COLOR EVEN FURTHER!
BEAUTIFUL COLOR IS ONE OF THE MOST IMPORTANT PARTS OF A TERRINE!
WH- WHAT AM I GOING TO DO?!
SOMA!
AH

NO!
RSTL
I CAN'T RELY ON SOMA FOR EVERYTHING.
FIRST, I HAVE TO CALM DOWN.
SHFF
I'M GOING TO GET THROUGH THIS...
CLUTCH
...AND DO IT ON MY OWN!
OKAY... WHAT CAN I DO TO PRESERVE THE CAULIFLOWER'S COLOR?
OH!
WAAAAH

POINT
YOU FAIL. NEXT!
NGH!
NOT BAD. YOU PASS.
SIP
SHFF
TINK

DONE!
SPARKLE
SPARKLE

BDMP
BDMP
SIGH
...

MEGUMI TADOKORO...
YOU FAIL.
RIGHT. IS THAT EVERYONE?
EVERYONE WHO FAILED, GATHER YOUR BELONGINGS AND WAIT IN THE HOTEL LOBBY-
UM, S-SIR?
M-M-MAY I ASK, UM...
WH-WHAT WAS WRONG WITH MY DISH?
WHEN YOU BOILED THAT BAD CAULIFLOWER...
...YOU USED WINE VINEGAR WITH IT, CORRECT?
VINEGAR BLANCHES INGREDIENTS. YOU USED IT TO PRESERVE THE CAULIFLOWER'S COLOR.
USING MORE VINEGAR IN THE BASE SEASONINGS OF THE DISH HIGHLIGHTED THE INHERENT SWEETNESS OF THE CAULIFLOWER.
THE SWEET VEGETABLES AND THE SLIGHT HINT OF SOUR VINEGAR MATCHED PERFECTLY TOGETHER, RESULTING IN AN EXQUISITE OVERALL TASTE TO THE DISH.
White Wine Vinegar
TH-THEN WHY DID YOU...?!

WHO SAID YOU WERE ALLOWED TO CHANGE MY RECETTE?
THE ENJOYMENT OF THIS PARTICULAR DISH WAS INTENDED TO COME FROM THE HARMONY OF SWEETNESS BETWEEN THE VEGETABLES CHOSEN.
WAS "ACCENTUATE WITH TARTNESS" WRITTEN ANYWHERE ON MY RECETTE? NO. IT WAS NOT.
WHAT YOU CREATED WAS PRACTICALLY A DIFFERENT DISH ENTIRELY.
IF YOU MAKE SOMETHING DIFFERENT FROM WHAT WAS SPECIFIED, OF COURSE YOU WILL FAIL.
HAVE I MADE MYSELF CLEAR?
WSH
NOT TO ME, SIR.
THAT WAS AN INEVITABLE SITUATION, RIGHT?
SOME OF THE VEGETABLES HAD STARTED GOING BAD, SO SHE HAD NO OTHER CHOICE.

BESIDES, WE'RE SUPPOSED TO BE GETTING TREATED LIKE YOUR EMPLOYEES, RIGHT?
IN THAT CASE, PROVIDING AND MAINTAINING THE INGREDIENTS IS THE RESPONSIBILITY OF THE HEAD CHEF.
TWITCH
TWITCH
IF ANYONE'S AT FAULT HERE, IT SHOULD BE THE HEAD CHEF.
THAT'S **YOU.**
BAM
SHUT YOUR MOUTH!
JUST WHO DO YOU THINK YOU'RE GETTING LIPPY WITH, HUH?
WELL?!
HAH. SINCE YOU OBVIOUSLY DIDN'T UNDERSTAND, LET ME CLARIFY IT FOR YOU.
I **DELIBERATELY** INCLUDED THAT BAD CAULIFLOWER.
IT WAS A STEP TO HELP WEED OUT THE FAILURES.

CAULIFLOWER EXHIBITS ALL THREE MAJOR PROBLEMS WHEN IT COMES TO VEGETABLES: IT OXIDIZES EASILY, BRUISES EASILY, AND IS HARD TO PREPARE.
OF ALL VEGETABLES, IT IS THE ONE A CHEF HAS TO HANDLE MOST CAREFULLY.
YAMMER
!
I FAILED EVERY SINGLE DUNCE HERE WHO WAS STUPID ENOUGH TO LOSE THEIR COOL AND CHOOSE THEIR INGREDIENTS POORLY.
AND THAT INCLUDES THE SLOWPOKES WHO WEREN'T FAST ENOUGH TO GET THE GOOD ONES.
BUT TADOKORO TRIED TO MAKE UP FOR HER SLOWNESS BY COMING UP WITH A WAY TO–
I AM HEAD CHEF HERE!
THERE IS NO WAY THAT I WILL ALLOW MY RECETTE ...
...TO BE ALTERED BY SOME IDLE KITCHEN HAND!

SHFF
AND IF ANOTHER SIMPLE KITCHEN HAND LIKE YOU THINKS THEY CAN STEP IN AND DEFY ME...
...THEN HOW ABOUT I USE MY RIGHTS AS HEAD CHEF...
...AND FIRE YOU TOO!
!
WHY YOU-
SOMA, ENOUGH!
CLUTCH
IT'S OKAY.
IF YOU KEEP IT UP, THEY'LL KICK YOU RIGHT OUT WITH ME, SO YOU'D BEST STOP.
WHO CARES ABOUT THAT RIGHT NOW?!
EHEH HEH... I-IT'S OKAY, SOMA. R-REALLY.

DON'T YOU WORRY 'BOUT ME.
HONEST ... EHEH HEH...

'SCUZE ME, CHEF SHINO-MIYA!
ONE MORE THING.
WHAT, MONSIEUR YUKIHIRA.
DO YOU HAVE SOME OTHER PROB-LEM?
NO, NO PROBLEM. IT'S MORE OF A QUESTION.
DO CERTAIN TOTSUKI RULES STILL APPLY TO GRADUATES?
...
WHAT DO YOU MEAN?
A SHOKU-GEKI.

I'M CHALLENGING YOU.

IF I BEAT YOU...
...WILL YOU RESCIND TADO-KORO'S EXPULSION?
THE PERFECT RECETTE [END]

THANK YOU FOR PICKING UP *FOOD WARS!: SHOKUGEKI NO SOMA* VOLUME 3! ON THE NEXT PAGE STARTS A SPECIAL MANGA SHORT:

YOUR AND MY ROMANCE COUNSELING

SHUN SAEKI'S DEBUT WORK, IT APPEARED IN THE *JUMP NEXT!* 2011 SPRING ISSUE.

I HOPE YOU ENJOY THIS FUN STORY ABOUT HOW A FLUBBED ENCOUNTER LEADS TO AN AWKWARD FRIENDSHIP AND BUDDING ROMANCE!

ONE DAY, SOONER OR LATER...
...EVERYONE GETS HIT BY REALITY.
SPECIAL SHORT
YOUR AND MY ROMANCE COUNSELING
BASICALLY, THEY REALIZE INSTEAD OF PINING AFTER THE UNATTAIN-ABLE...
HOO! CHECK HER OUT!
LOOK AT THAT CLEAV-AGE... THOSE CURVES!
STILL...
...IT'S BETTER TO FIND AND DATE THE GIRLS YOU HAVE A REAL SHOT WITH.
THAT'S EASIER SAID THAN DONE.
IS SHE REALLY STILL IN HIGH SCHOOL?!
FRESH
Free Bracelet!

ME...
I JUST CAN'T SEEM TO GIVE UP ON MY CRUSH.
SPECIAL SHORT
YOUR AND MY ROMANCE COUNSELING
BY: SHUN SAEKI

DWAH?!
YOU IDIOT!
WHAT DO YOU THINK YOU'RE DOING?!
SHE'S STANDING RIGHT OVER THERE!
SLAM
HEY! IT'S NOT LIKE THESE WERE PEEP SHOTS. BESIDES, YOU WERE LOOKING AT IT TOO.
YEAH, BUT I HEARD THAT KAWAI WAS FORCED INTO IT.
PSST
PSST
FORCED?
APPARENTLY, SHE KNOWS THE EDITOR OF THIS MAGAZINE.
FRESH
Idol #28
THE GIRL WHO WAS SUPPOSED TO BE IN THAT SHOT CANCELED BECAUSE SHE WAS SICK, SO KAWAI GOT DRAGGED IN TO REPLACE HER.
HEH. YOU ALWAYS KNOW ALL THE DIRTY DETAILS ON HER.
SMIRK

*BOTH GIRLS HAVE THE KANJI FOR "RIVER" IN THEIR LAST NAMES.

YUI KAWAI, WITH HER BEAUTY, INTELLIGENCE, AND ETERNAL SMILE, IS ONE OF THE MOST POPULAR GIRLS IN SCHOOL.
RUMOR HAS IT ASUKA KAWASHIMA PLAYS AROUND...
...BUT SHE HAS A COOL BEAUTY TO MAKE ANY PRO MODEL JEALOUS!
SO YEAH. THE TWO GREAT RIVERS ARE SO FAR OUT OF OUR LEAGUE IT'S NOT EVEN FUNNY.
HEY...
IF I COULD GIVE UP ON HER, I WOULD.
BUT SOMEBODY KEEPS CLINGING TO THE CRUSH HE'S HAD ON KAWAI SINCE ELEMENTARY SCHOOL.
STAB
URK!
KAWAI AND I HAVE BEEN IN THE SAME SCHOOL SINCE ELEMENTARY.

EVER SINCE THEN, JUST ABOUT EVERY GUY HAS HAD A CRUSH ON HER AT SOME POINT.
I WAS NO DIFFERENT. BUT FORGET DATING HER...
I'VE BARELY EVEN SPOKEN TO HER.
IF YOU WANT TO GIVE UP, THERE'S ONE GREAT WAY TO DO IT.
WHAT'S THAT?
GO CONFESS TO HER... AND THEN WATCH YOURSELF CRASH AND BURN.
GETTING THE SMACKDOWN SHOULD KNOCK SOME SENSE INTO YOU!
SURE, YOU'RE GONNA FALL FLAT ON YOUR FACE, BUT YOU'VE GOTTA DO SOMETHING FOR IT TO COUNT AS PROGRESS.
HE DOES HAVE A POINT.
I DO WANT TO TRY GOING ON A DATE WITH A GIRL SOMEDAY...

I'M GOING TO CONFESS TO HER, EVEN THOUGH I KNOW I'M GONNA FAIL.
OKAY!

BUT, UH... I DON'T EVEN KNOW HER CELL PHONE NUMBER.
I HATE TO RESORT TO SOMETHING THIS LAME AND OLD FASHIONED...
KAWAI
ARGH! WAFFLING OVER IT ISN'T GOING TO SOLVE ANYTHING!
I have something important to tell you. Please come up to the roof after school.
Kobayakawa
KCHAK
AWAI
IF I WANT TO BREAK THE STATUS QUO...
...I JUST HAVE TO DO IT!

I WONDER IF SHE'LL ACTUALLY COME, THOUGH.
KAWAI IS PROBABLY LOOKING AT THAT NOTE LIKE, "THIS IS FROM KOBAYA-WHO?"
KACHUNK
KOBAYAKAWA?
SHE CAME!

BTAM
WHAT IS IT YOU HAVE TO TELL ME?
UM ...
I- I...
O-OKAY, I'M GONNA SAY IT. I'M GOING TO TELL HER!
BDMP BDMP BDMP BDMP BDMP BDMP BDMP
K- KA...
KA- WA-
MMMMM!
I DON'T COME UP TO THE ROOF THAT OFTEN.
BOY, THAT BREEZE FEELS GREAT.

BA-THUMP
I-I CAN'T!
THE WORDS JUST WON'T COME OUT!
?
B-BUT I HAVE TO SAY SOMETHING!
UM ...
T-TO TELL THE TRUTH, I UM...
THAT L-LETTER, UM... I-I PUT IT IN YOUR SHOE LOCKER BY MISTAKE!
AUGH! WHAT A SUCKY LIE!
BLANCH
...
THEN, UM... WHO DID YOU MEAN TO CALL UP HERE?
UHHH...
!
THE TWO BIGGEST IDOLS, KNOWN COLLECTIVELY AS THE TWO GREAT RIVERS...

I-I MEANT KAWASHIMA!
YOUR SHOE LOCKERS ARE, LIKE, RIGHT NEXT TO EACH OTHER!
I, UM... MUST'VE OPENED THE WRONG ONE BY MISTAKE!
FLAIL
OH, GOD... THIS IS GETTING WORSE AND WORSE!
BFFT!
AHA HA HA HA HA HA HA HA HA HA HA HA HA!
?!
DUN

WHA –?
HUH ?
AHA HA HA... OH GOD, MY SIDES... HEE HEE! MY SIDES HURT NOW... HA HA HA!
WHO MESSES UP SOME-THING LIKE THAT?
THAT'S SO ADORABLE!
HEE HEE
SHE CALLED ME ADORABLE!
THOUGH, UM... I'M NOT SURE I SHOULD BE HAPPY ABOUT WHY.
SO ANYWAY, HOW DID YOU FALL FOR ASUKA?
HUH ?!
TP
TP
TP
UM...
I-I CAN'T SAY...
LEAN
YOU CAN'T?

HMPH HMPH
YOU MAKE IT SEEM LIKE YOU'RE GOING TO CONFESS TO ME, BUT THEN YOU TELL ME IT'S FOR ASUKA?
THAT'S SO TOTALLY HORRIBLE OF YOU! I FEEL DUMPED!
I-I DIDN'T MEAN IT LIKE THAT AT ALL! HONEST!
SMILE
HEE HEE! JUST KIDDING.
C'MON, YOU CAN TELL ME WHY. 'KAY?
I JUST LOVE TALKING ABOUT ROMANCE AND RELATIONSHIPS WITH PEOPLE! ♡
DOUBLY SO IF IT'S ABOUT FRIENDS LIKE ASUKA.
...?
STILL, YOU PICKED HER, HEY?
YOU LUCKY GUY! ASUKA IS A REAL LOOKER, THAT'S FOR SURE!
YOU MUST'VE BEEN DISAPPOINTED TO SEE FRUMPY ME SHOW UP INSTEAD.
N-NO, NO!
YOU'RE REALLY CUTE, TOO, KAWAI-SAN.
NUDGE
NUDGE

WHAT?
HUH. YOU'RE SMOOTHER THAN I EXPECTED, YOU PLAYBOY.
SHE'S SO CUTE!
WAIT, DID I JUST SAY SOMETHING REALLY COOL?
UM...
NOT BAD! ♡
I KNOW!
SWFF SWFF
HOW ABOUT I HELP YOU?
HUH?

I'LL GIVE YOU SOME PERSONAL ROMANCE COUNSELING!
EVERYTHING YOU NEED TO KNOW FOR DATING ASUKA, I'LL TEACH YOU!
GAPE
STARE
WHAT, AM I NOT GOOD ENOUGH FOR YOU?
I MEAN, YEAH, I DON'T HAVE MUCH PERSONAL DATING EXPERI-ENCE...
...BUT I'VE HEARD LOTS OF PEOPLE TALK A WHOLE LOT ABOUT THEIRS!
SHE DOESN'T? THAT CAN'T BE RIGHT!
SOUND GOOD? OKAY! I'LL SEE YOU TOMOR-ROW!

WHOA...
I-I THINK I JUST GOT STUCK IN SOMETHING WAY BIGGER THAN I EXPECTED...
THE NEXT DAY...
MORN-IN'!
YAMMER
YAMMER
YAMMER
YAMMER
YO, KOBAYA-KAWA!
YIKES!
GLOOOOOM
WHAT HAPPENED TO YOU?! YOU LOOK TERRIBLE!
I DIDN'T SLEEP A WINK...
AH, SO SHE TURNED YOU DOWN LIKE WE THOUGHT?
UH, ACTUALLY ...
AHA!

LEAN
MORNING, KOBAYAKAWA!
AH!
G-GOOD MORNING.
?!
YAMMER
YAMMER
WHAT THE...? WHY IS KAWAI TALKING TO KOBAYA-KAWA?
WHAT COULD SHE EVER WANT WITH A SCHLUB LIKE HIM?
YAMMER
TH-THIS CAN'T BE HAPPEN-ING!
WHAT'S WRONG? YOU'VE GOT BAGS UNDER YOUR EYES!

PARDON US A MOMENT. I'M GOING TO BORROW KOBAYAKAWA HERE.
OH, GOD! THEY'RE TOUCHING ME!
HUG
UM, SURE ...
WHERE ARE WE GOING?
HEE HEE! OUT TO BATTLE PLAN!
NO WAY! THOSE TWO CAN'T SERIOUSLY BE-
YEAH, NO WAY.
HEY, ASUKA. WHAT DO YOU THINK OF THAT?
YAMMER
YAMMER
HUH.
...
TOTALLY BAD TASTE.

AH, SO YOU DIDN'T SLEEP WELL?
TH-THAT'S RIGHT, KAWAI-SAN.
HOLD ON, WHY ARE YOU BEING SO FORMAL AND POLITE?
HUH?
WE'RE THE SAME AGE.
W-WELL, UM...
TALKING TO A PRETTY GIRL LIKE YOU MAKES ME NERVOUS, A-AND I'M FORMAL WHEN I'M NERVOUS...
SKRITCH
SKRITCH
STARE
YOU KEEP SLIPPING NICE COMPLIMENTS INTO EVERYTHING YOU SAY SO NATURALLY.
ARE YOU SURE YOU'RE NOT GOOD AT THIS STUFF AND JUST HIDING IT?

N-NO! I-I JUST BLURTED OUT WHAT I WAS REALLY THINKING...
THERE YOU GO AGAIN!
GIRLS ARE WEAK TO THAT KIND OF SMOOTH TALK!
NUDGE
NUDGE
GEEZ. IF YOU'RE *THIS* GOOD, WHAT DO YOU NEED MY HELP FOR?
I-I'M NOT GOOD! I SWEAR!
PLEASE HELP ME!
HEE HEE! OH, ALL RIGHT.
I'LL MEET YOU AGAIN AFTER SCHOOL FOR MORE PLANNING!
2-2

...
NEVER IN A MILLION YEARS DID I THINK IT WOULD REALLY, TRULY WORK OUT.
HUH?
WHAT, DID YOU NOT JUST MAKE ONE OF THE SCHOOL'S TWO BIG IDOLS YOUR OWN PERSONAL GIRLFRIEND?!
HECK, NO!
SHE JUST AGREED TO GIVE ME ADVICE ON STUFF.
ADVICE? ON WHAT?
UH... ROMANCE.
ROMANCE ADVICE FROM YOUR CRUSH?
HAH! ARE YOU REALLY THAT DUMB?
ARGH! HEARING THAT FROM HIM MAKES ME EVEN MADDER!
I KNOW IT'S STUPID!

AFTER THAT...
...WE BOTH STARTED STAYING AFTER SCHOOL ON OUR FREE DAYS TO GO OVER ADVICE ON ROMANCE AND DATING.
TALK NATURALLY DRIFTED FROM THAT TO MORE NORMAL TOPICS, INCLUDING GOSSIP...
WHAT ?!
BAM
YOU SAW THAT MAGAZINE PICTURE ?!
UM, Y-YEAH...
NOW IT'S GOTTEN TO THE POINT WHERE WE JUST HANG OUT AND CHAT LIKE FRIENDS.
I'VE GOTTEN BETTER AT BEING LESS FORMAL TOO.
I WISH...
FORGET IT EXISTED! NO, FORK OVER THE MAGAZINE FIRST!
I-I CAN'T !
IT BELONGS TO A FRIEND...
AUGH! THAT OLD MAN! I'VE BEEN SO EMBAR-RASSED THANKS TO HIM!
...THE DAYS WOULD GO ON LIKE THIS FOREVER...
OH, YEAH! THAT!
I STILL REMEMBER THAT LIKE IT WAS YESTERDAY!
GAH! YOU DO?!

WELL, YEAH!
YOU WERE DEAD LAST IN THAT SPRINT WHEN EVERYBODY IN FRONT OF YOU TRIPPED OVER EACH OTHER, ALLOWING YOU TO GET FIRST PLACE.
THINKING ABOUT IT, THAT WAS PROBABLY MY CROWNING ACHIEVEMENT IN LIFE.
I STILL KEEP THE FIRST-PLACE MEDAL IN A SAFE PLACE.
AHA HA HA HA! A SPORTS FESTIVAL IN ELEMENTARY SCHOOL WAS YOUR CROWNING ACHIEVEMENT?
HA HA, YEP! THAT'S ALSO WHEN YOU STARTED GETTING REALLY POPULAR WITH ALL THE GUYS.
HUH? NO WAY! I'VE NEVER BEEN THAT POPULAR.

NO, FOR REAL! YOU WERE!
EVERY GUY I KNEW HAD A CRUSH ON YOU.
STARE
EVERY GUY?
DOES THAT MEAN ...
...YOU DID TOO?

UM! W-W-WELL...
I, UH...
BLUSH

GOOD GRIEF.
IT'S AT TIMES LIKE THIS WHEN YOU NEED TO PULL OUT THOSE CHAT TECHNIQUES WE TALKED ABOUT!
EVEN IF IT'S A LITTLE WHITE LIE...
...GIRLS PAY REALLY CLOSE ATTENTION TO STUFF LIKE THAT.
HUH?
IT, UM... WASN'T A LIE.
I SAID IT!
TOO LATE!
WITH TIMING THAT SLOW, IT JUST SOUNDS LIKE A JOKE.
O-OH...
UM, ANYWAY... THERE'S SOMETHING I'VE WANTED TO ASK YOU.
REALLY?
ASK AWAY!

KA-WAI...
HOW COME YOU'VE NEVER HAD A BOYFRIEND?
HUH?
UM... HAD ONE? I-I'M NOT DELIBERATELY *N-NOT* HAVING ONE...
I'D LOVE TO HAVE A BOYFRIEND, I-IF I COULD FIND ONE.
BUT IF I'M GOING TO PICK SOMEONE, I-IT SHOULD BE SOMEONE I COULD REALLY LOVE WITH ALL MY HEART, DON'T YOU THINK?
BLUSH
I KNOW THIS SOUNDS KINDA ODD, BUT I'VE HAD A LOT OF PEOPLE CONFESS TO ME.
NO DUH!

AT FIRST, I TURNED THEM DOWN BECAUSE I DIDN'T KNOW ANY OF THEM WELL...
...BUT THEN I STARTED TO THINK THAT IF I GAVE THEM A CHANCE, I MIGHT GROW TO LIKE THEM.
BUT THAT'S THE LAST I EVER HEARD FROM ANY OF THEM.
BUT BY THAT POINT, EVERYONE WAS ALREADY STARTING TO DATE OTHER GIRLS.
SO THAT'S WHY UP TO NOW...
...I'VE HAD ZERO EXPERIENCE ACTUALLY GETTING A BOYFRIEND.

B-BUT THAT CAN'T BE RIGHT!
IT'S TRUE! I TOLD YOU, REMEMBER?
I'VE HEARD ABOUT ROMANCE FROM A LOT OF PEOPLE, BUT I DON'T HAVE EXPERIENCE MYSELF.
BUT...

SOMEDAY, I'D LIKE TO FIND SOMEONE I CAN REALLY LOVE...
...AND FIND OUT WHAT TRUE ROMANCE IS LIKE.
WSH
A-AND WHEN THAT TIME COMES, I'LL GIVE YOU ANY ADVICE YOU NEED!
WHAT?
I MEAN, YOU'RE SUCH A BIG HELP TO ME RIGHT NOW...
...SO WHEN THAT TIME COMES, I WANNA HELP YOU BACK!

...
THAT'S A PROMISE, OKAY?
SHF
YEAH, I'LL PROMISE.
BUT, THE DAY I HAVE TO GIVE YOU ADVICE...
...IT'S PROBABLY GOING TO HURT SO MUCH, I'LL FEEL LIKE DYING.

BY THE WAY...
WHEN DO YOU PLAN ON CONFESSING TO ASUKA?
URK!
UM, E-EVEN THOUGH I HAVEN'T REALLY TALKED TO HER MUCH YET?
WELL ...
THAT PART IS UP TO YOU, I GUESS.
RIGHT, UM...
SHE'S BEEN SO NICE ABOUT GIVING ME ADVICE TOO. IT'D BE WRONG FOR ME TO NOT GO THROUGH WITH IT.
BUT... ONCE I'VE DONE THAT...
OKAY! I'LL CONFESS TO KAWASHIMA TOMORROW!
EEE! ♡

NICE DECISIVE-NESS!
THAT'LL NET YOU A WHOLE LOT OF POINTS WITH A GIRL.
...WILL THIS RELATIONSHIP WE HAVE BE OVER?
NUDGE NUDGE
STILL, TOMORROW? DOESN'T IT MAKE YOU NERVOUS BEING THAT SOON?
WELL, YEAH... MY HEART IS THUDDING ALREADY.
OKAY, THEN.
LET'S DO A PRACTICE CONFESSION!
HUH?

RIGHT NOW! READY, GO!
TA-DAH! IT'S TOMORROW AND ASUKA STANDS BEFORE YOU!
GRIN
GRIN
I KNOW I'M NOT AS CUTE AS ASUKA, SO CUT ME SOME SLACK, OKAY?
GRIN
STUTTER
UMM ...
STUTTER
STUTTER
I-I, UH...
LOOSEN UP A LITTLE.
THIS IS JUST PRACTICE, YOU KNOW.
C'MON.
THAT'S EASY FOR YOU TO SAY.
C'MON, DO IT!
BUT THE ONE I REALLY LIKE ISN'T HER...
IT'S YOU.
UMM...

YUI KAWAI.
I'VE LOVED YOU...
...FOR A REALLY LONG TIME.

UM...
KOBAYA-
KAWA?

YOU CONFESSED USING MY NAME.
WHAT?!
I MESSED UP!
GEEZ!
THAT'S THE ONE THING YOU REALLY DON'T WANT TO DO TOMORROW, OKAY?
SKRITCH
SKRITCH
CRAP! I ACCIDENTALLY SAID WHAT I REALLY FEEL!
BLUSH

WELL, GOOD LUCK.
I'M SURE EVERYTHING WILL GO JUST GREAT FOR YOU.
YEAH. THANKS FOR EVERY-THING.
SHFF
BYE!
SEE YOU LATER!

TIME PASSED...
KAWASHIMA
BAM
I have something important to tell you. Please come up to the roof after school.
-Kobayakawa

...
KOBAYA-KAWA.
HE'S...
...REALLY GOING TO CONFESS TO HER.

KACHUNK
THERE SHE IS!
WELL?
WHAT'D YOU WANT TO TALK ABOUT, KOBAYA-KAWA?
AND MAKE IT QUICK, 'KAY? I WANNA GO HOME.
WSH
...

BDMP
KAWA-
SHIMA...
BDMP
BDMP
BDMP
BDMP
BA-THUMP
I...
BA-THUMP

I'M IN LOVE WITH SOMEBODY ELSE.
BA-THUMP

I LIED TO THAT PERSON AND TOLD HER I HAD A CRUSH ON YOU.
I'D LIKE TO APOLOGIZE TO YOU FOR ANY MISUNDER-STANDING THAT MIGHT'VE CAUSED.
I'M SORRY.
BOW
...
HUH.
REALLY.
NOW I GET IT.
KAWA-SHIMA?

NOTHIN'. IT'S JUST THIS KINDA SITUATION IS WHERE PEOPLE CONFESS TO ME, Y'KNOW?
I'D BEEN THINKING ALL DAY HOW BEST TO TURN YOU DOWN GENTLY.
...
SO YOU DON'T NEED TO APOLOGIZE TO ME OR ANYTHING.
OKAY. LET ME REPHRASE IT, THEN.
THANK YOU.
I'M GLAD...
...THAT YOU BOTHERED TO COME AT ALL.
...
IT WAS JUST A WHIM.
SEE YA.
ASUKA!

HE'S REALLY A GREAT GUY! HONEST!
OKAY, SO HE CAN BE A LITTLE WUSSY AND FLAKY AT TIMES, BUT HE'S SWEET AND FUNNY!
YOU'VE GOT TO BELIEVE ME! HE'S A GOOD GUY!
OKAY, OKAY! I GET IT.
I'LL AT LEAST LISTEN TO HIM.
YOU PROM-ISE?
BECAUSE HE'S SUPER NICE!
GIGGLE
AH, WELL.
NEXT TIME...
...MAKE SURE YOU CONFESS TO THE RIGHT PERSON, 'KAY?
!

BTAM
KAWAI IS GOING TO BE SO DISAPPOINTED...
UM, LET ME GET RIGHT TO THE POINT. HOW'D IT GO?
WELL ...

SHE TURNED ME DOWN, JUST LIKE I EXPECTED.
COMPLETELY FLAT. I HAD NO CHANCE.
I GUESS THIS IS IT FOR OUR TIME TOGETHER...
THANK YOU FOR EVERY-THING.
I'LL NEVER FORGET HOW MUCH YOU HELPED ME.
SO, UM... SEE YA.
WAIT.
DO YOU REMEMBER THE PROMISE YOU MADE?
HUH?
UM...

I THINK...
...I'VE DEVELOPED A CRUSH ON SOME-ONE.
GONG
WHAT?! WHO?!
BLUSH
TH-THAT'S STILL A SECRET.
MUTTER
WHOEVER IT IS, I'LL HATE 'IM FOREVER!
...
SLUMP
MUTTER

SO THIS TIME...
...I'D LIKE YOU TO GIVE ME SOME ROMANCE ADVICE, OKAY?
SPECIAL SHORT – YOUR AND MY ROMANCE COUNSELING [END]

SIDE STORY - CUOCO IN ITALIA
BAR
TAKUMI? W-WOULD YOU, UMM...
...GO ON A DATE WITH ME?
YOU'RE AS ADORABLE AS EVER, TAKUMI.
WOULD YOU LIKE TO COME HAVE FUN WITH ME TODAY?
MWAH
TAKUMI.
HOW ABOUT I SHOW YOU SOMETHING THAT'S FUN AND FEELS REALLY GOOD?

Trattoria Aldini
SÍ, GRAZIE. (THANK YOU VERY MUCH.)
I'M VERY FLATTERED.
BUT I'M AFRAID I HAVE WORK THAT I MUST ATTEND TO.
MY APOLOGIES FOR THE WAIT.
TUNK
BUON APPETITO! (ENJOY!)
TAKUMI HAS GOTTEN BETTER.
AND YOU HAVE ISAMI TOO.
IT LOOKS LIKE ALDINI'S FUTURE IS IN GOOD HANDS. RIGHT, CHEF?

YES. EVEN IN MY EYES AS THEIR FATHER...
...THEY'RE BOTH EXCELLENT CHEFS.
BUT TAKUMI...
THERE'S JUST SOMETHING COLD ABOUT HIM.
IN A FEW YEARS, HE'LL LIKELY SURPASS ME IN SKILL...
...BUT BEYOND THAT, HE'S YET TO FIND ANY FURTHER GOAL TO SET HIS SIGHTS ON.
WHAT HE NEEDS...
...IS A RIVAL TO COMPETE AGAINST.

SIDE STORY [END]

'EKI BEGINS
A SHOKU-GEKI?
HA! I HAVE FOND MEMORIES OF THAT WORD.
ACCEPT IT...
... SHINO-MIYA.
IT WAS A RECKLESS CHALLENGE...
BUT FOR THE SAKE OF A FRIEND...
YOU AREN'T SOME-ONE...
...WHO DESERVES TO GET KICKED OUT OVER SOMETHING LIKE THAT.
I...
I DON'T EVEN KNOW HOW TO START APOLO-GIZIN'...

THE SHOKU
LET'S DO THIS, CHEF TADOKORO!
RIGHT!
...THEY STAND AND FIGHT!
FOOD WARS!: SHOKUGEKI NO SOMA V4
ON SALE FEBRUARY 2015!

You're Reading in the Wrong Direction!!

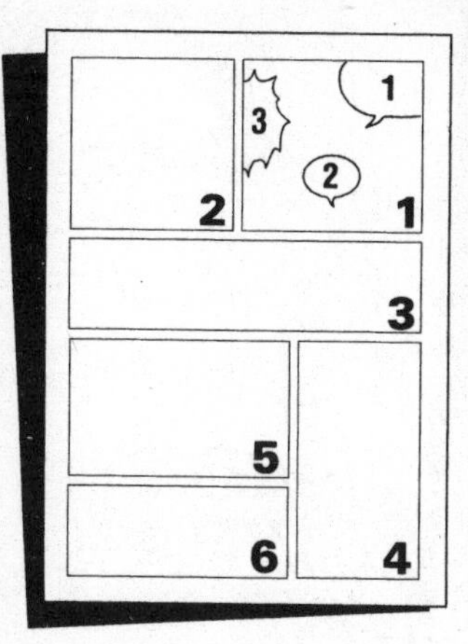

Whoops! Guess what? You're starting at the wrong end of the comic!

...It's true! In keeping with the original Japanese format, **Food Wars!** is meant to be read from right to left, starting in the upper-right corner.

Unlike English, which is read from left to right, Japanese is read from right to left, meaning that action, sound effects and word-balloon order are completely reversed... something which can make readers unfamiliar with Japanese feel pretty backwards themselves. For this reason, manga or Japanese comics published in the U.S. in English have sometimes been published "flopped"—that is, printed in exact reverse order, as though seen from the other side of a mirror.

By flopping pages, U.S. publishers can avoid confusing readers, but the compromise is not without its downside. For one thing, a character in a flopped manga series who once wore in the original Japanese version a T-shirt emblazoned with "M A Y" (as in "the merry month of") now wears one which reads "Y A M"! Additionally, many manga creators in Japan are themselves unhappy with the process, as some feel the mirror-imaging of their art skews their original intentions.

We are proud to bring you Yuto Tsukuda and Shun Saeki's **Food Wars!** in the original unflopped format.

For now, though, turn to the other side of the book and let the adventure begin...!

—Editor

321
THE STORY OF GOD
THE WORLD AND YOU

10 Publishing
a division of 10 of those.com